The General
Will Is Citizenship

The General Will Is Citizenship

Inquiries into French Political Thought

Jason Andrew Neidleman

ROWMAN & LITTLEFIELD PUBLISHERS, INC.
Lanham • Boulder • New York • Oxford

ROWMAN & LITTLEFIELD PUBLISHERS, INC.

Published in the United States of America
by Rowman & Littlefield Publishers, Inc.
4720 Boston Way, Lanham, Maryland 20706
http://www.rowmanlittlefield.com

12 Hid's Copse Road
Cumnor Hill, Oxford OX2 9JJ, England

British Library Cataloguing in Publication Information Available

Library of Congress Cataloging-in-Publication Data

Neidleman, Jason Andrew, 1970–
    The general will is citizenship : inquiries into French political thought / Jason Andrew Neidleman.
        p. cm.
    Includes bibliographical references and index.
    ISBN 0-7425-0788-2 (alk. paper) — ISBN 0-7425-0789-0 (pbk. : alk. paper)
        1. General will. 2. Citizenship—France—History—18th century. 3. Rousseau,
    Jean-Jacques, 1712–1778—Contributions in political science. 4.
    France—History—Revolution, 1789–1799—Influence. 5.
    Republicanism—France—History—18th century. I. Title.

JC328.2.N45 2001
323.6'01—dc21   00-031103
Printed in the United States of America

⊗™ The paper used in this publication meets the minimum requirements of American
National Standard for Information Sciences—Permanence of Paper for Printed Library
Materials, ANSI/NISO Z39.48-1992.

Contents

Acknowledgments

This book is the product of years spent in the intellectually vibrant environment of Harvard University. I cannot possibly articulate the vast number of ways I benefited from my time at Harvard, but I must acknowledge several individuals. Stanley Hoffmann introduced me to French political thought, encouraged me to undertake this project, and provided much needed support. I am also indebted to Richard Tuck and Peter Berkowitz, who supplied helpful criticism and encouragement. On a less personal level, I am grateful for two Andrew W. Mellon fellowships, which afforded me the time to complete the manuscript.

I have benefited from the advice of Harvey Mansfield, Seyla Benhabib, and Pratap Mehta and from the various seminars and colloquia that these individuals organized. I wish also to thank friends and colleagues like Chad Noyes, Benjamin Berger, Andrew Sabl, Patchen Markell, Jennifer Pitts, Peter Cannavò, Sankar Muthu, Arash Abizadeh, Michaele Ferguson, Chris Brooke, and all of the members of the political theory workshop in the Government Department at Harvard.

Patrick Riley gave me faith in my enterprise, by way of his work and camaraderie, and by linking me in spirit to Judith Shklar, whose work on Rousseau redoubled by affection for him. Many thanks also to Sanford Lakoff, who read the manuscript with careful attention and provided nuanced comments and criticisms.

I am indebted to Mary Carpenter of Rowman & Littlefield, whose enthusiasm for this project has helped sustain it, and to Rose Marye Boudreaux, whose copyediting produced a much improved manuscript.

For the past decade, I have been inspired by ongoing, spirited conversations with Geoff Berman, Colin Starger, and John Chalcraft and by the love and affection of my wife, Nicole Nourmand.

The book is dedicated to my parents, who have been tolerant, supportive, and loving at all the right times.

Chapter 1

The State of Citizenship in Contemporary Democratic Theory

We have Physicists, Geometricians, Chemists, Astronomers, Poets, Musicians, Painters: we no longer have citizens.

—Jean-Jacques Rousseau, *First Discourse*

When Rousseau proclaims citizens extinct, he does not mean to suggest the demise of people who call themselves citizens or even people who might properly (though conventionally) be called citizens. Rather, he pronounces the extinction of citizens worthy of the name, the extinction of citizens who do more than simply inhabit or retain a status. The U.S. Census Bureau has determined that 2,500 inhabitants make a city. For Rousseau, a specified number of inhabitants might make Phoenix, Arizona, or Laredo, Texas, but a city worthy of the name must have more than inhabitants with the status of citizenship. Its inhabitants must practice citizenship.

This book constructs a revitalized conception of citizenship, with connotations beyond plain membership or status. First, it makes a theoretical claim about the proper framework for theorizing citizenship. This claim lays the foundation for a normative defense of republican citizenship, but it also bears on liberal conceptions of citizenship, republicanism's chief rival. Indeed, the model of citizenship outlined in this work places burdens on any account of citizenship, whether it be liberal, republican, libertarian, or other.[1] Chapters 2 through 8 construct a picture of republican citizenship, grounded in the general will. In this introduction, I take up the more basic, theoretical problem of outlining a framework for theorizing citizenship.

What does it mean to say "the general will is citizenship," as I do in the title of this work?[2] By claiming the general will is citizenship, I mean to suggest that one can come to possess a robust framework for thinking about citizenship if one can come to terms with the meaning of the general will in eighteenth- and nineteenth-century French political thought. Jean-Jacques Rousseau, for whom the general

1

will was the central political concept, defined it variously as the will of the individual qua citizen (as opposed to the will of the individual qua man), as the common good, and, frequently, he defined the general will by what it is not—in opposition to private will or the will of all.[3] All of these definitions are accurate, but none capture what I take to be the essence of the general will—namely, the way it embodies the tension between what I will call "popular will" and "rational will." Rousseau tries to combine or reconcile popular and rational will in his grand idea of the general will, which incorporates commitments to both voluntarism and virtue, to both individual autonomy and the rationalization of will. Rather than think of the general will as a specific concept or formula for legitimacy, I interpret it as a way of thinking about a tension that I take to be intrinsic to egalitarian politics—the tension between popular will and rational will. I do not insist that Rousseau intended the general will to be understood in this manner, nor do I claim that it is the only way of understanding it. I do claim, however, that it is the best way of understanding the general will, if one hopes either to fully appreciate the force of Rousseau's political theory or to develop a defensible framework for theorizing citizenship.

Rousseau, of course, claimed that the general will did far more than simply capture the tension between popular will and rational will. He believed that the general will resolved that tension. His most famous claim to that effect comes in Book II, chapter iii of *The Social Contract* where he distinguishes between the general will and the will of all.

> There is often a great difference between the will of all and the general will. The latter considers only the common interest; the former considers private interest, and is only a sum of private wills.[4]

This argument has baffled Rousseau's interpreters, none of whom have successfully drawn a definitive distinction between the general will and the will of all. I believe that the distinction fails in *The Social Contract*, as it does in all attempts to transcend the tension between popular will and rational will.[5] Democratic societies value both autonomy and rationality, but they can never close entirely the gap between the two. They require abstract principles of justice and legitimacy, with which they can never feel entirely secure. If popular sovereignty is to be truly respected as the only legitimate political authority, the authority of formal or procedural constraints on popular will must always be tenuous. Yet, popular will must be constrained or rationalized in some fashion if ochlocracy is to be avoided. The general will aspires to a synthesis of rational will and popular will but never gets there, settling instead for a state of perpetual striving, and this activity—this striving for a reconciliation of popular will and rational will—is the essence of what I will call citizenship. Citizenship, on this account, emerges from the inexorable political dialectic between popular will and rational will. The practice of citizenship combines popular assertions of authority with the attempt to

cultivate a collective identity and a shared set of principles, intended to generalize or rationalize popular will.[6] This dialectic between popular will and rational
will is also what I take to be the essence of the general will in French political
thought—which accounts for the claim that the general will is citizenship.

From a theoretical standpoint, the question of the tension between popular will
and rational will can be approached on a couple of levels. Philosophers have long
argued over the sources of authority for truth claims. To put the complicated matter bluntly, some have retained an account of universal reason, open to all those
who will consult it, regardless of place and time. Others have argued for the contextualizing of truth claims, describing them as reflective of a particular social
consensus, and, therefore, subject to revision.[7] This is, for the most part, not the
level at which I address the tension between popular will and rational will.
Rather, I claim that, regardless of one's epistemology, students of politics must
confront the political problem of the perpetual gap between popular will and rational will, the gap between what citizens ought to will and what they actually
will. They must confront the simple political fact that they may find the results of
popular decision making abhorrent, judged by their standards for legitimacy
and/or justice. Whatever the set of rights and duties one lays out, whatever the deliberative procedures one outlines, there will always be the possibility that actual
expressions of popular will might challenge basic tenets of justice and legitimacy.[8] Consequently, egalitarian societies will always balance popular will and
rational will, striving to respect popular decision making while searching for
ways to ensure its rationality. Committed to both a respect for popular will and to
certain limitations on it, egalitarian societies can never totally reconcile popular
will and rational will.

This tension, which I take to be intrinsic to all egalitarian politics, places certain burdens on attempts to theorize citizenship. If crucial issues are left open to
popular decision making, outcomes might be irrational. On the other hand, if constraints are placed on popular decision making, there will be costs to popular sovereignty. Neither will it be possible resolve the problem through the imposition of
"democratic" constraints on popular decision making, for that maneuver presumes that the epistemological dispute over truth claims has been resolved.[9] That
is, it assumes that certain truths can be discerned independent of the consensus
that emerges in any given society. Unconvinced by objective claims to universal
truth, we might be tempted to resort to contextualizing truth claims. However, if
our concerns are political, it quickly becomes clear that this theoretical move is
no more defensible than the appeal to transcendent, universal truths. William Galston illustrates the problem:

> When we are faced with evils like Hitlerism, Stalinism and apartheid, it is not enough
> to say that these practices violate *our* shared understandings; systematic public evils
> challenge the very validity of our principles, which therefore require a defense that
> transcends interpretation.[10]

In a postmetaphysical age, pre-political claims to truth become increasingly less convincing, and popular will becomes the only legitimate arbiter of validity claims. Democracy becomes synonymous with politics. As Michael Walzer puts it, "Democracy is . . . *the political way* of allocating power; every extrinsic reason is ruled out." [11] However, as Galston's words illustrate, this conception of politics concedes too much to the potentially despotic vagaries of popular will. Neither need we think only of Adolf Hitler, Joseph Stalin, and apartheid. We take similar stands with respect to (at least some of) the rights protected in the Bill of Rights. We want to argue that there are certain limitations on what any democratic majority can legitimately decide. These limitations may emerge from a shared understanding, but they must be grounded in something higher if they are to trump future shared understandings, as they are intended to do. Egalitarian societies are caught in a predicament: they require a set of abstract principles, with which they can never feel totally secure. Neither appeals to the sovereignty of popular will nor to rational restrictions on it resolve the tension that is at the heart of egalitarian politics. Political theorists must learn to thrive within the tension between popular will and rational will, while looking skeptically on claims to have resolved it.

Throughout this work, I will be occupying the space between these two concepts—between popular will and rational will. I recognize that the very mention of "rational will" raises many eyebrows, as it should, since the idea joins a concept with connotations of unchanging, noncontingent universality (the rational) to a concept that is subject to whimsy or arbitrariness (will). This book attempts to come to terms with the centrality of this paradox for democratic societies. I seek to show, through explorations in French political thought, how the notion of a rational will is simultaneously discomforting and indispensable. Though one rarely encounters theoretical opposition to the abstract notion of popular sovereignty, in practice, liberal democracies always restrict popular will in the name of something like rationality. Indeed, the core of the contemporary debate between liberals and republicans revolves around the restrictions placed upon popular will.[12] As Galston puts it, "Liberals are willing to restrict democratic authority in order to reduce the risk of democratic tyranny." For the republican, on the other hand, "the reverse is true: he is willing to risk democratic tyranny to avoid restricting democratic authority."[13] However, both liberals and republicans sit somewhere between unmediated democratic authority and the ostensibly rational restrictions placed upon it. That is, they both sit somewhere between rational will and popular will, which means that they both leave something to the discretion of citizens (though republicans obviously leave more than liberals). Neither can afford to neglect this space in which lies the practice of citizenship. Obviously, one must become increasingly concerned with the activity of citizens, the more discretion one assigns to democratic authority. Nonetheless, as liberals have come to understand, a strict insistence on limited government and formal rights does not absolve one of the responsibility for thinking about citizenship.[14]

In the remainder of this introduction, I offer an account of the centrality of citizenship to egalitarian politics (section I). I then describe the shortcomings of the manner in which currently popular schools of political theory approach the tension between popular will and rational will (section II), and, finally, I argue that a concern for the practice of citizenship must play a role in any convincing attempt to address the tension between popular will and rational will (section III).

I. A REVIVED CITIZENSHIP

Recently, there have been a number of calls from the left for a revival of citizenship, such that one political theorist has pronounced a "new gospel of citizenship."[15] In the past, the left has generally viewed formal rights and proceduralism as allies. Repulsed by the moralism of conservatives and radical leftist plans for the creation of the "new man," postwar leftists have often shied away from offering an account of the character of citizens. Of late, however, it has become clear that leftists need to pay attention to this issue. Having realized the costs involved in ceding this terrain to the Right, some on the Left have turned to a revitalized conception of citizenship as a way of setting foot on it. Citizenship appeals to leftists because it incorporates the goals of inclusion and social justice while offering a locus of unity in otherwise diverse societies.

Chantal Mouffe writes that citizenship "might provide the rallying cry of all democratic forces in the attempt to defeat neo-liberalism." However, she continues, "the question we need to ask is: 'What kind of citizen?'"[16] This book offers an answer to Mouffe's question by following the path of the general will through eighteenth- and nineteenth-century French political thought. One conceptual difficulty of focusing on citizenship is that the idea itself is so broad that it might be understood to encompass any issue in political philosophy. I have attempted to describe citizenship via the general will, which is to say via the process of striving for a reconciliation of rational will and popular will. However, it is helpful to situate this account of citizenship within the more traditional definitions of it.

The starting point for most contemporary discussions of citizenship is T. H. Marshall's 1950 essay, "Citizenship and Social Class," which divides citizenship into three parts: civil, political, and social.

> The civil element is composed of the rights necessary for individual freedom—liberty of the person, freedom of speech, thought and faith, the right to own property and to conclude valid contracts and the right to justice. . . . By the political element I mean the right to participate in the exercise of political power, as a member of a body invested with political authority or as an elector of the members of such a body. By the social element I mean the whole range from the right to a modicum of economic welfare and security to the right to share to the full in the social heritage and to live the life of a civilised being according to the standards prevailing in the society.[17]

For Marshall and those who have embraced a model of citizenship along these lines, citizenship is a status, as opposed to a practice. This understanding of citizenship contains neither an account of a practice, nor of a state of mind, nor of a sense of attachment. It includes a network of rights, the accompanying duty of respect, and possibly some social entitlements. It excludes the Aristotelian notion of citizenship as ruling and being ruled in turn, as well as the Rousseauean notion of citizenship as identification with a community and dedication to the common good.

In contemporary discourse, there is sometimes a conflation of citizenship as legal status and citizenship as a practice, but we can profit from distinguishing clearly between the two. Citizenship as status is a formal category, lacking substantive connotation, while citizenship as a practice requires some normative account of motivation, identification, and participation.

This being the case, calls to a revival of citizenship as a practice face the daunting challenge of accommodating the substantial pluralism that now characterizes most liberal democracies. On the one hand, it might be argued that the need for a locus of unity grows as societies become increasingly diverse. On the other hand, the fact of pluralism is often portrayed as an insurmountable barrier to the cultivation of a shared identity. Pluralism simultaneously intensifies the imperative to find new sources of social cohesion and undermines the possibility of doing so. Consequently, Eammon Callan asks, "How can we honour both the commitment to a shared political morality and the accommodation of pluralism that is commonly in tension with that morality?"[18] As we shall see in the ensuing chapters, this is the question for which Rousseau believed the general will to be an answer. We need not go as far as Rousseau went, or even as far as contemporary communitarians might go, in cultivating a shared morality. Nonetheless, I shall argue that modern democracies do need to be able to speak of a political community if they aspire to the goals of inclusion, social justice, and self-government.

It is often said, following Benjamin Constant, that republican citizenship, along the lines captured by Rousseau's general will, has been vanquished, vanquished not so much by a superior alternative as by the empirical reality of social differentiation and political pluralism. Consequently, pluralists have been at pains to articulate an account of the practice of citizenship. Even Michael Walzer, a pluralist with a keen interest in reviving citizenship, expresses pessimism: "We are, I think, more civil and less civically virtuous than Americans once were. The new balance is a liberal one and there can be little doubt that it fits the scale and complexity of modern society and the forms of economic organization developed in the United States in the twentieth century."[19] Any conception of citizenship as a practice, that is, any conception beyond citizenship as status, bumps up against other political ideas—community, the common good, the common interest, and so on—ideas which in and of themselves have come to sound increasingly implausible.[20] Pluralists call these ideas monism, which they define as the notion that there could be a value that always takes precedence over other values.[21]

Republicans have a response here, and it has been well articulated by Walzer, Callan, Richard Dagger, Jean Elshtain, Benjamin Barber, and others.[22] First of all, the fact of pluralism need not become hegemonic. In other words, while pluralism places significant constraints on the kind of social unity that can be cultivated consistent with a respect for difference, it does not rule out the possibility that individuals might come to assign value to their shared role and identity as citizens. Second, even if pluralism always undermines attempts to articulate a common identity, polities may find that their goals cannot be accomplished in its absence. The claim here (which I will develop throughout the book) would be that societies must cultivate citizenship even if the goal of unity can never be fully attained, for it is through the pursuit of a shared identity that democracies attain the goals of inclusion, social justice, and self-rule.[23]

If pluralists fail to prove the obsolescence of active citizenship, they succeed in demonstrating the need for a chastened citizenship. Rousseau's ideal of the total subordination of private will to the general will cannot be sustained in large, differentiated, modern societies. As we shall see in the ensuing chapters, Rousseau himself evinced awareness of this problem. Citizenship cannot mean that one always thinks as a citizen; rather it must make the more modest demand that one give priority to one's identity as citizen some of the time. Just as pluralism need not become hegemonic, so too of citizenship. Citizenship or the general will is one imperative, but it ought not be the only one, particularly in today's liberal democracies, where private life offers more and more opportunities for fulfillment. Citizenship is one aspect of our identity but it can no longer be the only one, and it probably never could have been, despite Rousseau's assertions to the contrary. No, the practice of citizenship, if it is to flourish in the twenty-first century, must find a way of meeting Callan's challenge. That is, it must honor the commitment to a shared political morality while accommodating the pluralism that is commonly in tension with that morality.

II. THE TENSION BETWEEN POPULAR WILL AND RATIONAL WILL, OR WHAT POLITICAL THEORISTS WOULD LIKE TO DO BUT CAN'T

The French idea of the general will profoundly captures the tension between popular will and rational will, a tension that is intrinsic to egalitarian politics. Formal rights and institutions can effectively address this tension, but only a concern for the character of citizens can approach a reconciliation of it. In this section, I consider two schools of political thought that attempt to close the gap between popular will and rational will with arguments that do not depend on an account of citizenship. First, I examine Rawlsian liberalism or political liberalism,[24] and then I apply a similar critique to Habermasian discourse ethics and its Anglo-American offspring, deliberative democracy. I acknowledge the pitfalls involved in addressing these well-developed, internally diverse, sophisticated schools of politi-

cal thought in this very general way. The best defense I can give for doing so will
have to be the plausibility of the argument I develop. At this point, I will note that,
viewed from the perspective of citizenship, political liberalism and deliberative
democracy seem more similar than different. While political liberals and deliberative democrats differ over the proper constraints on popular decision making and
over the space in which it takes place, both focus almost exclusively on procedures and institutions while paying far less attention to the character of citizens.
[25] In this section, I show how, despite their ambitions, these schools of political
thought fail to reconcile popular will and rational will. Moreover, all formal or
procedural accounts of the tension between popular will and rational will must inevitably succumb to a similar critique. The choice must be made, either to live
with this problem, or to address it by attending to the challenge of reconciling individual and collective interests—the challenge of cultivating civic virtue without undermining personal liberty.

Political Liberalism

Both John Rawls and Jürgen Habermas construct systems of constraints and conditions, intended to ensure the rationality of democratic decision making, while
respecting the autonomy of each citizen.[26] For Rawls, political discourse must be
"reasonable," whereas Habermas avoids placing constraints on the substance of
political discourse, focusing instead on the fairness of the *process* by which decisions are made. Each understands his own views as more modest than the other's,
Habermas because his position is purely procedural, and Rawls because his theory constrains discourse in a much smaller sphere of political life than Habermas's.[27] Nonetheless, both attempt to respect popular will and individual autonomy while placing constraints on discourse. Habermas cedes authority to the
democratic process that Rawls wants to constrain. Despite this important difference, both Habermas and Rawls aspire to a reconciliation of popular will and rational will, and both fall short for similar reasons.

   Rawls insists that liberalism be "political," which means that it should not concern itself with "which moral judgments are true."[28] It should restrict itself to two
specifically political questions. First, "what is the most appropriate conception of
justice for specifying the fair terms of social cooperation between citizens regarded as free and equal, and as fully cooperating members of society over a
complete life, from one generation to the next?" Second, "what are the grounds
of toleration so understood and given the fact of reasonable pluralism as the inevitable outcome of free institutions?"[29] By calling his liberalism political, Rawls
asserts that the answers to these questions can be formulated without recourse to
metaphysics or what Rawls calls "comprehensive doctrines." In other words,
Rawls believes that the only acceptable principles of justice will be those that can
be settled on by all citizens, regardless of their personal comprehensive doctrine.
Liberals must not invoke a comprehensive conception of what is of value in

human life or ideals of personal virtue and character. They must affirm basic rights and liberties, but they must do so in a way that does not presume the falsity or validity of any particular comprehensive doctrine. Rawls often describes this principle as the priority of the right over the good.[30]

Only through a political conception of justice, one that prioritizes the right over the good, can citizens expect to find a set of principles that they can all accept.[31] In this manner, societies can build an "overlapping consensus," an agreement on basic principles of justice, which we might also call a reconciliation of popular will and rational will. However, Rawls acknowledges, indeed Rawls makes central to his argument, a condition for achieving this kind of consensus—citizens must be "reasonable." Rawls finds the essential force of his argument in this idea; it is the "reasonable" that gives Rawls his leverage on the problem of reconciling popular will and rational will.

Rawls defines the reasonable as "the willingness to propose and abide by fair terms of social cooperation among equals" and "the recognition of and willingness to accept the consequences of the burdens of judgment."[32] He distinguishes the reasonable from the rational, which "applies to a single, unified agent with the powers of judgment and deliberation in seeking ends and interests peculiarly its own."[33] Rational agents are simple utility maximizers or ends-seekers. They lack the underlying sensibility that causes individuals to "engage in fair cooperation as such, and to do so on terms that others as equals might reasonably be expected to endorse."[34] The rational and the reasonable constitute independent faculties for Rawls, such that there is no sense in which one can be derived from the other.

The classification of human beings as rational ends-seekers has a certain plausibility, and, regardless of its limitations as a general description of human motivations and actions, it seems to describe at least some portion of human behavior. The notion of human beings as reasonable, in the Rawlsian sense, is more problematic.[35] While some, even many, individuals may be largely motivated by a desire to engage in fair cooperation under the burdens of judgment, many others are not. If this is the case, a fact-value gap opens up between what I have called popular will and rational will. Indeed, Rawls has been widely criticized for "smuggling in some *ex ante* limitations on the process of public deliberation,"[36] as one critic puts it. Rawls's definition of the reasonable excludes the sincere and the devout; it dismisses potential disagreement on fundamental questions of justice by presuming that all people share a set of principles.[37] Rawls does not seek broad-based agreement; indeed he hopes only to "narrow the range of disagreement,"[38] but he seeks agreement nonetheless. My interest lies not in disputing the set of issues around which Rawls seeks agreement; rather, I wish only to show how this kind of agreement cannot be assumed. Despite Rawls's narrowing of the field of inquiry, the gap between popular will and rational will persists. Agreement, even of Rawls's modest kind, can only be cultivated through an emphasis on citizenship—through a concern for the character and values of citizens.

Rawls expects citizens to argue reasonably when they are discussing constitutional essentials.[39] If they do, Rawls believes that the liberal principles of justice "tend to shift citizens' comprehensive doctrines so that they at least accept the principles of a liberal constitution."[40] But what is to say that citizens will argue reasonably? Thomas Nagel concedes that this question depends on motivational psychology, an account of which neither he nor Rawls is willing to offer.[41] Brian Barry concedes that his liberal theory of justice is contentious, which is to say that some people will not like it.[42] Ronald Dworkin understands that he cannot expect his account of liberalism to be accepted, so he must settle for the weaker claim that it could be accepted.[43] If we take these theorists of liberalism at their word, we may begin to wonder about the conditions under which their principles actually could, or even would, be accepted. This should cause us to think about citizenship. Whatever one's principles of political right, of justice and legitimacy, one will have to address the gap between those principles themselves and the willingness of citizens to support and uphold them. This gap between popular will and rational will can only be addressed by attending to citizenship.

Deliberative Democracy

Like political liberalism, deliberative democracy seeks a theoretical reconciliation of popular will and rational will. It wants to simultaneously honor expressions of popular will and maximize the chances of rational outcomes. Moreover, it believes that the measures taken to rationalize will need not coerce or marginalize popular will. For this to be the case, all participants in deliberation need not *actually* affirm the deliberative procedures, but it must at least be *possible* for them to affirm these procedures (without jettisoning their essential worldviews). In this section, I contend that deliberative democrats advance a partial set of constraints on popular decision making, to which not all actors will be able to agree. This should not count as an argument against deliberative democracy; rather it shows deliberative democracy's limitations—its inability to reconcile popular will and rational will on a purely theoretical level. To foreshadow the argument of section III, we might distinguish between *theoretical* attempts to reconcile rational will and popular will (political liberalism and deliberative democracy) and *practical* strategies of reconciliation (citizenship). Neither approach reaches the ideal of total reconciliation, but citizenship comes up short for practical reasons and not as a result of a theoretical shortcoming.

Of course, deliberative democrats would dispute this charge, though they typically agree that political liberalism succumbs to it. Like so many others, they accuse Rawls of not so surreptitiously incorporating a substantive conception of the good into his doctrine of the reasonable. Deliberative democrats argue that Rawls ascribes to citizens a set of preferences and characteristics that arise only contingently, if they do at all, through the process of democratic will formation.[44] These constraints on deliberation illegitimately presume a "higher-ranking moral law," as Habermas puts it.[45] "Democratic procedure forms the only postmetaphysical source of legitimacy."[46] Despite their emphasis on public deliberation and their repudiation of any authority emanating from outside that deliberation, deliberative democrats in no way eschew the project of reconciling rational will and popular will. Indeed, Habermas claims to have an account of "the legitimating force of a discursive process of opinion- and will-formation, in which the illocutionary binding forces of a use of language oriented to mutual understanding serve to bring reason and will together—and lead to convincing positions to which all individuals can agree without coercion."[47] Habermas hopes to generate rational outcomes while minimizing the constraints on deliberation. He "can leave more questions open [than Rawls can] because he entrusts more to the *process* of rational opinion and will formation."[48] Liberals rightly note that entrusting more to the process of will formation risks a variety of unsavory outcomes. Predictably, debate among deliberative democrats has often revolved around the issue of how these outcomes might be avoided. Constraints on deliberation might be the only way to restrict tyrannical majorities, but embracing these constraints seems to undermine the animating force of deliberative democracy, which has always insisted that democratic deliberation forms the only source of authority. Moreover, accepting constraints on deliberation leaves the deliberative democrat vulnerable to the kind of critique they themselves deploy against political liberalism. There will be no way out of this bind, just as there was no way out of it for political liberalism. Deliberative democrats ultimately constrain popular will in ways of their own, ways which resemble Rawls's use of the "reasonable."

Deliberative democrats share Rawls's constructivist method, asking, much as he did, "what we can all agree to if we engage in a mutual search for justification."[49] By contextualizing truth claims, the deliberative democrat believes that the cognitive model of truth might be salvaged.[50] In this manner a far-reaching moral principle such as Kant's categorical imperative can be reformulated to include not what can be willed as a universal law, but what can be willed in agreement.[51] In addition to relaxing the standards for truth claims, deliberative democrats are modest about the depth of consensus they pursue. They seek agreement on procedures alone, out of a recognition of the limited possibilities for consensus in large, differentiated societies.[52] The basic principles for which deliberative democrats seek consensus are embodied in Habermas's principle D, which stipulates that "only those norms can claim to be valid that meet (or could meet) with the approval of all affected."[53] From this principle, Habermas generates criteria for judging the legitimacy of deliberation: among other things, there must be a symmetrical distribution of chances to speak, all participants must have the right to question the assigned topics of conversation, and, perhaps most significantly, discourses "require a form of communication that allows only the rationally-motivated force of the better argument to persist."[54]

Whereas Rawls applies the principles of public reason to a relatively limited sphere of interaction, deliberative democrats apply their principles to the entirety of what they call the "public sphere," which includes schools, churches, the media, and the variety of civic associations that pervade civil society. They see in this sphere of political life a forum for the exchange of views and, most importantly, for the development and transformation of preferences.[55] Deliberative democrats fault most of contemporary political theory for proceeding from "the methodological fiction of an individual with an ordered set of coherent preferences."[56] For them, it is vitally important to remember that individuals form and transform their preferences through the deliberative process. Both Kant's (and in some sense Rawls's) moralism and Rousseau's civic republicanism throttle deliberation by imposing extra-deliberative sources of authority. Kant's universal maxims and Rousseau's civil religion constrain the options available to deliberating agents in a manner offensive to the deliberative democrat's sensibilities. They hope to find a basis for agreement without appeals to foundational knowledge that could dictate which worldviews are correct.

Rawls sought something similar but ceded less to the open-ended process of will formation. By locating the sphere of deliberation in the public sphere as a whole and encouraging the introduction of all kinds of opinions, deliberative democrats believe they have articulated a theory of democracy that truly respects popular will. However, they also lean heavily on some assumptions about the rationality of popular will. By locating the process of will formation in the whole of the public sphere, they open themselves up to potentially illiberal outcomes. Some argue that reasoned decision making is actually quite unlikely to be found in the associations that make up the public sphere, which tend to be, and are often intended to be, partial advocates for the interests of a particular group.[57] Moreover, deliberative democracy's refusal to constrain deliberation further exposes it to unpleasant outcomes. Nor can this problem be remedied through the application of ground rules for deliberation, for they undermine the respect that deliberative democracy wants to pay to popular will.

I do not wish to challenge the normative appeal of deliberative democracy — or of political liberalism, for that matter. I wish only to show why neither overcomes the tension between popular will and rational will. Deliberative democrats make several claims about the ways in which their theories reconcile popular will and rational will but, ultimately, none of them succeed. They argue that individuals form preferences through the process of deliberation, which may go some way toward diffusing the tension between popular will and rational will but, as we have seen, it in no way assures that the outcomes of deliberation will be salutary.

As a reaction to this problem, deliberative democrats introduce the idea of democratic constraints on deliberation, which, they argue, rationalize deliberation without cost to democracy. So, for example, Amy Gutmann and Dennis Thompson argue that "extreme nondeliberative steps may be justified as necessary steps to deliberation."[58] The problem with this argument is that it rests on an elision between a particular view of deliberative democracy and a decision made by means of deliberative democracy.[59] It occludes the deliberative process itself with constraints that are justified in the name of deliberation. Even if constraints on deliberation ultimately improve it, it is to claim that this improvement comes without cost to the process of deliberation. We may agree with Gutmann and Thompson that "deliberation does not have priority over liberty and opportunity,"[60] but we ought not pretend that prioritizing a conception of these values—even when doing so improves the outcomes of deliberation—in no way undermines the process of democratic deliberation itself. In fact these constraints on deliberation force deliberative democrats into a tautology. If the democratic sovereign is the only legitimate political authority, by what authority may constraints be placed on their deliberation?

This paradox confronts all egalitarian political theory. Rousseau makes it the starting point of his political thought, which is what I find most appealing about his republicanism. But this is jumping ahead. I want to say something more about the way the tension between rational will and popular will plays out in deliberative democracy. Some deliberative democrats may resist Gutmann and Thompson's defense of significant, substantive restraints on deliberation. Habermas, for example, has a much leaner criterion for legitimate deliberation, captured by the "discourse principle" (D). For Habermas, D provides the justification both for popular sovereignty and for a collection of rights, which follow, on his account, "simply from the application of the discourse principle to the medium of law."[61] The discourse principle, it in turns out, implies a whole "system of rights," including individual liberties, rights of association, legal protection, rights to political participation, and even the provision of a respectable standard of living.[62] In other words, the same principle that yields respect for popular will also produces a variety of rational constraints on it.

This, I believe, assigns too much power to D. For Habermas, D follows naturally from the structures of argumentation themselves and is implicit in any discourse. This allows him to build constraints on popular will into his definition of democracy. However, in so doing, he, like Gutmann and Thompson, occludes the distinction between a particular decision about democracy and the process of arriving at a decision democratically. His account of democracy becomes substantive as opposed to purely procedural (which is, incidentally, not an indictment of it in and of itself). One could think of a variety of reasons to honor popular will that need not necessitate an acceptance of D or the system of rights that follows from it—any interest-based argument for democracy would fit the bill.

To make the matter more concrete, we might note that many citizens may find the discourse principle itself controversial, and many others are certain to question the notion that it implies the system of rights Habermas outlines. Indeed, Habermas recognizes that the acceptance of D depends on the general acceptance of the idea of impartiality. His claim, however, is that "the idea of impartiality is rooted in the structures of argumentation themselves and does not need to be brought in from the outside."[63] There may be something to this claim, but it is problematic in that it rests on the assumption that all citizens identify with Habermas's "structures of argumentation." Many citizens choose dogma over deliberation. The only way to address this issue, to move people away from dogmatism and toward deliberation, is to think about the character of citizens.

Seyla Benhabib acknowledges the problem deliberative democrats face: "either the ideal communication is defined so narrowly as to be meaningless or broadly which involves controversial substantive premises."[64] Deliberative democrats criticize Rawls for overdetermining the outcomes of will formation, which inclines them toward leaving things undetermined. However, they soon recognize the dangers of this approach and pursue some combination of the substantive and the procedural. This remains unsatisfying however, because, for every concession that is made to substantive outcomes there is a cost to procedure, and vice versa. For the most part, political liberalism and deliberative democracy try to wriggle out of this dilemma without resorting to an account of the character of citizens. They pursue a theoretical reconciliation of rational will and popular will and throw their hands in the air when it comes to the cultivation of citizens who actually subscribe to the principles they advocate. Once it becomes clear that the tension between rational will and popular will is intrinsic to egalitarian politics, we may wish to abandon the notion that it can ever be overcome, and look toward the possible ways in which it might be mitigated through an emphasis on citizenship. Rather than pursue a theoretical reconciliation of the tension and ignore the available practical possibilities, we ought to concede the intractability of the theoretical conflict and think about the pragmatic strategies available for addressing it.

III. ADDRESSING THE TENSION BETWEEN POPULAR WILL AND RATIONAL WILL, OR WHAT POLITICAL THEORISTS OUGHT TO DO BUT WON'T

In section II, we saw how political theorists fall short in their efforts to reconcile the tension between popular will and rational will. Here, the case will be made that political theorists ought to turn their attention to the practice of citizenship and the character of citizens. Political theory has historically endeavored to answer two questions: what is justice, and how can the principles of justice be put into practice? Those inclined toward political philosophy will distinguish between, say, principles of political right[65] and the conditions for putting those principles into practice. Those with a more social-scientific orientation may systematize these issues into the categories of "political institutions" and "political culture." In either case, both questions remain present and pressing, and political theorists need to keep both questions in mind.

Nevertheless, as we have seen, a substantial portion of contemporary political theory eschews the second question, opting to concentrate all of its attention on the first. Here, I refer to my discussions of political liberalism and deliberative democracy, which have been justly criticized for focusing almost exclusively on the criteria and procedures of political legitimacy, while paying scant attention to the circumstances, norms, values, and virtues that contribute to the flourishing of their principles.

Having said this much, I should note that there have been attempts to fill this gap. There are friendly critics of liberalism who have attempted to recuperate a teaching of virtue, present, they claim, in the liberal tradition.[66] There are perfectionist liberals who endorse the political cultivation of a particular type of individualism and autonomy.[67] There are political and social conservatives who bemoan the lack of attention liberal societies pay to cultural questions, and there are the communitarians, who emphasize culture, custom, and virtue as critical components of both the principles of political right and of the conditions for putting those principles into practice. This dual concern for both principles of political right and for the conditions under which they flourish is also characteristic of each of the thinkers under consideration in this book. Indeed, the French idea of the general will is appealing as a model of citizenship precisely because it encompasses issues of political culture or identity, as well the principles of political right.

In this introduction, I have not disagreed with the substance of the arguments offered by either political liberals or deliberative democrats. I have not disagreed with their arguments so much as characterized them as contentious doctrines that must be actively defended or propped up through a focus on the character of citizens. As Galston notes, "very few individuals will come to embrace the core commitments of liberal society through a process of rational inquiry."[68] The schools of thought I have considered here limit themselves to an account of the principles of political right and, for the most part (exceptions are noted below), they resist excursions into questions of citizenship. Political theorists constantly accuse each other of utopianism, a charge frequently applied to those in favor of a revival of citizenship. However, partisans of citizenship ought to throw the charge right back and ask how citizens can be expected to adhere to liberal and/or democratic principles if societies fail to cultivate the appropriate set of norms and virtues.

In fairness, both liberals and deliberative democrats have acknowledged this point and have begun to address what I have called citizenship. Both are reluctant to do so, and for good reason, since a collective concern for the character of citizens poses obvious risks to individual autonomy. Ultimately, however, in democratic societies, the sovereign people will act as the ultimate source of authority. No externally conceived procedural constraint on popular will can eliminate the risk posed by a tyrannical majority. Consequently, no political theory can afford to ignore the question of citizenship.

An Alternate Liberalism

Contemporary liberals have generally shied away from the question of citizenship, leaning on the Lockean doctrine that the care of souls is not the task of the state. However, in spite of this basic doctrine, some liberals have come to accept the necessity of cultivating the conditions necessary to the flourishing of liberal regimes. As Ronald Terchek and Peter Berkowitz have shown, this revived concern for the character of citizens is as much a recovery as it is a revival.[69] Terchek has found in some of the canonical works of liberalism what he calls "anxious" liberalism, which emphasizes the virtues requisite to a flourishing liberal society. Likewise, Berkowitz has illustrated the centrality of virtue to the liberalism of Thomas Hobbes, John Locke, Immanuel Kant, and John Stuart Mill. Even Rawls acknowledges the need to cultivate a certain set of virtues in the citizenry—"the duty to listen to others and a fairmindedness in deciding when to accommodate."[70]

For liberalism, however, the problem cannot be rectified this simply. Berkowitz explains the dilemma: "liberalism depends on virtues that, according to its own tenets, fall outside its strict supervision and that it cannot always summon and that it might even undermine."[71] Indeed, one of the basic doctrines of liberalism is its reluctance to address questions of character—of the beliefs, values, and virtues of citizens. Liberals have of late come to recognize the ways in which they depend on certain social and cultural conditions. However, this realization has furnished them with no resources to cultivate these conditions.

Once liberals acknowledge the importance of the character of citizens, they have two options. One option would be to acknowledge the importance of a certain set of social and cultural conditions, while insisting that liberalism lacks the resources to cultivate them. This would compel liberals to sit in a potentially unsatisfying but theoretically defensible position. The pathologies characteristic of liberal societies—narcissism, self-absorbed materialism, political disengagement, economic exploitation, factionalism, and so forth—would be judged a price worth paying. Liberals would simply argue that the costs to personal liberty involved in the cultivation of citizens cannot be justified by the progress that could be made toward a reconciliation of popular will and rational will. On the other hand, they may wish to go on the offensive, abandon their preference for neutrality, and actively cultivate a certain set of values, beliefs, and virtues in citizens.[72] This option, I believe, would require them to become republicans, at least to a degree, and they would have to face many of the same objections that republicans face. Indeed, Berkowitz notes that it becomes necessary to distinguish between cultivation and coercion and to determine how a set of virtues might be cultivated consistent with a respect for basic liberty and equality.[73] These are precisely the problems with which republican theorists begin, and liberalism's willingness to engage them shrinks one important disagreement between the two doctrines.[74] Ideally, the account of the general will presented in the ensuing chapters will help these converging camps address the tension between coercion and cultivation, between virtue and voluntarism, or, as I prefer to put it, between popular will and rational will.

Deliberative Democracy and Citizenship

Habermas insists that discourse ethics is a strictly formal or procedural theory.[75] However, it does depend on the deliberation of citizens, and it requires that their deliberation adhere to certain criteria—even that they engage in "ideal role-taking," which requires them to adopt a particular orientation toward conceptions of justice.[76] Some may dispute the centrality of deliberation itself to democratic politics, and the account of the general will presented in this book will do just that. However, for now, I wish to say something more about my internal critique of deliberative democracy and the ways in which deliberative democrats have attempted to respond to it.

Though deliberative democrats have largely abstained from proactively addressing the question of citizenship, they have identified some social and cultural conditions necessary to the flourishing of deliberation. John Dryzek, for example, briefly considers the conditions under which deliberation is fostered.[77] Likewise, Habermas acknowledges that rational morality depends on "convivial socializing processes" and has always understood the threat posed by market-oriented, strategic logic to political discourse in the public sphere.[78] Bohman, for his part, worries about the threat that globalization may pose to democratic deliberation.[79] Simone Chambers deals squarely with the problem, by qualifying her support for more deliberative institutions with the caveat that "all such initiatives will fail to produce a discursively formed public opinion if citizens are unwilling to or uninterested in acting discursively."[80]

Concerns of this sort, though few and far between in the literature, are laudable. Bohman goes so far as to claim that deliberative democracy's concern with feasibility demonstrates that deliberative democracy has "'come of age' as a complete theory of democracy rather than simply an ideal of legitimacy."[81] This kind of triumphalism is premature. Deliberative democracy's concern for feasibility strengthens the theory, but it places it in the same awkward space occupied by liberals who acknowledge the variety of social and cultural preconditions necessary to the flourishing of their principles. Neither school of thought possesses the resources to cultivate the very preconditions they identify as necessary. As Benhabib puts it, "discourse ethics requires the utopian projection of a way of life in which respect and reciprocity reign."[82]

Among deliberative democrats, Amy Gutmann's *Democratic Education* offers the most ambitious attempt to articulate a strategy for securing the social and cultural conditions for the flourishing of democratic deliberation. An examination of her argument illuminates many of the issues raised thus far.

Democratic Education, Gutmann writes, provides an account of citizenship that reinforces the image of citizenship presented in *Democracy and Disagreement*. Whereas *Democracy and Disagreement* focuses on how citizens should deliberate, *Democratic Education* examines the conditions under which citizens are likely to deliberate in *Democracy and Disagreement*'s preferred manner.[83] In the book, Gutmann outlines a set of principles or beliefs, which must be incorporated into the educational process if a deliberative democracy is to flourish. This, however, is not her principal concern; rather she focuses principally on the question of who should have the authority over education in a democracy. Gutmann's analysis is driven by a rigorous, thorough, intellectually honest desire to attend to both of these issues—to both the substance of educational policy and the process by which it is made. She writes,

> A democratic state of education recognizes that educational authority must be shared among parents, citizens, and professional educators even though such sharing does not guarantee that power will be wedded to knowledge.[84]

Acknowledging this point, it seems to me, starts one on the path to republicanism, understood as a doctrine of popular sovereignty and civic virtue. For the republican, virtue is the only democratic insurance against the abuse of authority. Gutmann does not follow this republican trajectory. Instead, she conditions her embrace of democratic control on a set of formal constraints on the exercise of sovereign power.[85]

As she and Thompson do in *Democracy and Disagreement*, Gutmann defends these constraints on democratic decision making in the name of democracy itself. Likewise, we appeal to our previous response. While we must acknowledge that democratic procedures can generate results that are destructive of democracy, Gutmann's argument rests on a elision of the question of who decides with the question of what is decided. We cannot disagree with Gutmann's claim that "citizens and public officials can use democratic procedures to subvert democracy,"[86] but this does not permit us to defend the following contradiction in terms: "Democratic control is worth defending, but not if its results are repressive or discriminatory."[87] To place limits on democratic decision making is to transform it into something else—some hybrid of popular sovereignty and the sovereignty of something else—reason, a set of principles, or something else. Since this added source of sovereignty takes precedence whenever it conflicts with popular will, democracy *tout court* may not the best word to describe this regime.

Gutmann's defense of so-called "democratic" constraints on democracy elides questions of procedure with questions of substance. It is rendered coherent only if our defense of democracy rests on the view that the activity of democratic governance yields desirable outcomes, judged by some external standard. If we understand the principle of popular rule to mean that democratic procedures are the only legitimate method for settling on a set of political principles, Gutmann's conclusion becomes incoherent. In Gutmann's democracy, the people decide, but only so long as they make the right decision. Meanwhile, those who have their will trumped are left to wonder who created the criterion for the right decision. They had assumed their will was sovereign.

Gutmann's attitude to this problem is not cavalier; her book's great virtue lies in the extent to which she struggles with this problem. Her inclinations tend always toward democratic control, and she places restrictions on it extremely reluctantly and cautiously. Nonetheless, she writes "we know the market and pure democracy cannot decide education."[88] Gutmann's democracy is not pure because pure democracy is incapable of constraining democracy in its own name.[89] Her democracy is modified, quite literally, by deliberation. Deliberation constrains democracy—in its own name, of course—such that its decisions will not be discriminatory or repressive. These constraints may well be salutary, but they do not come without cost to the process of democratic decision making.

It is not difficult to think of cases in which we might wish to overturn decisions made by democratic majorities, nor must we struggle to find democratically generated decisions that might subvert democracy itself, for example, the electoral victory of *Le Front Islamique du Salut* in Algeria in 1990. Nevertheless, Gutmann's attempts to limit democracy in its own name fail. Limits on democratic decision making must be generated, or at least authorized, by the sovereign. In democracies, this means constraints on democracy must be authorized by the people—that is, the people must constrain themselves. Unfortunately, they might equally choose to remove these constraints. The trouble with theorizing constraints on sovereign power is that no source of authority exists to authorize those constraints. This is why Plato's ideal required philosophers to assume sovereign control, why Rousseau needed a legislator to ensure the rationality of the general will, and why Locke sanctioned an appeal to heaven when sovereign power became arbitrary. If political power is to be constrained, it must be constrained by something outside of itself—a philosophy, a legislator, the will of God, or what we post-Kantians call reason, rationality or, in Gutmann's case, norms of deliberation. Who will enforce these constraints? Gutmann, it seems clear, realizes that democratic citizens must constrain themselves. This being the case, the competence, integrity, and virtue of citizens are the only guarantees that the democratic sovereign will serve the common good. Gutmann recognizes the importance of the character of citizens—she devotes an entire book to the subject—but she refuses to make the success of democratic societies dependent of the character of their citizens. She opts instead for formal or procedural safeguards on citizen deliberation.

It is at this juncture, I believe, that one ought to consider republicanism's theoretical advantages. We have seen how Gutmann's appeals to democratic constraints on democracy yield a theoretical impasse. Arriving at this impasse is not a problem. Refusing to acknowledge it is. The impasse, I have tried to show, is a product of the noble attempt to honor popular sovereignty and rationalize it. It is an intrinsic part of egalitarian politics. Failing to acknowledge it produces the types of theoretical incoherencies examined in this introduction. Accepting this impasse alerts one to the importance of citizenship in democracies.

CONCLUSION

Most political theorists hesitate to address the question of citizenship, of how civic virtue can be cultivated without betraying formal principles of political right. Their hesitance is commendable, in a sense, for it evinces an awareness of potential risks to personal freedom. Liberals have persuasively argued for a strict separation between the public and the private, out of an understanding of the evils that might be justified through the blurring of that divide. However, there is a cost attached to the refusal to cultivate citizenship, a cost that Rousseau illustrates as well as anyone. In the chapters that follow, I describe Rousseau's account of citizenship, its potential pathologies, and the possibilities for reviving it under modern conditions.

I undertake this project by taking a journey through the history of ideas, one idea in particular—the general will. In every account of the general will explored in this work, we will find a confrontation with both of the fundamental questions of political theory—what are the principles of political right? and how can they be put into practice? I hope to show that the general will overcomes the complacency characteristic of political theory that ignores questions of citizenship in favor of an exclusive focus on the principles of political right. Because it emphasizes the manner in which citizens acquire the habits, norms, and values necessary to support free institutions, the general will contains the resources to confront the tension between popular will and rational will. My aspiration is that the appropriations of, responses to, and reactions against the general will discussed in this book will contribute to a model of citizenship, sensitive both to the need for a shared identity and to the pluralism that characterizes modern societies.

NOTES

1. For an analysis of these different conceptions of citizenship, see David Miller, "Citizenship and Pluralism," *Political Studies* 43, no. 3 (September 1995): 432–50.

2. I borrow this phrase from Stephen Ellenburg, *Rousseau's Political Philosophy: An Interpretation from Within* (Ithica, N.Y.: Cornell University Press, 1976), 107. To say that the general will is citizenship does not, of course, imply that an account of the general will addresses all questions of citizenship. For example, the general will in the context of eighteenth- and nineteenth-century France speaks only indirectly to issues like the naturalization of immigrants, rights of minors, and similar debates over the citizenship status of various members of society. Nonetheless, the general will does provide a general framework from conceptualizing the rights, duties, identity, and education of citizens.

3. See chapters 3 and 4.

4. Jean-Jacques Rousseau, *On the Social Contract with Geneva Manuscript and Political Economy*, ed. Roger D. Masters, trans. Judith R. Masters (New York: St. Martin's, 1978), 61.

5. I make this argument in chapter 3.

6. In contrast to formal or procedural constraints on popular will, republican citizenship tries to rationalize will without formally constraining it. By cultivating a common identity and consensus on basic principles of justice and legitimacy, popular will and rational will might be reconciled without recourse to institutions grounded in an authority higher than the actual deliberation of a democratic body. We must ask, first, if this approach actually respects popular will more than formal or procedural constraints do, and, second, whether

or not the generalization of will ought to be equated with the rationalization of will. Both of these questions shall be evaluated in the ensuing chapters.

7. Countless works could be cited here. For an argument on behalf of the contextual-izing of truth claims, see Richard Rorty's *Philosophy and the Mirror of Nature* (Princeton, N.J.: Princeton University Press, 1979). For the counterclaim, see Thomas Nagel's *The Last Word* (New York: Oxford University Press, 1997), and for an attempt to find a post-metaphysical foundation for truth claims, see Jürgen Habermas's *The Philosophical Dis-course of Modernity* (Cambridge, Mass.: MIT Press, 1987), and *Moral Consciousness and Communicative Action* (Cambridge, Mass.: MIT Press, 1990).

8. Simone Chambers writes, "That historically specific understandings can be justi-fied on non-contingent ahistorical grounds (natural rights theory, neo-Kantianism, and so on) is not a reason why they *will* continue; it is only a reason why they perhaps *ought* to continue." See Simone Chambers, "Discourse and Democratic Practices," in *The Cam-bridge Companion to Habermas*, ed. Steven K. White (New York: Cambridge University Press, 1995), 245.

9. The claim is sometimes made that popular decision making might be justifiably constrained without an appeal to an authority outside of the values, norms, and traditions of a particular society. Proponents of this position envision the possibility of overruling the will of a voting majority through an appeal to something within the culture itself. As I note below, this begs the question as to why established values and norms should trump the newly developed will of an actually existing citizen body. (One can imagine for oneself the scenarios under which progressive decision making would be desirable, by which I mean decision making that violates established values and norms). This position may be an accurate description of the way in which societies actually restrict popular will, but it cannot serve as a justification for restricting popular will for there is no compelling a pri-ori reason to elevate established norms and values over progressive ones.

10. William A. Galston, *Liberal Purposes: Goods, Virtues, and Diversity in the Liberal State* (New York: Cambridge University Press, 1991), 156 (hereafter cited as *Liberal Pur-poses*).

11. Michael Walzer, *Spheres of Justice* (New York: Basic, 1983), 51 (italics in original).

12. The prevalence of various connotations of the terms "liberalism" and "republican-ism" demands that I specify the sense in which I use these terms. Both liberalism and re-publicanism grow out of a belief in the basic liberty and equality of all human beings. I understand liberalism broadly, as the doctrine that sovereign power ought to be limited for the sake of individual liberty. Republicanism, by contrast, I take to be the doctrine that popular participation in governance is a constituent element of political liberty and the best safeguard against the abuse of public power. I take liberalism's chief tenets to be a strict insistence on the distinction between public and private and a repudiation of paternalism. Republicanism, on the other hand, emphasizes self-rule and civic virtue. Note that these characteristics of republicanism and liberalism reflect areas of emphasis and sometimes disagreement, not necessarily antagonism. In other words, liberals may assign some value to self-rule and civic virtue, just as republicans tend to be wary of the dangers of pater-nalism and the politicization of private affairs. The schools of thought are distinguished by the ways in which they balance these values against one another.

13. Galston, *Liberal Purposes*, 54.

14. Galston, *Liberal Purposes*, and Peter Berkowitz, *Virtue and the Making of Modern Liberalism* (Princeton, N.J.: Princeton University Press, 1999).

15. Benjamin R. Barber, preface to *A Passion for Democracy* (Princeton, N.J.: Princeton University Press, 1998), ix. See also *Dimensions of Radical Democracy: Pluralism, Citizenship, Community*, ed. Chantal Mouffe (London: Verso, 1992) (hereafter cited as *Dimensions of Radical Democracy*), and *Theorizing Citizenship*, ed. Ronald Beiner (Albany, N.Y.: SUNY Press, 1995). Robert Bellah asks, "Is it possible that we could become citizens again and together seek the common good in the post-industrial, postmodern age?" See Bellah, *Habits of the Heart: Individualism and Commitment in American Life* (Berkeley: University of California Press, 1985), 271. It should be noted that the newness of this new gospel might be questioned. See for example, Robert Nisbet, *Twilight of Authority* (New York: Oxford University Press, 1975), which defends a similar revival of citizenship.

16. Mouffe, "Democratic Politics Today," preface in *Dimensions of Radical Democracy*, 3–4.

17. T. H. Marshall, "Citizenship and Social Class," in *Citizenship and Social Class* (London: Pluto, 1992), 8.

18. Eammon Callan, *Creating Citizens: Political Education and Liberal Democracy* (Oxford: Clarendon, 1997), 10.

19. Michael Walzer, *Radical Principles: Reflections of an Unreconstructed Democrat* (New York: Basic Books, 1980), 68. In a later essay, Walzer becomes even more pessimistic: "Citizenship is unlikely to be the primary identity or the consuming passion of men and women living in complex and highly differentiated societies, where politics competes for time and attention with class, ethnicity, religion and family, and where these latter four do not draw people together but rather separate and divide them. Separation and division make for the primacy of the private realm." See Walzer, "Citizenship" in *Political Innovation and Conceptual Change*, eds. Terence Ball, James Farr, and Russell L. Hanson (New York: Cambridge University Press, 1989), 218 (hereafter cited as "Citizenship"). It should be noted that Walzer, despite his pessimism, has offered an account of citizenship and pluralism in *What It Means to Be an American* (New York: Marsilio Publishers, 1992).

20. See Andrew Vincent and Raymond Plant, *Philosophy, Politics, and Citizenship: The Life and Thought of the British Idealist* (Oxford, U.K.: Basil Blackwell, 1984), 162–83.

21. See John Kekes, *The Morality of Pluralism* (Princeton, N.J.: Princeton University Press, 1993), 20.

22. See Walzer, *What It Means to Be an American*; Callan, *Creating Citizens*; Richard Dagger, *Civic Virtues: Rights, Citizenship, and Republican Liberalism* (New York: Oxford University Press, 1997) (hereafter cited as *Civic Virtues*); Jean Elshtain, *Democracy on Trial* (New York: Basic, 1995); and Benjamin Barber, *A Passion for Democracy*, and *Strong Democracy: Participatory Politics for a New Age* (Berkeley: University of California Press, 1984).

23. Beyond this point in the book, I will use the term "citizenship" to refer to republican citizenship, or active citizenship, or citizenship as a practice. Citizenship, in this sense, implies a preferred way of identifying with the community and participating in it. It contrasts with the idea of citizenship as a legal status *tout court,* which abstains from offering an account of how citizenship ought to be exercised.

24. Here, I discuss "political liberalism," a particular version of what I broadly defined as "liberalism" in note 12. Some of my arguments with respect to political liberalism do not apply to all versions of liberalism, broadly understood. Elsewhere in the book, I speak more generally about liberalism and my conclusions can, likewise, be generalized.

25. In claiming that political liberals and deliberative democrats address the tension between popular will and rational will without attending to the character of citizens, my claim is not that these theorists have nothing to say about the subject. Both deliberative democrats and political liberals have had something to say about the circumstances under which their abstract principles will flourish. Indeed, a few have focused on the values, beliefs, and virtues of citizens. However, they have failed to explain how the sort of citizenship they describe can be cultivated consistent with their abstract principles of justice and legitimacy. (These matters are discussed in section III.) Describing preconditions to the flourishing of a set of principles is necessary but not sufficient. Political theorists must do more. We must describe not only the type of citizen capable of putting our preferred principles into practice, but also the political practices that might produce citizens of that type without undermining justice, legitimacy, or personal liberty.

26. See especially John Rawls, *Political Liberalism* (New York: Columbia University Press, 1993), and two works by Jürgen Habermas, *Between Facts and Norms* (Cambridge, Mass.: MIT Press, 1996), and *Moral Consciousness and Communicative Action*.

27. See Habermas, "Reconciliation through the Public Use of Reason: Remarks on John Rawls's Political Liberalism," *The Journal of Philosophy* 92, no. 3 (March 1995): 109–31, and Rawls, "Reply to Habermas," *The Journal of Philosophy* 92, no. 3 (March 1995): 132–80.

28. Rawls, *Political Liberalism*, 30.

29. Rawls, *Political Liberalism*, 3, and 5–6. Rawls writes that the answer to these questions lies in his two principles of justice: "a. Each person has an equal claim to a fully adequate scheme of equal basic rights and liberties, which scheme is compatible with the same scheme for all. . . . b. Social and economic inequalities are to satisfy two conditions: first, they are to be attached to positions and offices open to all under conditions of fair equality of opportunity; and second, they are to be to the greatest benefit of the least advantaged members of society."

30. Rawls, *Political Liberalism*, 175–76.

31. Rawls, *Political Liberalism*, 97.

32. Rawls, *Political Liberalism*, 94, 55. Rawls defines the burdens of judgment as "the sources of reasonable disagreement . . . among reasonable persons." Already we see how Rawls's conception of the reasonable begs the question. It rests on an unacknowledged substantive account of what constitutes reasonable argumentation. The reasonable is defined as respect for reasonable disagreement among reasonable persons—a hardly satisfactory reconciliation of the tension between popular will and rational will, for we are immediately inclined to inquire who or what will deem an opinion "reasonable."

33. Rawls, *Political Liberalism*, 50.

34. Rawls, *Political Liberalism*, 51.

35. Thomas Nagel distinguishes between the personal standpoint and the impersonal standpoint, both of which form constitutive aspects of the human thought process. See Nagel, *Equality and Partiality* (Oxford, U.K.: Oxford University Press, 1991) chap. 2. Nagel and Rawls make a compelling point, but it may not be compelling to all democratic citizens, or even to most. What Rawls and Nagel describe may be a plausible account of rational will, but it cannot reconcile popular will and rational will. To do this, liberals would have to go on the offensive and embrace the cultivation of the kind of citizens who would subscribe to their principles. This, however, takes liberals into an area they prefer to avoid. Indeed, liberalism acquires much of its persuasive force by refusing to enter this space.

36. James Bohman, "Survey Article: The Coming of Age of Deliberative Democracy," *The Journal of Political Philosophy* 6, no. 4 (1998): 409. Below, I show how deliberative democracy (which Bohman defends) also succumbs to this critique.

37. For this critique, see David Miller, "Citizenship and Pluralism," 432–50, and Leif Wenar, "*Political Liberalism:* An Internal Critique," *Ethics* 106 (October 1995): 32–62.

38. Rawls, *Political Liberalism*, 18.

39. The same could be said of liberals like Ronald Dworkin and Brian Barry. Dworkin encourages citizens to take a different "liberal perspective" in public life from the "personal perspective" that governs their private life, and he describes "our personal perspective as everything the liberal perspective is not." See Dworkin, "Foundations of Liberal Equality," in *Tanner Lectures on Human Values* (Salt Lake City: University of Utah Press, 1990), 11: 12, 14. These may be worthy ideals, but many citizens do not accept them. If they are required as preconditions to political deliberation, many people and points of view will be excluded. If so, we will need some account of how they are to be excluded consistent with a respect for democratic decision making. Similarly, Brian Barry asks that citizens be impartial, while conceding that impartiality "does not play a central role . . . [in] common-sense moral thinking." See Barry, *Justice as Impartiality* (Oxford: Clarendon Press, 1995), 19 (hereafter cited as *Justice*). We must either justify the exclusion of those who reject justice as impartiality and explain the process by which they will be excluded or suggest a process by which citizens might come to value impartiality. The latter option demands an account of citizenship.

40. Rawls, *Political Liberalism*, 163.

41. Nagel, *Equality and Partiality*, 23.

42. Barry, *Justice*, 122.

43. Dworkin, *Tanner Lectures*, 100.

44. See Seyla Benhabib, "Deliberative Rationality and Models of Democratic Legitimacy," *Constellations* 1, no. 1 (1994): 32 (hereafter cited as "Deliberative Rationality"); Habermas, *Between Facts and Norms*, 457; and Bernard Manin, "On Legitimacy and Political Deliberation," *Political Theory* 15, no. 3 (August 1987): 351.

45. Habermas, *Between Facts and Norms,* 457.

46. Habermas, *Between Facts and Norms*, 448.

47. Habermas, *Between Facts and Norms*, 103. This is a way of understanding what Habermas hopes to achieve by bringing together facticity (*Faktizität*) and validity (*Geltung*), terms he uses throughout *Between Facts and Norms,* published in German under the title *Faktizität und Geltung.*

48. Habermas, "Reconciliation through the Public Use of Reason," 131.

49. Benhabib, *Situating the Self* (New York: Routledge, 1992), 28.

50. See Habermas, *Moral Consciousness and Communicative Action*, 56.

51. Habermas, *Moral Consciousness and Communicative Action*, 67.

52. Habermas writes, "as interests become differentiated, the scope of action in the interest of the whole becomes ever more general and abstract." *Moral Consciousness and Communicative Action*, 205.

53. Habermas, *Moral Consciousness and Communicative Action*, 93.

54. Habermas, "Toward a Communication-Concept of Rational Collective Will-Formation. A Thought Experiment," *Ratio Juris* 2, no. 2 (July 1989): 152. As we shall see, the deliberative democrats' idea of the "force of the better argument" cannot be understood in purely procedural terms. Who or what will distinguish between Habermas's rational motivation and, say, demagoguery or ideology, in the old Marxist or Gramscian sense? Haber-

mas has a splendid body of work that describes how rationally motivated outcomes might be distinguished from ideological or demagogically inspired ones. This, however, is not the point. Without a socially entrenched, substantive account of what would constitute a rationally motivated argument, as opposed to a tendentious, ideological, biased, or irrational one, the idea that the force of the better argument should prevail lacks all coherence. Of course, the notion that there might be substantive constraints on deliberation violates the essence of deliberative democracy. For Habermas's account of the distinction between rationally motivated deliberation and ideologically or irrationally motivated deliberation, see *The Structural Transformation of the Public Sphere* (Cambridge, Mass.: MIT Press, 1989), *Legitimation Crisis* (Boston: Beacon, 1975), and his essays "Technology and Science as 'Ideology,' " from *Toward a Rational Society* (Boston: Beacon, 1971), and "Further Reflections on the Public Sphere" in *Habermas and the Public Sphere*, ed. Craig Calhoun (Cambridge, Mass.: MIT Press, 1992).

55. Jon Elster, introduction to *Deliberative Democracy* (New York: Cambridge University Press, 1998). See also Manin, "On Legitimacy and Political Deliberation," 349.

56. Benhabib, "Deliberative Rationality," 16.

57. See, for example, Evan Charney, "Political Liberalism, Deliberative Democracy, and the Public Sphere," *American Political Science Review* 92 (March 1998): 97–110.

58. Amy Gutmann and Dennis Thompson, *Democracy and Disagreement* (Cambridge Mass.: Harvard University Press, 1996), 135. They endorse the substantive principles of "basic liberty, basic opportunity, and fair opportunity," as "components of the *content* of deliberation [italics added]," 348.

59. Jeremy Waldron makes this argument in the context of an article on judicial review. "Judicial Review and the Conditions of Democracy," *The Journal of Political Philosophy* 6, no. 4 (1998): 344.

60. Gutmann and Thompson, *Democracy and Disagreement,* 17.

61. Habermas, *Between Facts and Norms,* 122.

62. Habermas, *Between Facts and Norms*, 122–23.

63. Habermas, *Moral Consciousness and Communicative Action,* 76.

64. Benhabib, *Situating the Self,* 29. Clearly true of deliberative democracy, this claim could also be applied convincingly to all egalitarian political theory.

65. The full title of Rousseau's *Social Contract* is *On the Social Contract or Principles of Political Right. (Du Contrat social; ou Principes du droit politique).*

66. See Macedo, *Liberal Virtues*; Galston, *Liberal Purposes*; and Berkowitz, *Virtue and the Making of Modern Liberalism.*

67. See Joseph Raz, *The Morality of Freedom* (Oxford: Clarendon, 1986).

68. Galston, "Civic Education in the Liberal State," in *Liberalism and the Moral Life*, ed. Nancy L. Rosenblum (Cambridge, Mass.: Harvard University Press, 1989), 91.

69. Ronald J. Terchek, *Republican Paradoxes and Liberal Anxieties: Retrieving Neglected Fragments of Political Theory* (New York: Rowman & Littlefield Publishers, Inc., 1997), and Berkowitz, *Virtue and the Making of Modern Liberalism.*

70. Rawls, *Political Liberalism*, 217. See also Rawls, *A Theory of Justice* (Cambridge, Mass.: Harvard University Press, 1971), pt. 3, chap. 8.

71. Berkowitz, *Virtue and the Making of Modern Liberalism*, 16.

72. Berkowitz, *Virtue and the Making of Modern Liberalism*, 191.

73. Berkowitz, *Virtue and the Making of Modern Liberalism*, 191 and 177. According to Berkowitz, liberal democracy should address a series of questions, among them: "How

can schools contribute to liberalism's need for individuals who can govern themselves well? What is to be done to defend our character and our communities against a commercial culture that is both an expression of and a threat to our liberty?" This focus is laudable; however, I see no way these questions could be addressed without drawing on the resources of republicanism.

74. Liberals and republicans will, of course, continue to disagree over questions such as the definition of freedom, the proper relationship between individual and society, and the centrality of civic participation to human flourishing.

75. Habermas, *Moral Consciousness and Communicative Action*, 103.

76. See Thomas McCarthy, *Ideals and Illusions* (Cambridge, Mass.: MIT Press, 1996), 184.

77. Jon Dryzek, *Discursive Democracy: Politics, Policy, and Political Science* (New York: Cambridge University Press, 1990), 78.

78. Quoted in Veit Bader, "Citizenship and Exclusion: Radical Democracy, Community, and Justice. Or, What Is Wrong with Communitarianism?" *Political Theory* 23, no. 2 (May 1995): 233. For Habermas's account of threats to the integrity of the public sphere, see n54.

79. Bohman, "Survey Article: The Coming of Age of Deliberative Democracy."

80. Chambers, "Discourse and Democratic Practices," 247.

81. Bohman, "Survey Article: The Coming of Age of Deliberative Democracy," 401.

82. Benhabib, *Situating the Self*, 38. Habermas also acknowledges the dilemma: "The emergence of legitimacy from legality admittedly appears as a paradox only on the premise that the legal system must be imagined as a circular process that recursively feeds back into and legitimates *itself*. This is already contradicted by the evidence that democratic institutions of freedom disintegrate without the initiatives of a population *accustomed* to freedom. Their spontaneity cannot be compelled simply through law; it is regenerated from traditions and preserved in the associations of a liberal political culture. Legal regulations can, to be sure, take precautions that keep down the costs of the civic virtues that are called for, ensuring that only small price hikes are necessary. The discourse-theoretic understanding of the system of rights directs our attention to both sides. On the one side, the burden of legitimation shifts from citizens' qualifications to legally institutionalized procedures of discursive opinion- and will-formation. On the other side, the juridification of communicative freedom also means that the law must draw on sources of legitimation that are not at its disposal." See Habermas, *Between Facts and Norms,* 130–31.

83. See the preface in Gutmann, *Democratic Education* (Princeton, N.J.: Princeton University Press, 1987).

84. Gutmann, preface in *Democratic Education*, 42.

85. Gutmann, preface in *Democratic Education*, 44–45.

86. Gutmann, preface in *Democratic Education*, 14.

87. Gutmann, preface in *Democratic Education*, 71.

88. Gutmann, preface in *Democratic Education*, 127.

89. Gutmann, preface in *Democratic Education*, 72.

Chapter 2

The General Will:
Rousseau's Procedural Argument

Nowadays, Rousseau's general will is approached more as an example of what is wrong with republicanism than as an example of what is right about it. Many of Rousseau's critics assert that his general will cedes too much to popular will by emptying it of all content and, thereby, leaving it vulnerable to usurpation by despotic forces. Others claim that Rousseau's endorsement of political indoctrination and civic virtue unduly restricts popular will. The fact that Rousseau managed to provoke these opposite criticisms is itself intriguing. Ultimately, both criticisms prove to be accurate in some sense, but both also miss something essential about the general will—the way it encapsulates the inexorable political tension between popular will and rational will. For Rousseau, it was insufficient to assert that whatever the people will is right. Although he does say "the general will is always right," he also says that only the general will is rightfully sovereign. The people always want what is good for themselves, but they do not always see it, which is to say that they do not always see the general will. From the fact that the general will is always right, it does not follow "that the people's deliberations always have the same rectitude. . . . The people is never corrupted, but it is often fooled."[1] In striving to both respect popular will and rationalize it, Rousseau's general will issues in a paradox. As Hans Barth puts it, "Everyone's will must be respected, but everyone must also will what is general."[2] Addressing this paradox will take Rousseau beyond the question of the abstract principles of political right, to the social and cultural question of how to cultivate citizens who embrace those principles.

At the outset of *The Social Contract*, Rousseau misleadingly claims to be concerned only with the "principles of political right"—the subtitle to the work. He begins book I, chapter i with an obfuscation: "Man was/is born free, and everywhere he is in chains. . . . How did this change occur? I do not know. What can make it legitimate? I believe I can answer this question" (I, i, 46). Rousseau presents *The Social Contract* as an argument about legitimacy, but, unless he has in-

27

troduced a radically new definition, his argument pushes far beyond the question of legitimacy to the broader questions of human happiness and flourishing. His political philosophy is so revolutionary precisely because it extends the boundaries of politics beyond questions of legitimacy to incorporate the ethical and moral dimensions of the human experience that form the conditions for happiness—"the aim of every sensitive being."[3] While previous modern thinkers had been satisfied with the more modest goal of comfortable self-preservation, Rousseau approaches politics in the manner of the ancients, with an eye toward the highest peaks of human excellence.[4] We must, therefore, resist the commonly held belief that "Rousseau's question is not what the best political order is but what can make society legitimate."[5] On the contrary, the general will will do much more than set out standards of political legitimacy. It will tackle the question that Rousseau himself specified as the paramount question of politics—how to create the best men.[6]

It is, perhaps, unnecessary for political theory to produce an answer to the question of how to create the best human beings. It may even be the case that political theory ought to insist that the question not be asked, or at least that it not be pursued with much zeal. Nonetheless, a political theory that aspires to be comprehensive must do more than describe standards for political legitimacy. A comprehensive theory of politics must address two questions: what are the principles of political right, and how can those principles be put into practice? Unlike much contemporary political theory, which focuses almost exclusively on the former question, the majority of Rousseau's work addresses the latter. With the notable exception of book I of *The Social Contract* and a few chapters of books II, III, and IV, Rousseau's political writings emphasize the virtues, strategies, norms, and customs that combine to form the foundation of a thriving, stable, free republic.[7] I believe this explains, at least partially, why many of Rousseau's readers detach the formal, procedural argument of *The Social Contract* from the rest of his political writings. Though this can be a useful exercise, ultimately, Rousseau's procedural argument—his "principles of political right"—can only be understood within the context of his political theory as a whole.

We can particularize the two questions just posed with two parallel questions that incorporate Rousseau's "general will," an idea which, when fully explained, yields a theory of republican citizenship: what is the general will? and how can it be made dominant? Answering the first question is what I propose to do in this chapter; the second question (along with the complicated relationship between the two) provides subject for chapter 3.

Because the general will represents so much—"the articulation of an entire patriotic ethos,"[8]—it is difficult to specify exactly what it includes and excludes. Most readers agree that the general will embodies the essence of Rousseau's political philosophy, and few doubt its significance in the history of ideas, both as a theoretical justification of popular sovereignty and as an influence on later political thinkers and actors. However, despite the consensus on the importance of the general will, the term itself says something different to most readers, depending on their context, agenda, and predisposition. To a certain extent, these different readings are unavoidable, and, as Judith Shklar warns, it would be both "vain and illiberal to assume that one's own reading is the only right one."[9] Still, this remains the business of political theorists, and this book requires an initial audacity, an asserted interpretation of the intent and meaning of Rousseau's general will. A foundation of this kind is necessary in order to understand precisely the ensuing appropriations, distortions, and alterations that make up the legacy of the general will in the French political tradition.

Most significantly, there has been a tendency for students of Rousseau's thought to understand him through the lens of later historical developments, rather than on his own terms. Psychologically, it tends to be almost impossible to remove the clutter of nineteenth- and twentieth-century terror, nationalism, totalitarianism, multiculturalism, and globalization to see clearly through to Rousseau's original, and self-consciously historically embedded ideas. As W. T. Jones writes, Rousseau's critics have often "anachronistically assumed him to be interested in the problems that interest them and have not asked themselves what problem concerned him."[10] The clearest example has been the debate pitting Rousseau, the liberal individualist, against Rousseau, the proto-totalitarian collectivist. This battle of one-dimensional distortions mirrors the foolish ideological bipolarity that dominated international politics between 1945 and 1989. One hopes, with Iain Hampsher-Monk, that the collapse of that bipolarity on a political level will remind us of how crude an exercise it has been in the struggle to do justice to Rousseau's thought.[11] The underlying assumption of this project is that there is much to be gained, both in terms of our understanding of Rousseau and in terms of our approach to politics in general by distinguishing clearly between the general will as conceived by Rousseau and the general will as appropriated by later political thought and movements. In order to make these distinctions, however, it is necessary to specify that which resists specification, namely what Rousseau means by the "general will."

As a beginning, I want to move deliberately through the formal argument Rousseau advances in *The Social Contract,* reading generously, under the assumption that Rousseau wrote carefully and was aware of at least some of the gaps, contradictions, and paradoxes that readers have long discerned in his work. In chapter 3, I will draw out some of the implications of these difficulties.

I. TAKING MEN AS THEY ARE

Most readers interpret the society depicted in *The Social Contract* as utopian. Interestingly, Rousseau introduces Book I of the work by describing his project in a way that belies this reading. He writes, "I want to inquire whether there *can be* a legitimate and reliable rule of administration in the civil order, taking men *as they are* and laws as they can be. I shall try always to reconcile in this research what right permits with what interest prescribes, so that justice and utility are not at variance" (Rousseau's italics) (I, introduction, 46). Rousseau vows to take men "as they are" and not as they *could* be—an unexpected formulation from a supposed utopian. Moreover, he indicates that interests prescribe certain principles of right, implying that politics must be theorized with respect to the actual, already existing interest of citizens.

In any association of people, according to Rousseau, there exists a general will; it is general with respect to the entirety of that association, though it is particular in relation to a larger body.[12] Every political community will have a general will that reflects its particular culture, history, and geography. Moreover, every member of a political community who has not alienated himself from the community shares this will. It is the will that members have qua citizens, as opposed to the will that they may have qua private individuals. What is important to emphasize is that all individuals have this will automatically, so to speak, by virtue of their membership in the political community. This characteristic of "men as they are" is the foundation from which Rousseau attempts to develop principles of political right. In this way, the general will *is* citizenship; it is the will members have as citizens, the will that they acquire when they enter society and develop an interest in the perpetuation of the apparatus of their continued existence and freedom.

In addition to his or her private interest, members of society develop an interest grounded in their identity as part of a collective body. Though these different interests can come into conflict, the general will is not a "higher" will, but rather "a will that ordinary people pursuing basic interests have."[13] In other words, it is not the sacrifice of self-interest to the common good or the subordination of the individual to the city. It is the very real interest that individuals have in the perpetuation of the conditions necessary to their freedom. The general will does not require citizens to ascend to a higher level of consciousness or excellence. Neither does it demand that they sublimate their personal interest into some collective faculty or high idea. As Patrick Riley writes, "it is only metaphorically that will can be spoken of as general. No act of philosophic imagination can conjure up anything but a personal will."[14] If principles of political right can be developed based on each citizen's personal, self-acknowledged interest, Rousseau will have succeeded in reconciling "what right permits with what interest prescribes."

II. THE CONTRACT

Unlike life in, say, Thomas Hobbes's state of nature which is famously "nasty, brutish and short," Rousseau depicts the life of pre-political human beings as uneventful, self-sufficient, and peaceful.[15] It is only through increasingly differentiated human interaction that men begin to dominate one another. The solution to this problem will be a "social contract" just as it had been for Hobbes, but this social contract will be substantially different. For Rousseau, Hobbes's social contract merely entrenched societal oppression and inequality—conditions that Hobbes had mistakenly attributed to natural man. Hobbes and the other state of nature theorists "continually speaking of need, greed, oppression, desires, and pride transferred to the state of Nature ideas they had taken from society; they spoke of Savage Man and depicted Civil man."[16] Consequently, although they believed themselves to be solving the problem of exploitation through the transfer of man from the state of nature to civil society, they were actually entrenching and legitimizing the inequities characteristic of modern societies.

Rousseau targeted the natural law theorists' version of the social contract, which he viewed as a fraud, imposed by the powerful (the rich) on the powerless (the poor). By assuming a natural right to property, natural law theorists conceived of politics as a means of safeguarding the possessions one has prior to entering the social contract. For Rousseau, this account reflected neither an accurate account of the right to property (which he viewed as wholly social) nor the interest of the majority of citizens who were either compelled or simply duped into accepting their own subjugation.[17]

It is helpful to situate Rousseau's repudiation of the natural law tradition within the Genevan political context, which seemed never to be far from his mind. Much has been made of Rousseau's devotion to his homeland, particularly of his controversial habit of signing his political writings with the appellation "citizen of Geneva."[18] Despite his professed love for his homeland,[19] Rousseau's attitude toward the Geneva regime was ambivalent, as Helena Rosenblatt has shown in a study of Rousseau and Genevan politics.[20] Rousseau was born into a bourgeois family in Geneva, to a father who was active on behalf of his class in its aspirations to full political equality. During Rousseau's lifetime, Genevan politics was dominated by the struggle between the bourgeois class, which sought full political rights, and the patrician class, which hoped to maintain its hold on power. Though we are currently likely to connect natural law ideology with the bourgeoisie, it was actually the patriciate that embraced natural law doctrine in eighteenth-century Geneva. The patricians deployed social contract theory as a means of preserving the status quo and resisting popular demands for democratization.[21] The patricians tried to make the case that government should be left to the "experts," as they immodestly called themselves, by making the measure of political legitimacy the extent to which the sovereign power safeguards the rights individuals have by nature.[22] The people's interests were relevant to be sure, but their *will* was not, and their interests could be most effectively managed by the patriciate. As Rosenblatt writes, "Modern natural law theory supplied . . . a means to depoliticize liberty, in other words, to dissociate it from political participation."[23]

Rousseau expressed outrage at this logic in his *Letters Written from the Mountain,* where he condemns Geneva's ruling council for devoting itself to "preserving the instrument of [its] usurpations."[24] This kind of corruption will follow inevitably, according to Rousseau, unless the social contract places a premium on incorporating the will of every member of society. For Rousseau, the social contract must produce "a form of association that defends and protects the person and goods of each associate," but it must do more than that. It must also ensure that each associate "uniting with all, nevertheless obeys only himself and remains as free as before" (I, vi, 53). This condition can be satisfied if, and only if, every member of the sovereign body participates in political decision making. If not, some faction of society will inevitably dominate over others, producing relations of dependence, which are, for Rousseau, incompatible with freedom. It is critical for Rousseau that no member of society be dependent on another. Here again, it is worth recalling *The Second Discourse,* specifically Rousseau's description of the proliferation of *amour-propre*, which has rendered man dependent on forces deadening to the soul. "We have enslaved ourselves to the sciences and the arts and to customs, and yet we call it freedom."[25] Through a socially produced system of *manières* and inequality, people had subordinated themselves to their own vanity and passions and had been subordinated by the institutions of inequality. The social contract must solve this problem of dependence: "In the relations between man and man the worst that can happen to one is to find himself at the other's discretion."[26]

Ironically, for man to overcome the dependence produced by modern society and to reclaim his natural freedom, he must give himself over entirely to the state, subordinating his private will to the general will. Only by retaining nothing for himself, by alienating himself and all of his rights to the community, can he recover the freedom imperiled by civilization. Rousseau prescribes "the total alienation of each associate, with all his rights to the whole community. . . . Each of us puts his person and all his power in common under the supreme direction of the general will; and in a body we receive each member as an indivisible part of the whole" (I, vi, 53). This will avoid the problem of dependence, since if "each gives himself to all, he gives himself to no one" (I, vi, 53 and II, xii, 77). The rights that man has by nature have all been alienated, but a stronger freedom, one resilient to the particularizing influences of *amour-propre* and inequality, has been embodied in the general will. Unlike previous accounts of the social contract, which he viewed as cloaks used to legitimize the inequitable distribution of power and wealth, Rousseau aspires to eliminate inequities. Because everything is alienated to the community at the outset, no associate is in a position of domination with respect to any of the others.

This pushes Rousseau beyond the principle of consent, which had been the moral foundation for previous social contract theories. For Rousseau, consent can be consistent with inequality and dependence; it can be a compromise between particular wills that does little more than legitimize the domination of one individual or group of individuals by another. Something stronger is required:

> Dependence on men, since it is without order, engenders all the vices, and by it, master and slave are mutually corrupted. If there is any means of remedying this ill in society, it is to substitute law for man and to arm the general wills with a real strength superior to the action of every particular will.[27]

Consent, though necessary to legitimacy, is insufficient. Full political legitimacy demands the subordination of private interest to the general will. For Rousseau, the natural right to all things must be alienated, along with all other rights, so that a transformed conception of rights and freedom can be made secure under the dominion of the general will. This deviates substantially from the traditional social contract, which was an attempt to minimize the portion of man's natural freedom that he would have to relinquish upon entering society. John Locke, for example, demanded that associates alienate only that portion of their liberty necessary to protect the rights of each. For Locke, individuals enter the social contract in order to prevent others from infringing on the freedom they have by nature. Rousseau's individual, by contrast, *acquires* freedom through the social contract. Consequently, whereas Locke's individual alienates as little as possible to the community, Rousseau's alienates everything.

Having said that, it is crucial to note that the transformation of man into citizen is not total. Rather "everything that is not of the essence of the social compact is set aside" before "each of us puts his person and all his power in common under the supreme direction of the general will" (I, vii, 55). [28] Rousseau recognizes not only that the private will exists, but also that it is stronger than the general will. His intention in *The Social Contract* is not to wholly overwhelm it, and it is certainly not to do away with the distinction between particular and general as the Jacobins will try to do. Eliminating the distinction means that everything becomes political; nothing can be private, and the general will becomes a will to all things. However, for Rousseau, the general will is only the will that one has as citizen; it is the will that pertains to issues of common concern—the will that is political. The idea of alienating oneself and all one's rights applies only to everything political. People enter society, Rousseau writes, to assure the "goods, life, and freedom of each member by the protection of all." [29] Assuring these things is the task of politics, and, therefore, the domain of the general will. As we will see in chapter 3, just what this task involves is ambiguous and problematic. For now it is sufficient to note that Rousseau is quite clear in specifying limitations on the scope of the general will (for example, I, vi, 53, and II, iv, 62).

III. FORCED TO BE FREE

Having drawn a preliminary, hazy boundary for the general will, Rousseau proceeds to a discussion of its application. While there may be limitations on the scope of sovereign power, Rousseau foresees no need for limitations on its application (I, vii, 55). He explains,

> the sovereign, formed solely by the private individuals composing it, does not and cannot have an interest contrary to theirs. . . . the sovereign power has no need of a guarantee toward the subjects, because it is impossible for the body ever to want to harm all its members, and we shall see later that it cannot harm any one of them as

an individual. The sovereign, by the sole fact of being, is always what it ought to be
(I, vii, 55).[30]

In equating the sovereign with the general will, Rousseau idealizes sovereign
power, and this allows him to be sanguine about the absolute power he says the
body politic holds over its members (II, iv, 62). Because the sovereign is nothing
other than the entire body of citizens, citizens are alternately sovereign and subject. This means the actions of the sovereign can never be unjust, since no one
would favor doing harm to himself. Such is the logic that Rousseau presents. It is
a logic that has been justly attacked by critics such as Isaiah Berlin, who points
out that the "sovereignty of the people could easily destroy the sovereignty of individuals."[31] Rousseau was not unaware of these risks, but, characteristic of his
political philosophy as a whole, he feared that any limitation on the power of the
sovereign body would be exploited by particular interests that would threaten the
supremacy of the general will. Ironically, Rousseau felt that absolute sovereignty
was the best way to prevent the abuses of authority that his critics assign to him.
Rousseau believed that nothing could secure freedom and well-being better than
the will of an uncorrupted sovereign body. No benefit from an institutional check
on sovereign power could possibly justify a limitation on the expression of the
people's will. Threats to the republic come then, not from the thorough and forceful application of the general will—not from the sovereign in relation to the subjects—but from particular or private wills—from the subjects in relation to the
sovereign. Rousseau writes,

> each individual can as a man, have a private will contrary to or differing from the
> general will he has as a citizen. His private interest can speak to him quite differently
> from the common interest. . . . And considering the moral person of the State as an
> imaginary being because it is not a man, he might wish to enjoy the rights of the cit-
> izen without wanting to fulfill the duties of a subject, an injustice whose spread
> would cause the ruin of the body politic (I, vii, 55).

Consequently,

> in order for the social compact not to be an ineffectual formula, it tacitly includes the
> following engagement, which alone can give force to the others: that whoever refuses
> to obey the general will shall be constrained to do so by the entire body (I, vii, 55).

At this point in the argument, Rousseau has claimed first, that the general will reflects the interest of each citizen; second, that individuals possess a separate, private interest that they are frequently tempted to place above their interest as a citizen; and third, that when individuals do attempt to subvert the general will with
their private will, they shall be constrained by the sovereign power. If we recall
that the general will is manifested as legislation, as the rule of law, Rousseau's argument can be put as follows: all citizens should be compelled by society to obey
laws they had a say in establishing.

If legislation is not rightfully established; that is, if the sovereign power does not embody the general will, Rousseau states emphatically that there is no obligation to obey. At the outset of the book, in language similar to that used in the passage just quoted, Rousseau writes, "If I were to consider only force and the effect it produces, I would say that as long as a people is constrained to obey and does so, it does well; as soon as it can shake off the yoke and does so, it does even better" (I, i, 46). Rousseau's argument is that people ought to overthrow a government that usurps the general will, while they ought to be constrained from subverting laws that are democratically and legitimately established.

The account I have just given is not standard, although I believe that it would be had Rousseau written simply, "whoever refuses to obey the general will shall be constrained to do so by the entire body." However, he added an infamous clause. He wrote "whoever refuses to obey the general will shall be constrained to do so by the entire body; *which means only that he will be forced to be free*" (italics added) (I, vii, 55). Given the controversy that the phrase "forced to be free" has inspired, it is ironic that Rousseau depreciated its importance by prefacing it with the word "only." It is unlikely that Rousseau would have failed to realize that the notion that people could be forced to be free would seem counterintuitive to most people, particularly since he had argued earlier that where force rules, there is no duty (I, iii, 48).[32] Yet, he tacks on the phrase as if it were the obvious and natural conclusion to the argument he had made up to that point. Ultimately, I believe that the phrase "forced to be free"—though not an especially salutary formulation—is consistent with Rousseau's arguments against tyranny and oppression. We have already begun to see why; however, to fully understand, one must continue on to the argument that immediately follows in the text.

IV. CIVIL FREEDOM

Up to this point in the argument, we have seen how forced obedience to laws rightfully established can be consistent with freedom. However, had Rousseau intended to express only this, he could have stated simply and uncontroversially that citizens be forced to obey the law. Instead, he went so far as to claim that this constraint was not only consistent with their freedom but generative of it. For this to make sense, we must grasp Rousseau's various definitions of freedom.

Pre-social man, according to Rousseau, possesses natural freedom, a right to all things, which is limited only by the force of the individual. It is this freedom that previous social contract theorists had sought to safeguard. For them, natural freedom can be preserved in social life, if citizens are willing to alienate a small portion of it to the sovereign. The sovereign, in turn, ensures that no group or individual violates the natural rights of any others. All of this is insufficient for Rousseau. First, he understands natural freedom to be the freedom of the savage, of pre-social man. Once men enter society, natural freedom is surrendered. Second, if citizens fail to alienate their natural freedom to the social body, patterns of subjugation, inequality and dependence will quickly develop. For Rousseau, the chief threat to freedom comes from factions within the social body and the relationships of dependence that inevitably accompany them. This is why Rousseau concludes the chapter on sovereign power as follows,

> whoever refuses to obey the general will shall be constrained to do so by the entire body; which means only that he will be forced to be free. *For this is the condition that, by giving each citizen to the homeland, guarantees him against all personal dependence; a condition that creates the ingenuity and functioning of the political machine, and alone gives legitimacy to civil engagements which without it would be absurd, tyrannical, and subject to the most enormous abuses* (italics added) (I, vii, 55,).

Without obedience to the general will, to the laws established by the sovereign body as a whole, Rousseau fears that a space will open for factions or individuals to exercise nonconsensual, oppressive authority over their fellow citizens. Only by making the authority of the general will absolute can the citizen be protected against the personal dependence that inevitably arises when factions gain political power. This is the basis for civil freedom.

Rousseau describes civil freedom as living within the parameters of the general will and connects it with moral freedom—which he defines as obedience to the law one has prescribed for oneself (I, viii, 56). If freedom is understood this way, whoever acts to subvert the general will by succumbing to particular interests, commits a crime not only against the state, but against himself as well, and—as one commentator puts it—"is riddled with contradictions."[33] This view is a moral view of freedom, inextricably connected to a conception of justice. It is not surprising, therefore, that Rousseau introduces his discussion of civil freedom with a description of the transition from the state of nature to civil society: "This passage from the state of nature to the civil state produces a remarkable change in man, by substituting justice for instinct in his behavior and giving his actions the morality they previously lacked" (I, vii, 55). Certain advantages of natural freedom are forfeited in this transformation, but life in civil society offers far greater benefits for the development of moral faculties and noble sentiments (I, viii, 56).[34]

In subordinating private interest to the general will (that is, entering civil society) natural freedom and an unlimited right to everything is exchanged for civil freedom and socially sanctioned proprietorship (I, viii, 56). Natural rights are assimilated by the general will and reconstituted as civil rights, through the transfer of authority from any and all parts of the social body to the whole. This authority is then manifested in the general will and the laws that express it. It is the will of all members because it wills the conditions necessary to protect them against the influence of particular wills that tend toward inequality, privilege, and dependence. If civil freedom is living under laws one has prescribed for oneself, the general will must create the conditions in which citizens will not be victimized by personal dependence. As indicated above, Rousseau believed that the chief threats to personal freedom came from forces operating in society rather than from the state or from an external power.

Rousseau's solution is to eliminate personal dependence by making citizens dependent on the community as a whole. Only through the sovereignty of the general will—the will of members qua citizens—can freedom be protected from the particularizing effects of private will—the will of members qua men. Rousseauean democracy cannot be libertarian because if people lived exactly as they pleased, they would imperil the conditions for self-government. Without a sense of shared purpose, people inevitably slip into relationships of dependence that undermine freedom. Isaiah Berlin's distinction between negative and positive liberty illuminates this tension, in as much as positive liberty addresses the question of self-government while negative liberty refers to the extent of government interference with individual agency.[35] The difficulty for the realization of freedom, on Berlin's account, is that negative and positive are inherently at odds, yet, are both ends in themselves. Berlin formulates this conflict as a zero-sum game in which some negative liberty is sacrificed to positive liberty, and he clearly believes Rousseau has sacrificed far too much.

While Rousseau, like Berlin, understands liberty to consist of conflicting tendencies, he implicitly rejects the possibility of strictly separating the two. For Rousseau, it is insufficient to think of negative liberty outside the context of self-government, whereas for Berlin, sovereignty need not reside in the people for negative liberty to be maximized. While the absence of government interference alone satisfies Berlin's criteria for freedom, Rousseau worries about individuals enslaving themselves and each other through passions, appearances, opinions, and relationships of domination. Rousseau and Berlin agree that negative and positive liberty are theoretically distinguishable and usually conflictual, but they disagree as to whether one is possible without the other.

Berlin writes, "to manipulate men, to propel them towards goals which you—the social reformer—see, but they may not, is to deny their human essence."[36] Rousseau feared just this kind of political usurpation, whereby an individual or faction would impose its (private or corporate) will on the people. Only an account of legitimacy that requires the participation of all citizens in political decision making (positive liberty) could possibly safeguard against this unsavory eventuality. If we understand the actualization of Rousseauean freedom to require an uncomfortable synthesis of negative and positive liberty, Berlin's highly influential indictment loses at least some of its force. Berlin's argument rests on the existence of a clear-cut distinction between the will of what he has here called the "social reformer" and the will of the people. The problem with Berlin's charge (when considered in relation to Rousseau) is that Rousseau means to contest its very terms. By insisting that the general will include the voice of every individual, Rousseau wants to attack the distinction between the will of the sovereign or, to use Berlin's language, the will of "the social reformer" and the will of indi-

viduals. Rousseau understands the general will to be each individual's will, such
that the sovereign does not "propel" men in the coercive, external sense that
Berlin implies. On the contrary, to the extent that the general will dominates, the
constraints the sovereign places on individual actions are self-imposed, and necessary to the freedom of every individual. This is how Rousseau arrives at the
seemingly oxymoronic notion of forcing someone to be free. The individual right
to do whatever we want, whenever we want (as long as it does not undermine the
rights of others) oversimplifies the complicated question of human freedom.
Berlin's distinction comes up short, for example, in any one of the many possible
circumstances under which an agent's actual choice does not reflect what he or
she truly wants.[37] This judgment need not involve us in the pretense to know people's true desires; rather we need only think of the ways in which one's actions
might undermine one's own, self-acknowledged goals. For Rousseau, those who
subvert the general will (that is, break the law) must be constrained, not as a limitation on their freedom, but as an element of it. Real freedom requires both positive and negative liberty, and this combination may be problematic when the two
types of liberty conflict. This, however, is an essential part of political life and
not, as Berlin suggests, a denial of human essence.

From this it should be clear that we must resist C. E. Vaughan's claim that, while
Locke's social contract is "expressly devised to preserve and confirm the rights of
the individual," Rousseau's "is an extreme form of collectivism. A more complete
contrast is hardly possible to conceive."[38] As with Locke, and other liberal thinkers,
the individual is at the center of Rousseau's political philosophy. While it's true that
"the right of the individual must be subordinate to the right of all" (I, ix, 58), this is
only justified by the result it produces for individuals. It is only due to the depraved
state of modern society that freedom cannot be reestablished other than through total
alienation. While it's true that some of Rousseau's political prescriptions imply an
"extreme form of collectivism," these prescriptions can only be understood in conjunction with his concern for the freedom and welfare of individuals. Total alienation
is made necessary by the particularizing forces of modernity that tend inexorably toward tyranny; it is the only way for the individual to regain the liberty that he has
lost to *amour-propre,* dependence, and institutionalized inequality.[39]

V. PRIVATE WILL AND GENERAL WILL

Following the chapter on civil freedom, Rousseau describes the convention of
proprietorship as an example of the manner in which natural rights are reconstituted as civil rights, and, with that, he concludes Book I. The latter halves of
Books II, III, and IV (on the Legislator, the degeneration of government, and civil
religion) address the problem of making the general will dominant and, as such,
will be discussed in chapter 3. For now, I will concentrate on what remains of
Rousseau's procedural description of the principles of political right.

Rousseau begins Book II with a clarification of the relationship between private and general will. Whereas the private will tends toward preferences and individual or corporate interests, the general will tends toward equality and the common good (II, i, 59). Therefore, "the general will alone can guide the forces of the State" (II, i, 59). However, private will is not transcended and, though Rousseau is not always clear on this point, it is not even transformed. Rousseau is ambiguous about the possibility for agreement between private and general will. Here he writes,

> if the opposition of private interests made the establishment of societies necessary, it is the agreement of these same interests that made it possible. It is what these different interests have in common that forms the social bond, and if there were not some point at which all the interests are in agreement, no society could exist (II, i, 59).

This agreement of private interests is similar to what Rousseau (in just two chapters) will call the will of all—defined as the sum of private interests (II, iii). At this point, Rousseau clarifies the relationship between private will and the general will with the claim that, though there may easily be coincidental agreement between private will and the general will, it is impossible for this agreement to be "lasting and unchanging. For the private will tends by its nature toward preferences" (II, i, 59). Here, Rousseau appears to be arguing, on the one hand, that there is some agreement between particular wills, by which the general will is generated. On the other hand, he maintains that private will, though it may temporarily coincide with the common good, will eventually subvert it, due to its intrinsic tendency toward preferences for some part of the society at the expense of the whole.

This tendency toward preference explains why Rousseau writes that there is "*often* a great difference between the will of all [the sum of private wills] and the general will . . . which considers only the common interest" (italics added) (II, iii, 61). Rousseau's distinction between the general will and the will of all raises a question that has long vexed Rousseau's readers. Is the general will different (in kind) from particular will—that is, is it an entirely unique kind of will—or is it the agreement of private interests, rightly understood? Given the argument at the beginning of Book II, the latter alternative seems persuasive, especially considered in conjunction with the elaboration Rousseau offers in chapter iii, where he argues that, if one takes the sum of private wills, one can "take away from these *same wills* the pluses and minuses that cancel each other out, and the remaining sum of the differences is the general will" (italics added) (II, iii, 61). If this is true, the general will is the sum of particular wills. However, it is not just any sum of particular wills, but rather a particular sum of particular wills— namely, that sum that considers only the interest common to each of the individual, particular wills. Though this explanation is something of a circumlocution, I believe it is sustainable.[40]

The process of taking away the "pluses and minuses" from the sum of particular wills defines the sphere of the general will, as I argued in section II, whereby that which does not bear on the collective interest is excluded. Rousseau clarifies his meaning with the claim that the general will is created by opposition to the private interest of each (II, iii, 61). If one insists on operationalizing the concept, it is useful to understand the general will as that which is left over when the private wills of each cancel each other out (II, iii, 61).[41] Consequently, the sphere of politics expands to the extent that private wills correspond, reaching perfect unity only where the citizen has learned to will privately in a way that corresponds exactly to the general will.

The fact that the general will is a particular sum of particular wills also has the implication that the general will must be personal and general at the same time; it must spring from the personal will of each member and can only be a collective faculty in that it is shared by all. Rousseau eschews the language of transformation and even of private subordination to the public interest. Instead, he focuses on reconciling inclination to duty—not in a Hegelian transcendence of a contradiction, but in a more straightforward, socially engineered coincidence of private and public demands.

VI. JURISDICTION OF THE GENERAL WILL

Having specified the character of the general will, Rousseau proceeds to a discussion of its limits (II, iv). At first it appears as though there are no limits on the scope of sovereign power: "Just as nature gives each man absolute power over all his members, the social compact gives the body politic absolute power over all its members, and it is this same power, directed by the general will, which as I have said bears the name sovereignty" (II, iv, 62). However, while there is, in one sense, no limit to the power of the general will, there are substantial limits on its jurisdiction and content. Most importantly, the general will is uniquely political, and, therefore, it can only express itself in laws that are generated from the sovereign as whole and applied to each citizen identically. "The general will should be general in its object as well as in its essence."[42] Its dictates are legitimate only to the extent that they emerge from a strictly democratic process of decision making, through which the voice of every citizen is taken into account.

Rousseau notoriously leaves the content of the general will largely unspecified, as he must if he is to respect popular will—the values, norms, and traditions that will undoubtedly vary for different societies in different times and places. However, he does note that the general will tends constantly toward equality (since it incorporates the voice of every citizen) and can only manifest itself through laws that apply equally to all citizens. By limiting the general will in this way, Rousseau limits the power of the state over the individual. Any matter relating to a particular individual or object falls outside the jurisdiction of the general will. Because the general will must originate from the sovereign body as a whole and apply to all equally, it does not, in theory, and should not, in practice, threaten the rights of minorities. This, I believe, is Rousseau's meaning when he writes that "it is no longer necessary to ask whether the law can be unjust, since no one is unjust toward himself" (II, vi, 66). If laws must meet with the consent of the entire sovereign body, legislation that singles out a particular group or individual is automatically incompatible with the general will, and will be opposed by those disadvantaged by it as well as by those acting out of respect for the common good.

In this chapter, Rousseau also reemphasizes that,

> in addition to the public person, we have to consider the private persons who compose it and whose life and freedom are naturally independent of it. It is a matter then of making a clear distinction between the respective rights of the citizens and the sovereign, and between the duties that the former have to fulfill as subjects and the natural rights to which they are entitled as men (II, iv, 62).

Rousseau reiterates the claim he made in describing the social contract—namely, that whatever does not touch the needs of the collective must be left to the members' private will. However, in the next paragraph, he includes an important addition: "It is agreed that each person alienates through the social compact only that part of his power, goods, and freedom whose use matters to the community; *but it must also be agreed that the sovereign alone is the judge of what matters*" (italics added) (II, iv, 62).

In other words, there is no strict way of knowing beforehand where the line will be drawn between that which touches the needs of the collective and that which is left to private will. This difficulty exists, I believe, for all societies that try to maintain a distinction between public and private, even those that adhere strictly to the natural law tradition.[43] The division of public and private is a tool used to maximize freedom, and there is no reason to believe that Rousseau's less rigid approach to the problem maximizes freedom any better or worse than a doctrinaire legalistic or liberal approach. There is no need here to reel off the many ways in which traditional conceptions of the public/private divide have been exposed as oppressive.[44] While the social contract itself is neutral, it can only be just if the contractees are situated equally. If not, the social contract will merely entrench the inequality of the society on which it is superimposed. As I have noted, a strict distinction between public and private may be the best response to threats from the overextension of public authority. However, if threats to freedom come primarily from within civil society itself, a less formalistic approach may be desirable. Societies must constantly ask whether freedom is best served through the limitation of public power or through its forceful application to sites of oppression. Suffice it to say that a measure of indeterminacy in how the public and private are defined by different societies may be just as likely to support freedom as to undermine it.

VII. FORMULATION OF THE GENERAL WILL

The last step in Rousseau's procedural argument is an account of the process by which sovereign power is exercised. "The sovereign, having no other force than the legislative power, acts only by laws; and since the laws are only authentic acts of the general will, the sovereign can only act when the people is assembled" (III, xii, 99). None of this should be shocking, given Rousseau's argument up to this point. It should be noted, however, that Rousseau's insistence on the participation of all citizens precludes the assumption of legislative power by parties, particular groups, or revolutionary clubs that claim to speak for the people. Any part of the political body is liable to abuse sovereign power, but the political body as a whole will not, according to Rousseau, since "no one is unjust toward himself."

Previously, Rousseau had insisted that the general will emanate from the sovereign body as whole and express the will of the people as a whole. Does Rousseau mean to suggest that all acts of the sovereign body require unanimous consent? In Book IV, chapter ii, he explains, "There is only one law that, by its nature, requires unanimous consent. That is the social compact" (IV, ii, 110). Majority rule will have to suffice for all other sovereign acts, however, "The more harmony there is in the assemblies, that is, the closer opinions come to obtaining unanimous support, the more dominant as well is the general will" (IV, ii, 109). The lack of unanimity in no way undermines the idea of the general will; the general will persists independent of the vagaries of public opinion, which may discern the general will with different degrees of alacrity depending on the virtue of citizens. In other words, though citizens know the general will that is theirs, they may do a better or worse job of subordinating their private will to it. Heterogeneity within a citizen body may limit the breadth or thickness of the general will, but all individuals and groups will possess a common interest and, therefore, a general will. This general will persists regardless of the extent to which individuals allow their differences, vanities, or ambitions to subvert their devotion to it.

In order to ensure that the general will is not corrupted in any way, Rousseau suggests a variety of procedural strategies. First, citizens must convene regularly, not to discuss or debate, but simply to indicate whether a proposed law "does or does not conform to the general will that is theirs"(IV, ii, 111). The guiding principle here is that citizens should be thinking not only of themselves (private will), but of themselves in their relation to the whole (general will). This occurs when each individual thinks for himself, insulated from the corrupting opinions of men motivated by *amour-propre* and self-interest. Here, Rousseau offers a microcosm of the story told in *The Second Discourse,* in which natural man's moral goodness was corrupted during the move from the state of nature to society. We should recall what Rousseau believed to be his great unifying principle: "Everything is good as it leaves the hands of the Author of things; everything degenerates in the hands of man."[45] When they formulate the general will, Rousseau wants citizens as close to their natural goodness as possible and as far away from the opinions of self-interested factions or individuals. As Ernst Cassirer puts it, "every individual is capable of discovering within himself by his own power the original pattern of humanity and of shaping that pattern out of his own self."[46] By delving into the fundamental, primordial, essential goodness human beings share, independently deliberating citizens will simultaneously make and discover their general will.[47] Something like this should characterize the voting process.

Unfortunately, people have a tendency to follow custom and not their own "genius," as Rousseau writes in *The First Discourse.* "How sweet it would be to live among us if the outward countenance were always the image of the heart's dispositions,"[48] which is to say that the heart's dispositions are good by nature and only become corrupt through interaction with other people. Excessive debate and discussion makes deliberation "opaque," such that it becomes more and more difficult to see through to the general will. [49]

Since the sovereignty of the general will is threatened by factions, inequality, and *amour-propre,* it will rarely be the case that the assembled citizens agree unanimously on legislation. Yet, to be legitimate, the general will must reflect the will of every citizen. Rousseau addresses this dilemma with the claim that "the citizen consents to all the laws, even to those passed against his will" (IV, ii, 110). How can this be the case? It turns out that each member need not favor the actual results of this process, they need only to have been included in it.[50] What makes the general will general is the common interest it embodies and the fact that it emerges from a process that includes every citizen; there is no requirement that every sovereign act reflect the expressed preference of every citizen. Though desirable, there can be no guarantee that all citizens will overcome *amour-propre* in favor of the general will. This allows Rousseau to claim that, "When the opinion contrary to mine prevails, that proves nothing except that I was mistaken, and what I thought to be the general will was not" (IV, ii, 111). For this to be true, Rousseau must be working with the assumption that there is a content to the general will that is independent of public deliberation.

Rousseau believes it to be extremely unlikely that any society will succeed in achieving perfect agreement, since private interests remain stubbornly present[51] (not because there is honest disagreement about the common good—a possibility that Rousseau does not acknowledge). In discussing the process by which the general will is formulated, Rousseau calls the general will an "opinion" (IV, ii, 111). In one sense, the general will is grounded in an objective interest that precedes political deliberation. In another, there must be a process by which this interest is embodied in legislation, and this process intrinsically involves opinion. Richard Dagger gets at this distinction by distinguishing between *the* general will and *a* general will. As he puts it, "a general will can be known only through counting votes, but votes are irrelevant to the general will."[52] The general will exists prior to deliberation and is not necessarily the policy that is decided upon (which could be a general will) but the policy that ought to be decided upon. A general will always has something of the will of all in it. That is not to say that it is simply an aggregation of private wills; rather, a general will falls somewhere in between, depending on the extent to which deliberation has been informed by private interest. Dagger's distinction is helpful, but it does not totally work. The understanding of the general will as a pre-deliberative idea captures something about it, but not enough. Even, *the* general will, if we continue to use Dagger's language for the time being, is in some sense, an aggregation of particular wills. That is to say, the general will depends, to some extent, on the actually expressed will of the citizenry. This, of course, undermines the distinction between the general will and the will of all. As we began to see earlier, the space between the general will and the will of all is not great. Previously, we saw how both were composed of particular, individual wills. Here we see how the general will that emerges from a process of deliberation never corresponds exactly to the general will that ought to emerge.

We can clarify this by disaggregating three connotations of unity contained within Rousseau's general will. (1) There is the general will that exists within any association. Rousseau posits this fact, under the assumption that there will be a set of interests shared by all members of any association.

(2) Since all individuals have a private will, different from that which they share as members of an association, there arises the challenge of coordinating individual wills on matters political, such that each member wills the general will. Citizens must be willing to subordinate their private interests to their public interest. Rousseau suggests various strategies to accomplish this, some of which have been discussed here, others that will be discussed in chapter 3.

(3) The general will should be as expansive as possible, consistent with the individual freedom of each member. As we have seen, Rousseau limits the political to the common—the general will must originate from all and be applied equally to all. However, whenever possible, society should seek to expand the scope of the political; it should endeavor to diminish private differences and build on commonalities, such that the sphere of the political (the common) is enlarged. This is advantageous, primarily because it insulates individuals from the threats of *amour-propre* and private relationships of domination, but also because it increases the odds that citizens will successfully coordinate their wills on political matters.

These three impetuses toward unity, which are typically conflated and usefully disaggregated, are already present in Rousseau's procedural argument, though they remain somewhat latent. Rousseau develops them in addressing the question of how to make the general will dominant. For this, we must look beyond Rousseau's procedural argument, toward what he says about the viability of republican citizenship.

NOTES

1. Rousseau, *On the Social Contract with Geneva Manuscript and Political Economy*, ed. Roger Masters (New York: St. Martin's, 1978), 61, hereafter cited as *The Social Con-*

tract. All subsequent quotations are from this edition and will be given within the text including book, chapter, and page number (for example, II, iii, 61).

2. Hans Barth, "Volonté générale et volonté particulière chez J. J. Rousseau," in *Rousseau et la Philosophie Politique* (Paris: Presses Universitaires de France, 1965), 47–48 (hereafter cited as "Volonté générale et volonté particulière").

3. Rousseu, *Émile*, in *Oeuvres complètes,* Collection Bibliothèque de la Pléiade (Paris: Gallimard, 1969), IV:814.

4. Rousseau writes, "It is no small thing to bring order and peace to all parts of the republic; but if one does nothing more, all this will be more apparent than real." See Rousseau, *On the Social Contract*, 216.

5. Hlail Gildin, *Rousseau's Social Contract* (Chicago: The University of Chicago Press, 1983), 145.

6. Rousseau, *The Confessions* (London: Penguin, 1953), 377.

7. Rousseau's *Letters Written from the Mountain* is something of an exception, given its substantial focus on Genevan political institutions.

8. Judith Shklar, "General Will," in *Dictionary of the History of Ideas*, ed. Philip P. Wiener (New York: Charles Scribner's Sons, 1973), 2:276 (hereafter cited as "General Will").

9. Shklar, preface to *Men and Citizens* (London: Cambridge University Press, 1969), vii.

10. W. T. Jones, "Rousseau's General Will and the Problem of Consent, *Journal of the History of Philosophy* 25 (January 1987): 105.

11. See Iain Hampsher-Monk, "Rousseau and Totalitarianism—with Hindsight?" in *Rousseau and Liberty*, ed. Robert Wokler (Manchester: Manchester University Press, 1995), 267–88 (hereafter cited as "Rousseau and Totalitarianism").

12. Glen O. Allen, "*Le Volonté de tous and le volonté général:* A Distinction and Its Significance," *Ethics* 71, no. 4 (July 1961): 264.

13. Shklar, "General Will," 278.

14. Patrick Riley, *Will and Political Legitimacy: A Critical Exposition of Social Contract Theory in Hobbes, Locke, Rousseau, Kant, and Hegel* (Cambridge, Mass.: Harvard University Press, 1982), 112 (hereafter cited as *Will and Political Legitimacy*). Also writing on Rousseau, Shklar notes, "Men cannot be moved by anything but their interests; their self-preserving instincts and their will cannot respond to anything that ignores and defies these." See Shklar, *Men and Citizens*, 188.

15. See Rousseau, "Discourse on the Origin of Inequality among Men," in *The First and Second Discourses*, ed. Victor Gourevitch (New York: Harper and Row, 1986).

16. Rousseau, *The First and Second Discourses*, 139.

17. Helena Rosenblatt writes that it was Rousseau's intention to "invalidate the natural law theorists' highly acclaimed social contract." Rosenblatt, *Rousseau and Geneva* (New York: Cambridge University Press, 1997), 168–69. It is important to note, however, as Rosenblatt does, that, despite Rousseau's criticisms of various applications and manifestations of natural law, he never rejects the idea of natural law itself. Maurizio Viroli explains that Rousseau's argument "is about the place of natural law in the temporal order, and does not contest its superiority as a norm." See Viroli, *Jean-Jacques Rousseau and the Well-Ordered Society,* (New York: Cambridge University Press, 1988), 136.

18. See, for example, Christopher Kelly, "Rousseau and the Case for (and Against) Censorship," *The Journal of Politics* 59, no. 4 (November 1997). See also, Rosenblatt,

Rousseau and Geneva. James Miller's *Rousseau: Dreamer of Democracy* (New Haven, Conn.: Yale University Press, 1984) situates Rousseau's political thought within the context of eighteenth-century Genevan politics.

19. See the Epistle Dedicatory to the second discourse, in *The First and Second Discourse*.

20. Rosenblatt, *Rousseau and Geneva.*

21. Rosenblatt, *Rousseau and Geneva*, 101.

22. Rosenblatt, *Rousseau and Geneva*, 102.

23. Rosenblatt, *Rousseau and Geneva*, 127–28.

24. Rousseau, *Letters Written from the Mountain* (Paris: Seuil, 1971), 482.

25. Rousseau, *Discourses,* 5. For a discussion of the origins and implications of dependence see the "Discourse on the Origin of Inequality" and *Émile.*

26. Rousseau, "Discourse on the Origin of Inequality," 186.

27. Rousseau, "Émile," in *An Introduction to Émile or On Education*, ed. Allan Bloom (New York: Basic, 1979), 85.

28. Later, in chapter iv of Book II of *The Social Contract* entitled "On the Limits of the Sovereign Power," Rousseau writes, "But in addition to the public person, we have to consider the private persons who compose it and whose life and existence are naturally independent of it. It is a matter, then, of making a clear distinction between the respective rights of the citizens and the sovereign, and between the duties they have to fulfill as subjects and the natural right to which they are entitled as men" (II, iv, 62). He continues, "It is agreed that each person alienates through the social compact only that part of his power, goods, and freedom whose use matters to the community." Lest we begin to believe that Rousseau was a theorist of limited government, he adds that "it must also be agreed that the sovereign alone is the judge of what matters" (II, iv, 62).

29. Rousseau, "Discourse on Political Economy," 214.

30. Here, Rousseau refers to the argument he will make in Book II, chapter iv, "on the limits of the sovereign power." This argument depends on Rousseau's confidence in the rectitude of the general will, which, by definition, wills the common good. The problem is that this formulation occludes the space in which a debate over the appeal of limited government may occur. If it is assumed that the general will is the common good, then there will never be a need to consider limitations on sovereign power. However, we may want to take exception with this assumption. If we are skeptical about our ability to collectively determine the common good, we will want to institute limitations on sovereign power.

31. Isaiah Berlin, "Two Concepts of Liberty," in *Four Essays on Liberty* (Oxford: Oxford University Press, 1969), 163.

32. Rousseau writes in "The Geneva Manuscript": "You must think as I do in order to be saved. This is the horrible dogma that desolates the world." Rousseau, *The Social Contract*, 199.

33. Stephen Ellenburg, *Rousseau's Political Philosophy: An Interpretation from Within.* (Ithaca, N.Y.: Cornell University Press, 1976), 197.

34. This conclusion is something of a surprise, given the *Discourses'* condemnation of modern society and the exaltation of natural man.

35. Berlin, "Two Concepts of Liberty," 130.

36. Berlin, "Two Concepts of Liberty," 137.

37. Charles Taylor details the various ways in which this outcome might occur in "What's Wrong with Negative Liberty," in his *Philosophy and the Human Sciences: Philosophical Papers 2* (London: Cambridge University Press, 1985), 211–29.

38. C. E. Vaughan, introduction to *The Political Writings of Jean-Jacques Rousseau*, (Cambridge: Cambridge University Press, 1915), 1:48.

39. As with most attempts to distinguish between different intentions in Rousseau's system, Vaughan distorts Rousseau's political philosophy by insisting on the distinction between "Rousseau's early writings which assert the freedom of the individual and later ones which assert a radical collectivism." See Vaughn, *The Political Writings of Jean-Jacques Rousseau*, p. 5. The difference between Rousseau's argument in the *Discourses* and his argument in later political writings is one of theme and not of intention. The *Discourses* presents the problem that the later political writings are designed to remedy. The society outlined in *The Social Contract* is not a betrayal of his earlier allegiance to individual freedom, but, rather an account of the only political path to recapturing the freedom society has endangered.

40. Rousseau's use of the word "often" (*souvent*) in this passage would seem to confirm this reading. "There is *often* a great difference between the will of all . . . and the general will [italics added]." The word "often" indicates that, although social circumstances make it highly unlikely, it is possible that the general will and the will of all will be identical. Though the will of all is the sum of private wills, Rousseau implies that private will can be identical with the general will, when citizens equate their private good with the good of the whole.

41. In section VII of this chapter and in chapter 3, we will examine the advantages of minimizing the differences between private interests. For human beings to truly flourish in political life, this procedural safeguard is altogether insufficient. Realizing freedom through politics demands the cultivation of bonds of commonality, which allow for the legitimate expansion of the political sphere.

42. Rousseau, *Geneva Manuscript,* 175.

43. As Hampsher-Monk points out, "it simply is the case that the indeterminacy of natural law requires deliberation." See Monk, "Rousseau and Totalitarianism—with Hindsight?" 281–82.

44. Carole Pateman's *The Sexual Contract* (Stanford: Stanford University Press, 1988) shows how traditional conceptions of the social contract depend on sexual oppression. C. B. MacPherson's *The Political Theory of Possessive Individualism* (Oxford, U.K.: Oxford University Press, 1962) reveals the class-based inequality entrenched by the social contracts of Hobbes and Locke.

45. Rousseau, *Émile,* 137. Jean Starobinski writes that Rousseau "does not wish to give up the possibility of criticizing society for perverting human nature, but at the same time he wants to claim that man's original goodness remains unaltered." See Starobinski, *Jean-Jacques Rousseau: Transparency and Obstruction* (Chicago: University of Chicago Press, 1971), 20.

46. Ernst Cassirer, *The Question of Jean-Jacques Rousseau* (Bloomington, Ind.: Indiana University Press, 1963), 124.

47. The following chapter discusses the paradox involved in simultaneously making and discovering the general will.

48. Rousseau, *Discourses,* 5.

Chapter 2

49. Zev Trachtenberg, *Making Citizens: Rousseau's Political Theory of Culture* (New York: Routledge, 1993), 49.

50. Trachtenberg writes, "a set of goods can count as the common good even if not every member of society wants the good, but only if society takes everyone's wants into account in defining the general will." See Trachtenberg, *Making Citizens*, 22.

51. In *The Social Contract*, Rousseau acknowledges this in Book IV, chapter ii, as we have seen.

52. Richard Dagger, *Civic Virtues: Rights, Citizenship, and Republican Liberalism* (New York: Oxford University Press, 1997), 91.

Chapter 3

Rousseau and the Viability of Democracy

Rousseau's account of the procedural principles of political right is provocative, at times compelling, but it cannot stand on its own. Indeed, Rousseau, believed that no formal principles of political legitimacy could be defended without concurrent consideration of how human beings will be moved to observe those principles. In fact, it was this very issue upon which Rousseau distinguished his version of the general will from the reigning version, conceptualized by Denis Diderot in an entry of the *Encyclopédie*.[1] To some extent, Rousseau formulated his own contribution to the *Encyclopédie*, "Political Economy," as a criticism of Diderot's general will for its embrace of a cosmopolitan sense of justice—universally valid, with roots in the welfare of humanity as a whole.[2] Rousseau rejected the premise that there is a general will of humankind as a whole, and, more importantly for our purposes, he rejected Diderot's implied assumption that human beings will do the right thing if they know the right thing. It was empirically false to identify a "general will of the species," as Diderot had done, and counterintuitive to assume that this kind of cosmopolitanism could ever inform "thoughts and desires," as Diderot had prescribed.[3] Rousseau writes, "It is apparent from this what should be thought of those supposed cosmopolites who, justifying their love of the homeland by means of their love of the human race, boast of loving everyone in order to have the right to love no one."[4] The great failing of Diderot's general will, according to Rousseau, was not so much that it posited a "general society of mankind,"[5] but that it failed to address the question of how human beings are moved to observe principles of political right. If Diderot had attended to this latter concern, he would have understood the emptiness of the notion of a general will of all humankind.

Rousseau preferred a general will that both contrasts with particular will and, in some ways, remains particular itself. Rousseau's general will stands in between the particular and the universal, pursuing a modest unity of purpose and sentiment that does not attempt to push beyond the borders of a given society. It stands

49

in opposition to particularity and narrow self-interest and "moves toward univer-sality," as Patrick Riley puts it, "but has its reasons for not building *on* reason and for drawing up short at a more modest 'generality.'"[6] The most important of these reasons, I believe, is the resources a more modest generality provides for the cul-tivation of civic virtue.

Of course, this conception produces its own theoretical conundrums, as Rousseau himself understood (self-identifying as an *homme à paradoxe*). Indeed, the paradoxes and seeming contradictions in Rousseau's corpus have long puz-zled interpreters. One can begin anywhere—take the man himself, for example. In his *Confessions,* Rousseau admits that he is and always was a useless citizen. This would seem to be a problem since he had said in the *Discourses* that every useless citizen may be regarded as a pernicious man.[7] Rousseau avoids this fate by retreating into the pleasures of solitude, which, he asserts, are sweeter than any of the pleasures of political life.[8] Still, he spent many of his solitary days preoc-cupied with his reputation, struggling against the ostracism imposed on him by his contemporaries. The man who, more than any other modern political theorist, extolled the virtues of citizenship, who dreamt of having been born a Spartan or a Roman, failed to be a citizen of any *patrie* whatsoever. The man who wrote, "If only I had been born a Roman,"[9] failed even to be a Genevan.

In *Émile*, he asks his readers to forgive his paradoxes because, he claims, it is necessary to make them when one thinks. This should not absolve Rousseau from criticism for what can only be described as contradictions within his political the-ory. We might say that Rousseau failed to pay rightful homage to his own claims about paradox, often asserting that he had solved riddles as opposed to just illu-minating them. Consequently, we often find Rousseau staunchly committed to conflictual goals that cannot be entirely reconciled. Sometimes Rousseau leads us to believe that he intends these contradictions to reveal his essential teaching, while at other times he insists that he has reconciled the paradoxes of modern pol-itics. Whatever Rousseau's fundamental intentions were, it is my contention that the great political lesson made available by Rousseau's political theory lies in his paradoxes.

Many Rousseau scholars have postulated unifying ideas that might resolve the incoherencies in Rousseau's thought.[10] Instead, I embrace Rousseau's paradoxes (at least some of them) as reflective of basic tensions in egalitarian politics, and I go on the offensive against his critics. Rather than undermine their accusations of contradiction, I hope to show how Rousseau's contradictions illuminate fun-damental aspects of egalitarian politics. In so doing, it may be possible to put on the defensive those who aspire to a reconciliation of these tensions (as I argued in chapter 1). As Benjamin Barber writes, "My objective is not then to rescue Rousseau from his detractors, but to rescue his detractors from their own sparse vision."[11] This sparse vision stems from the misguided belief that egalitarian pol-itics can do without an account of citizenship—not just an account of the status or even the virtues of citizens, but an account of how these virtues can be cultivated consistent with formal principles of justice and legitimacy. The latter is precisely what Rousseau's general will provides.

Like most modern thinkers, Rousseau tried to simultaneously respect popular will and rationalize it. To accomplish, this he developed his great political idea, the general will, which embodies the paradox of willing a non-voluntaristic politics.[12] With the general will, Rousseau sought to preserve the spirit and virtue of antiquity, while respecting the individual rights cherished by the Enlightenment. Indeed, his general will combines (if paradoxically) much of what we find appealing about the modern age with much of what it lacks. In exploring this idea, I move beyond Rousseau's procedural argument, taking seriously his assertion that his writings ought to be interpreted as a unified whole. This, I believe, is the only way to fully understand Rousseau's general will, which incorporates both a procedural argument for political right and an account of the conditions necessary for putting those principles into practice. Because he inhabits this tension, Rousseau's description of politics produces a variety of well-known (and self-acknowledged) paradoxes. We might ask if it is possible to be an *homme à paradoxe* while simultaneously maintaining a coherent system of thought. Of course it is. It need only be that the world itself be replete with paradoxes, and this is a condition that Rousseau would have no trouble accepting. As Allan Bloom writes, "Rousseau's thought has an externally paradoxical character . . . but it is remarkably consistent, the contradictions reflecting contradictions in the nature of things."[13] Rousseau seeks neither to resolve these contradictions nor to surrender to them; rather, he theorizes within them, and, in so doing, produces the revelations about political life that account for his enduring influence. One may attempt to reconcile the contradictions in Rousseau or to use them as evidence of his ultimate incoherence, but, in so doing, Rousseau's essential teaching is obscured. The remainder of this chapter considers Rousseau's general will in this spirit, in an attempt to capture Rousseau's account of the struggle to cultivate citizenship while respecting individual rights.

I. FREEDOM AND MORALITY

I began the previous chapter by questioning the sincerity of Rousseau's self-imposed constraint from *The Social Contract*—that he would limit his inquiry to the question of legitimacy. In this chapter, we shall see how Rousseau's seemingly modest claim to show only what can make society legitimate, turns out to be a mammoth claim to communicate "truths that would make for the happiness of the human race."[14] The general will combines moral psychology and political theory to convey a complex picture of human flourishing, one that includes not only questions of legitimacy, but questions of justice and happiness as well. Rousseau's conclusions transcend the confines he establishes for them. This explains why it is so natural, yet so wrong, to read *The Social Contract* as a doctrine that "permits one to distinguish between a legitimate and an illegitimate political order not a just from an unjust one."[15] The book allows one to do both—"[it] is the transportation of the most essential individual moral faculty to the realm of public experience."[16] One should not make the mistake of reading *The Social Contract* outside of the context of Rousseau's writings as a whole. For Rousseau, the underlying question was always of the loftiest dimensions—how to reclaim man's natural goodness. Politics might be one way, and, on Rousseau's account, there are others as well, but none of them could ever be separated from morality.

This relationship between politics and morality, a relationship within which Rousseau always writes, worries liberal democrats while simultaneously haunting them. Rousseau confronted the tension between politics and morality, which can be alternately understood (in this case) as the tension between freedom and the conditions necessary for the viability of freedom. While, for earlier modern thinkers, freedom had taken the place of virtue as the chief concern of political philosophy, for Rousseau, freedom is intelligible only in conjunction with virtue. However, what makes him revolutionary is not simply his refusal to separate politics from morality—that alone would make him retrograde. What makes him revolutionary is the way he combines the moderns' emphasis on freedom and autonomy with the ancients' concern for virtue. Morality does not stand above freedom for Rousseau, as it had done for all previous thinkers. Allan Bloom writes, "For [Rousseau] freedom is the source of morality, as opposed to nature or revealed religion."[17] So, while Rousseau insists with the ancients that politics and morality must be linked, he insists equally stubbornly with the moderns that freedom be the cornerstone of politics.

Freedom is the source of morality; as Bloom says, however, morality is necessary for freedom as well. This is why the tension between morality and politics is a tension and can only be clarified (never resolved) by statements such as "for [Rousseau] freedom is the source of morality." It is true that Rousseau views freedom as a prerequisite for morality, but morality is also a prerequisite for freedom. This is both the most challenging and the most appealing characteristic of Rousseauean freedom—it demands both autonomy and virtue, two qualities that do not always sit comfortably side by side. Rousseau's attempt to fuse the two is the source of what Patrick Riley has called "Rousseau's circularities."[18] For Rousseau, the tension between morality and politics is intrinsic to political life itself and can only be eluded by ill-conceived attempts to separate moral psychology from political philosophy. Although this strict dichotomy has currently won the favor of many political theorists, it must not be allowed to contaminate our reading of Rousseau, who not only rejected the dichotomy, but theorized within the tension between its two poles.

The term "general will" itself encompasses so many of the tensions within Rousseau's conception of freedom. By using the word "will," rather than "spirit" or "interest," Rousseau emphasizes individual agency and decision making; and, by demanding that the will be made general, he confronts us with questions about the conditions necessary for freedom. Popular will must be respected, but it must also be rationalized or generalized. Rousseau expresses this problem by defining freedom as "my being able to will only what is suitable to me, or what I deem to be such, without external constraint."[19] (Note that this formulation leaves open the question as to which standards ought to determine "what is suitable.")

Had Rousseau been the authoritarian moralist many of his critics have made him out to be, he would not have made the general will the center of his political philosophy; instead, he could have opted for "common good" or "*esprit général,*" or he could have spoken of achieving perfect generality through a Platonic system of education.[20] Instead, he emphasized will, underlining the primacy of freedom in his political philosophy, even though, as indicated above, Rousseauean freedom is freedom of a particular kind—freedom as self-rule. Rousseau's focus on self-rule comes primarily from his preoccupation with the corruption prevalent in modern society and its effect on the viability of freedom. On Rousseau's account, it would be nonsensical to think about formal guarantees of personal autonomy, without simultaneously considering the social conditions required to exercise that autonomy.

The primary impediment to freedom in modern society is a socially produced system of *manières* and inequality, through which individuals have subordinated themselves to their own vanity and passions and have been subordinated by the institutions of inequality, which generates patterns of dependence that are incompatible with freedom. For freedom to prevail, inequality must be defeated. The barriers to "willing what is suitable . . . without external constraint" must be annihilated, and this is why the general will is general, why it targets the particular, why it is, in Shklar's words, "fundamentally a will against inequality." In order to will freely, individuals must be protected against the corrupting influences of *amour-propre, manières,* and institutionalized inequality. The general will attacks these forces, in the name of equality, and with the goal of enabling freedom.

The general will is a will against inequality and a will to freedom. It asks individuals to give themselves entirely to the state, because it is only through "excessive dependence on the city" that each citizen can be "in a position of perfect independence from all the others" (II, xii, 77). Modern patterns of inequality and dependence pose such a significant threat to individual autonomy that formal guarantees of personal liberty will be far from sufficient. These guarantees must be supplemented with an attack on the particularizing forces that threaten individual autonomy—which is to say that the general will must be made dominant or, put differently, that citizenship must be made compatible with autonomy.

II. AUTONOMY AND CITIZENSHIP

Rousseau's emphasis on the cultivation of citizenship has led many interpreters to conclude, as Tzvetan Todorov does, that "the principal object of Rousseau's political writings is not the life of the citizen but of the city."[21] Precisely the opposite is true, as I see it; the city (political community) is elevated in Rousseau, because it is only through the city that individuals can be emancipated from social tendencies toward dependence. This is not to say that Rousseau favors individuality or eccentricity, which would be farfetched given his emphasis on the necessity of a homogenizing process of socialization. However, Rousseau clearly believed that socialization is compatible with individual autonomy, and that individual autonomy is a prerequisite for freedom.[22] We should be wary of charges that Rousseau sacrificed the individual to the community; if anything, the opposite is more plausible—that his idealization of political life distorted it in the interest of the individual's well-being.

Indeed, Rousseau seems to believe that only an improbable, idealized picture of political life can guarantee individual autonomy. The general will itself can seem mythical, in the way it simultaneously embodies and/or emanates from the sovereign, the laws, customs, *mœurs,* justice, and voting majorities. As Frederick Neuhouser writes, "the general will is both the embodiment and a precondition for freedom."[23] For example, Rousseau seems to simultaneously claim that the sovereign has absolute power over its members, because whatever the sovereign dictates is the general will, and because the general will is that which is sovereign. Paradoxically, the general will stands both for that which the sovereign decides (popular will) and that by which the sovereign ought to decide (rational will); it originates both before and after the sovereign speaks. Only a felicitous coincidence between what the sovereign wills and what it ought to will can save political life from corruption.

Generally speaking, modern citizens have been corrupted, and their collective will reflects this corruption. Consequently, their freedom can only be recaptured if the popular will is generalized. Only after it has been made properly general, will sovereign power maximize freedom. Put alternately, men must become citizens, and that means that Rousseau must find a way to simultaneously preserve autonomy and inculcate virtue. Liberty means autonomy for Rousseau, in the sense that people are only free when they obey laws they give themselves.[24] Had this not been a central concern for Rousseau, he could have opted for an openly authoritarian approach to the cultivation of virtue; instead, he has to be more subtle, such that citizenship might be reconciled with individual autonomy. Rousseau asserts that no one should ever part with the freedom to make his own decisions, because "that is to renounce one's quality as a man."[25] This is why sovereignty cannot be surrendered to a king or aristocracy; that would mean surrendering the moral autonomy that makes human beings free. It also explains why the general will cannot be represented; doing so removes its active component, the willing, which is nothing less than the faculty of free and moral action. The paradox is that politics must simultaneously respect individual autonomy and cultivate the conditions for exercising autonomy. What Rousseau desired, to use Patrick Riley's phrase, is for "the generality of antiquity to be legitimized by consent."[26] This puts Rousseau in the awkward position of maintaining that individuals remain autonomous even when they consent to laws they have been conditioned to accept.

There will be no resolution to this paradox in Rousseau's work, only illumination of it. Some interpreters have tried to elude the tension by focusing on the formal side of Rousseau's argument, by reading *The Social Contract* as a procedural argument about the institutions necessary for political legitimacy. This conclusion is attractive in that it resolves some of the tensions in Rousseau's assertions about freedom; however, for reasons already given, it distorts Rousseau's intention. It simply cannot be made consistent with the claims Rousseau himself makes about the goal of politics and the aspiration to human fulfillment that underlies all of his writings. The hegemony of the general will involves much more than the institutions of self-government, and it is only with this in mind that it is possible to understand the intricacies and contradictions of Rousseauean freedom.

Rousseau does have a procedural argument, intended to secure the autonomous participation of every citizen in the articulation of the general will (as we saw in chapter 2). Citizens must convene regularly, not to discuss or debate, but to indicate "whether [the law] does or does not conform to the general will that is theirs" (IV, ii, 111). This falls well short of self-legislation, but Rousseau views it as participatory enough to qualify as consent and, therefore, preserve autonomy. By demanding that each member of the sovereign body participate, it becomes possible to call the decision produced by this process the general will. Thus, a set of judgments can be called the general will when the process of decision making incorporates the will of each member. The important implication here is that each member need not favor the actual results of this process, they need only to have been included in it (iv, ii, 110). This allows Rousseau to claim that "the citizen consents to all the laws, even to those passed against his will." If a citizen does vote in the minority, it never reflects honest disagreement; rather, it demonstrates only that this citizen was "mistaken" about the content of the general will.

To be mistaken, in Rousseau's terminology, is the equivalent of subordinating the general will to one's private will.[27] Political will must be rationalized or made general, according to Rousseau, and this rationalization comes at least as much from without as from within, which is the main reason why it will not do to say that Rousseau wants only to create the institutions for self-government. As Shklar notes, "once the Legislator has successfully rationalized personal will, the government does almost everything."[28] Once citizens have been taught to will generally, there is very little need for their active participation in policy making. The general will becomes evident, or transparent, to use Starobinski's language, such that the government, which, in Rousseau's system is nothing more than the executor of the sovereign's will, can simply enforce the laws. But if this is the case—if citizens must be made from denatured men—does it make sense to preserve the language of autonomy and will? Rousseau wants to condition citizens as much as is necessary to ensure that the general will prevails, but not so much as to prevent it from being formulated by autonomous agents.[29]

This tension recurs in the different images of authority presented by Rousseau. The Legislator in *The Social Contract,* the tutor in *Émile,* and Wolmar in *La Nouvelle Héloïse* all condition the will in an extremely subtle fashion, such that the subject of authority perceives himself to be acting of his own volition. The Legislator must be able to "persuade without convincing,"[30] as Rousseau puts it. The undemocratic role of the Legislator is difficult to reconcile with Rousseau's professed goals of liberty and autonomy. Again, Rousseau means to say something about the conditions necessary for free will. Unlike earlier liberals, Rousseau rejected the notion of a law of nature, of a morality inscribed naturally in each person; for him, morality depends on society. "It is certain that people are in the long run what the government makes them."[31] By nature man has only a self-absorbed primitive goodness, not the kind of moral awareness that can only be the product of socialization. This implies a new level of responsibility for politics, which must create social institutions that know how to denature human beings, to change human nature, such that the individual no longer feels whole outside of the political community.[32]

Since Rousseau views politics as a prerequisite for morality, there exists an imperative in his politics that is absent from previous social contract theory. This imperative produces many of the tensions in Rousseau's political philosophy and begins to explain his desire to temper modern autonomy with ancient virtue. The general will only prevails, according to Rousseau, when citizens feel a deep attachment to the fatherland and, therefore, to each other. Consequently, politics demands institutions that transform the totally self-interested goodness of natural man into the fraternally bound morality of the citizen. "It is not enough to say to citizens, be good, they must be taught to be so."[33] The voice of the citizens can only be considered the general will after the Legislator, customs, education, and civil religion have instilled in them a deep, emotional attachment to the fatherland—hence, Rousseau's belief that presiding over education is the state's most important business.[34] By almost whatever means necessary, whether it be through the Legislator, censorship, civil religion, or public festivals, men must be inspired with a patriotic zeal. Even Rousseau's warnings about the perils of sudden change reflect his paternalism. When he warns against giving the "governmental system any shock that is too sudden," because "citizens of a new type cannot be created overnight,"[35] one is struck more by Rousseau's claim that citizens can be created—that men can be made anew—than by his claim that customs must be respected.

Ideally, the project of transforming human nature will be accomplished by a great legislator—a Moses, Lycurgus, or Numa—who effectively creates a people through the substitution of civil right for natural right. In *The Social Contract,* Rousseau hopes for someone like the leader discussed in Plato's *Statesman,* "someone who saw all of men's passions yet experienced none of them . . . whose happiness was independent of ours, yet who was willing to attend to ours" (II, vi, 67). However, we have good reason to doubt the sincerity of this hope, both because Rousseau was extremely skeptical about the possibilities of a latter-day Moses, Lycurgus, or Numa, given the depraved state of modern society, and because Rousseau writes elsewhere that it would not be wise to depend on a great leader, and that good public mores will have to replace the genius of leaders.[36] After asserting the ideal of the Legislator, Rousseau begins more detailed discussions of the actually existing resources available to approximate that ideal. Custom and civil religion substitute for the Legislator in much of Rousseau's work, combining to produce a paradoxical synthesis of parochialism and toleration.

In his *Letter to d'Alembert,* Rousseau extols the value of public festivals in which "each sees and loves himself in the others so that all will be better united."[37] He wants to establish the primacy of this kind of absorption in the immediacy of total identification with the community. Rousseau's unification of parochialism and toleration is a kind of proto-Hegelian reconciliation of custom and reason, "single and universal," as Jean Starobinski puts it.[38] Custom becomes rationalized by its generality for Rousseau, by affecting moral conscience such that citizens voluntarily identify totally with the general will.

Similarly, Rousseau's civil religion is intended to cultivate the level of attachment to the community necessary to inspire civic virtue. Religion dominates Rousseau's writings, and, though it would be inaccurate to call him a Christian in any strict, doctrinal sense, he had a religious belief in the natural goodness of man, as well as in its political embodiment—the general will. Channeling religious enthusiasm into political life, as the ancients had done, can accomplish the Legislator's task of persuading without convincing. Accomplishing this, though, requires nothing short of a transformation of Christian principles, a transformation that understandably provoked charges of blasphemy from contemporaries, in spite of Rousseau's profound religiosity. Christianity, though it had been immensely successful at persuading without convincing, unfortunately did so in the name of the universal rather than the general. In other words, it generalized the will too much, such that men were no longer primarily attached to the fatherland or to politics at all. It divided man, creating competing allegiances to politics and religion, to this life and the next, so as to ensure that "the interest of the priest would always be stronger than that of the State" (IV, viii, 127). And for Rousseau, "Everything that destroys social unity is worthless. All institutions that put man in contradiction with himself are worthless" (IV, viii, 128). Moreover, the Christian virtues of passivity and other-worldliness threaten republican freedom, which must be aggressively asserted and militantly defended.[39]

Rousseau goes so far as to equate true Christians with slaves, lending a measure of credence to the charges of impiety directed at him.[40] He composed his *Letters Written from the Mountain* in response to these charges (though his largely instrumental appreciation of religion would seem only to feed the fires of criticism): "Religion is *useful* and even *necessary* to people, so far from attacking the principles of religion, [I] affirm them with all [my] power"[41]—the principles of religion, Rousseau affirms, the doctrine of Christianity, he does not. Whereas, for the priest, it matters a great deal that Christianity be true, for Rousseau, religion need only be persuasive. In fact, he equated a dogmatic insistence on Christian doctrine with fanaticism, which produces carnage rather than peace, intolerance as opposed to morality.[42] For Rousseau, there are only two possibilities. Either Christianity must be excluded totally from politics, or it must be made consistent with civic virtue.[43] Religion is crucial but only in that it must inspire morality and a willingness to sacrifice one's life for the fatherland. Under ancient paganism, religion served politics. The gods of the pagans were never jealous; they never demanded fidelity above and beyond fidelity to the laws. "Far from men fighting for the Gods, it was—as in Homer—the Gods who fought for the men" (IV, viii, 125). For the ancients, the allegiances demanded by politics and religion were congruent, but Christianity destroyed that congruence by introducing a God that demanded an allegiance above and beyond the interest of the fatherland.

In one sense, Rousseau admires the zealotry of religious fanaticism and wants to channel it into an emotional attachment to the fatherland. On the other hand, he knows that fanaticism divides society. Consequently, his civil religion is limited to a few positive principles: belief in divinity, the afterlife, the happiness of the just, the punishment of the wicked, and the sanctity of the social contract and its laws. The proscriptions number only one: intolerance (IV, viii, 131). The unlikely coupling of a spirit of tolerance with a religious devotion to the fatherland seems destined to self-destruct. Some see Rousseau's civil religion as an attempt at thought control, which it is, though one should not see it as only that.[44] For Rousseau, the paradox of an intolerant insistence on tolerance is the best safeguard against the emergence of an imperialistic, authoritarian religion, dangerous to personal freedom. The enthusiasm Christianity inspires can only be replaced with an equally enthusiastic civil religion. Consequently, what is properly understood as a secularization of the principles of religious salvation must also be perceived, in Starobinski's language "as a *sacralization* of the idealized forms of political life."[45] The general will, which originates (historically) as a Christian description of God's will, reclaims its sacredness in Rousseau's civil religion, a term that itself juxtaposes the sacred and the secular. Citizens must give themselves over to the general will with the same kind of religious devotion previously inspired by Christianity.

Whether it be through the Legislator, education, custom, or religion, there is a strong paternalistic side to Rousseau, one that often seems inconsistent with freedom. Ironically, for Rousseau, the only way to safeguard citizens' independence is by making them entirely dependent on the collective for their identity. Zev Trachtenberg argues that this paradox dooms Rousseau's project: "The cultural institutions [Rousseau] believes are needed to sustain society as it could be invalidate his explanation of how individuals can be free while they are obligated by law."[46] One may indeed be forced to this conclusion if one insists on interpreting the general will (and Rousseau's political philosophy as a whole) as a straightforward prescription for political action. If, on the contrary, one understands the general will as a ideal intended to illuminate the tensions and complexities intrinsic to political life itself, one is compelled to confront the intractable problem of how to secure the conditions for the viability of freedom in general without undermining the personal freedom of particular individuals. The general will must become the will of individuals (whether or not they initially adopt it as such), because it is the equivalent of the individual's will, at least in the sense that it wills the conditions necessary for the realization of freedom.

Rousseau's works should evoke skepticism toward totalitarian portrayals such as Lester Crocker's, which claims that Rousseau's philosophy "strips liberty of all meaning."[47] Consider, for example, Rousseau's insistence on individual autonomy, on Émile always doing what he wants to do, and his dismissal of "the idea that you must think as I do in order to be saved," which he sees as "a dogma that desolates the world."[48] On the other hand, Rousseau's works should equally evoke skepticism about these stated commitments to autonomy. He never explicitly rules out thought control when it comes to securing the conditions for freedom, and though he says that the truly free man does what he pleases, he also believes that the public "must be taught to know what it wants" (II, vi, 67). It is as if autonomy were nothing more than a prerequisite for legitimacy, and not ultimately crucial to freedom. So long as the individual believes himself to be willing his own ends, Rousseau is not bothered about whether he has been specifically conditioned to prefer those ends. He shares the ambivalence of his literary creation Claire, who tells Julie, "we are too educated . . . to allow ourselves to be governed by others and not educated enough to govern ourselves."[49]

Autonomy is necessary to freedom for Rousseau, but so far from sufficient, because he rejects the claim that the duty to obey can be derived from self-interest alone. Self-interest must be rationalized or made general for Rousseau, which takes him into areas of political philosophy commonly perceived as illiberal. It is tempting to dismiss Rousseau's politics based on these illiberal forays, but in doing so one runs the risk of becoming complacent about a conception of politics that wants to ignore the necessity of safeguarding the conditions for freedom. Rousseau carves out his theoretical space somewhere between liberalism and illiberalism, in the "middle of the totalitarian-liberal divide," as Hampsher-Monk puts it.[50] Forcing Rousseau to one side of this divide or the other forces him to take a side in a debate, the presuppositions of which he meant to contest. As Arthur Melzer argues, "Rousseau is neither radical democrat nor authoritarian, he is uniquely both; both the power of the state over individuals and the power of citizens over the state must be brought to a maximum."[51] It falls to us not to resolve this tension but to understand it. After all, were Rousseau's politics distinctly resolvable into one extreme or the other, he probably would not have had such an enduring influence, but, rather, would have fallen into obscurity as one-dimensional theorists of that kind usually do.

This does not entirely mute the force of the criticism that Rousseau puts personal freedom at risk by justifying the invasive application of public power. It may be the case that, in establishing the conditions for the viability of freedom, Rousseau goes beyond a framework for safeguarding individual autonomy, to the privileging of a certain subjective conception of happiness—one that endangers autonomous decision making in the name of its very protection. Charles Hendel argues that the general will has precisely this kind of transcendent claim to goodness, that it is a new version of Plato's idea of justice.[52] If Hendel is right, the general will becomes a metaphysical entity that must be discovered and that is not necessarily the will of each citizen. But this belies Rousseau's claim that the general will is possessed by all citizens. Perhaps the general will is not actually possessed by all, but only ideally possessed by them, which amounts to saying that the general will is not necessarily the policy decided on by public deliberation. As Crocker puts it, "the people's will and the general will aren't the same for Rousseau as they are in liberal societies."[53] In liberal societies men may decide, but for Rousseau men must become citizens before the general will becomes their own.

III. PARTICULARITY AND GENERALITY

By this point, it should be clear that the chief challenge to the dominance of the general will is the influence of particularity. Contemporary partisans of citizenship face this challenge in a new, more complicated guise. Today's pluralist societies make the impetus to overwhelm particularity indefensible. Consequently, Rousseau's political prescriptions are typically disavowed as intolerant of diversity. Rousseau, it is claimed, eviscerates pluralism and the public/private divide in the name of unity and homogeneity. However, Rousseau's response to particularity ought not be so speedily rebuffed.

Rousseau meets the challenge of diversity, or particularity, in two ways (neither of which have much of an initial appeal in an age of pluralism): sometimes he is eager to overwhelm it and sometimes he prefers to exclude it from the general will and, thereby, the political realm. The latter tendency appears inconsistent with the supreme task Rousseau assigns to politics—the creation of the best men—a goal that would seem attainable only through an extension of the political realm into the private sphere. Rousseau addresses this problem and, in the process, responds to the charge that his political philosophy leaves no space for difference.

It is of the utmost importance when considering the criticisms like Crocker's that one keep in mind the self-conceived limitations and applications of Rousseau's political theory. Much of the offense Rousseau has caused is largely the product of inappropriate extrapolations from some of his more utopian passages. When confronted with the actually existing societies of eighteenth-century Europe, Rousseau saw little hope for the realization of a free society along the lines he describes in *The Social Contract,* or even in the more modest *Government of Poland* and *Project for Corsica.* In most societies of Rousseau's age, the majority did not will in accordance with the general will. The consequence, from a Rousseauean perspective, is that these societies and the people in them were not free. Rousseau explains why people are in chains, but we should not take his explanation to be a prescription for homogenizing authoritarianism. Where possible, unity and patriotism should be cultivated, but Rousseau was awake (if not completely sensitive) to the obstacles posed by pluralistic societies. Depending on the issue, he will vacillate between accommodating difference and attacking it, generally according to whether he views it as dangerously divisive. So, for example, in the case of religion, diversity is manageable, while in the case of economic inequality, it must be mitigated.

Despite these subtleties, there is no doubting Rousseau's basic preference for unity. Rousseau saw unity in the goodness of natural man, whose simple, transparent needs and desires meant that he always wanted only what he could do and did only what he pleased. Whatever the accuracy of this view, it forms the foundation of Rousseau's critique of the divisiveness of modern society. United by nature, man becomes divided by what Judith Shklar calls a "semi-legitimate prison, half-natural and half-civic."[54] The goodness man has by nature must become virtue; otherwise he will always be divided between particular and general. The spectrum of Rousseau's works describes a variety of quests for unity, whether it be through solitude, education, or community. Self-sufficiency is the appeal of Émile's education, the life of Julie and Wolmar on their country estate, and Rousseau's solitary, philosophical reveries. Rousseau seeks to approximate the same kind of unity in political life, all the while aware of its utopian implausibility and of the likelihood that, ultimately, true unity can be attained only by withdrawing from society.

"Above all unite," is Rousseau's advice to Geneva in his *Letters Written from the Mountain*. "You are lost without resource if you stay divided."[55] Here Rousseau intends mainly to criticize the system of privilege dominant in Geneva, a more modest ambition than we typically understand by his language in *The Social Contract*. For example, in *The Social Contract,* Rousseau writes that individuals in a body politic, "have only a single will which relates to their common preservation and the general welfare" (IV, i, 108). The use of the phrase "single will," an infamous favorite of Maximilien de Robespierre's, seems to imply so much more than a critique of privilege or inequalities of wealth, or an impulse to patriotism—the kinds of unifying measures Rousseau favors in his specifically practical works. In *The Geneva Manuscript,* Rousseau goes so far as to call the sovereign body a "common self."[56] However, in considering the general will and questions of difference, it remains most fruitful to approach Rousseau with an appreciation of the tension between particular and general that inevitably characterizes political life and to avoid forcing him to one side of the distinction or the other.

In the previous chapter, I argued that the parameters of the general will can be specified by thinking of the general will as that which is left over when the private wills of each cancel each other out. Any matter relating to a particular individual or object falls outside the jurisdiction of the general will. Thus, in one sense, the general will implies what Alfred Cobban calls "the simple and easily defensible ideal that that which touches the whole community should be regulated by the whole community."[57] It would be inappropriate, however, to understand this hedge on state power as salutary from Rousseau's perspective. For Rousseau, restricting the domain of politics hinders man's quest for unity, forcing him to withdraw from politics to find true happiness. In fact, this limit on the jurisdiction of the general will must be read not merely as a safeguard for private interests, but also as an imperative to cultivate commonality, such that the sphere of politics can expand, consistent with the personal freedom of every citizen. Rousseau simultaneously limits political power to that which affects the whole community and advocates the expansion of all social institutions that enlarge the scope of that which affects the whole community.

Particularity will persist in even the most unified of societies. It is of the utmost importance, however, that it be excluded from political life. Rousseau insisted that civic life be a perfect unity, which meant not so much that particularity had to be eradicated, but that it had to be relegated to a nonpolitical sphere. But even outside of politics, this sphere of particularity continuously threatens to infiltrate the reign of the general will and the unity of the body politic.[58] Third-millennium societies like ours, with their various parties and interest groups, face tremendous difficulties, both in articulating a general will and in maintaining its superiority. The general will depends on a recognized common interest and on the exclusion of particularity, which implies that unity can only be *completely* recovered in politics when the citizen body is perfectly homogeneous. The most we can hope for in actually existing societies is to have two separate but equally robust spheres, one political and one private. It may be possible to construct two separate wholes, such that the human condition is divided but the human soul is not. After all, both the citizen of *The Social Contract* and the pupil in *Émile* pursue a similar kind of virtue, one through politics and one through education. Rousseau, though, is comfortable neither with the absorption of the private into politics nor with the notion that they can ever remain separate.

As we saw in chapter 2, Rousseau prefaces the total alienation of each associate, with the qualifier that "everything that is not of the essence of the social compact is set aside." Now, if the citizen body were perfectly homogeneous, nothing would have to be excluded from politics, because all things would be common, and would, therefore, fall under the scope of the general will. However, Rousseau knows that this is impossible, and he indicates as much in his many claims about the rights that people retain to all things that do not bear on the common. None of this denies the paternalistic implications of Rousseau's social prescriptions, specifically designed to enlarge the scope of the common. It does, however, refute the charges of interpreters who assert that Rousseau eliminates the distinction between public and private,[59] or that his ideal republic "is calculated to kill all privacy."[60]

What then does Rousseau mean by "everything that is not of the essence to the social compact"? The answer to this question, which is simply the members' differences, reveals the substance of the private sphere. The general will encompasses everything of concern to the collective as a whole and nothing more; consequently, differences among the members will have to be excluded from civic life to avoid the inevitably corrupting influence of particularity. The scope of the general will depends, therefore, on the degree of homogeneity within the political body. In societies like Sparta, the general will dominates all aspects of life, while in societies like our own, differentiation precludes the possibility of developing anything more than the thinnest version of a general will. So, Rousseau's respect for particularity is grudging; it would be inconsistent with freedom to overwhelm it, but society only flourishes when it is minimized.

Consequently, Rousseau pursues avenues for the cultivation of citizenship or unity that are consistent with autonomy and consent. While some differences can be tolerated, wide inequalities of wealth and privilege must be eradicated. As argued above, the social contract itself is formally neutral, in that all participate in its ratification. Unfortunately, the empirical conditions in a given society are typically unequal, such that the social contract has the effect of reifying preexisting relationships of dependence. For Rousseau these relationships are incompatible with freedom. "Tolerate neither opulent people nor beggars. . . . From the one come those who foment tyranny and from the other the tyrants" (II, xi, 75). Rousseau adds that cities should not be radically different from the countryside, and that distinctions should be based only on merit and not on the *droits honorifiques,* so prevalent in prerevolutionary France.[61] Inequalities of wealth and status introduce particularity and division into civic life, which makes formulating a truly general will impossible.

Similarly, Rousseau worried about political factions, which inevitably distort the general will through the tumult they incite in the sovereign body. Rousseau believed that the various divisions in society are not natural but, rather, the result of the continual comparison and conflict that occurs once people enter civil society. For example, with respect to religion, Rousseau writes, "As soon as peoples [sic] took it into their heads to make God speak, each made Him speak in its own way and made Him say what it wanted. If one had listened only to what God says to the heart of man, there would never have been more than one religion on earth."[62] Unfortunately, factions have distorted man's natural goodness, making it impossible for ordinary citizens to see past *amour-propre* to the general will. This is the source of Rousseau's antipathy for faction and even political debate. Fragmentation of the political sphere corrupts the purity of man's individual goodness by directing him toward the gaze of others as opposed to the good of the collective. "I believe that men's morals can be very accurately gauged by how much business they have with one another: the more dealings they have . . . the more contemptible they are."[63] For Rousseau, only when individuals deliberate on their own, away from the influence of particular associations, can they reach a decision consistent with the general will.

If there must be partial societies, "their number must be multiplied and their inequality prevented. . . . The general will always results from a large number of small differences" (II, iii, 61). In other words, differences that do persist cannot grow powerful enought to gain political relevance. In the case of inequalities of wealth and status, this distinction cannot be maintained; it would simply be impossible to formulate a general will in a society divided along class lines. However, with other differences, such as the specifies of religious doctrine, politics can maintain unity and respect diversity at the same time—as long as religious leaders do not attempt to exercise power over political matters. As Rousseau writes in his *Letter to Beaumont,* "religion never incites problems in a state unless the dominant party wishes to torment the weaker, or the weaker, intolerant by doctrine, cannot live in peace with those who are tolerant."[64] For Rousseau, particularity destroys the general will, but only if it infiltrates the political realm. If it can be kept out of politics, individuality and even association in the private sphere can coexist with generality in political life.

This compromise is a *modus vivendi* that Rousseau finds unsatisfying, so much so that he ultimately abandons politics as a vehicle for recuperating the perfect unity found in natural man. In one of his more frustrated moments, he wrote to Marquis de Mirabeau,

> In my old ideas the great political problem, which I compare to squaring the circle in geometry . . . : To find a form of government that puts the law above man. . . . If this form cannot be found, and I honestly believe it cannot, my opinion is that it is necessary to go to the other extreme and, in one stroke, to put man as high as possible above the law and to establish an arbitrary despotism—the most arbitrary that can be devised: I would like the despot to be God. In one word, I see no possible mean between the most austere democracy and the most complete Hobbism.[65]

If this is more than just a fleeting moment of frustration, the entire framework outlined in *The Social Contract* is called into question. Only the most austere republican virtue resembles the kind of unity and happiness attainable outside of politics, and Rousseau fears that virtue of this kind died with the onset of modernity. However, withdrawing from society has its drawbacks too, the most significant of which is that it is an option available only to exceptional individuals, or to children fortunate enough to have an expert tutor from birth. For most, man's natural goodness can only be recovered through republican virtue, though, even there, perfect unity is highly unlikely.

It is unlikely because private will never totally corresponds with the general will, or, put differently, the general will is rarely the equivalent of the will of all. The difference between the two, according to Rousseau, is that the former considers only the common interest, while the latter is nothing more than the sum of particular interests (II, iii, 61). Understanding the difference between these concepts illuminates Rousseau's understanding of the relationship between particular and general, between man and citizen. Unfortunately, as we saw in chapter 2, there is an ambiguity in Rousseau's treatment of this relationship. He sometimes implies that the general will transcends particular will, that it is an entirely unique kind of will. At other times, he talks about making the general will the equivalent of the will of all. It is unclear whether the general will is a perfect reconciliation of particular wills or a repression of particular will.

For Rousseau, the general will is indestructible; it persists in the conscience of all citizens, even when they themselves act against the collective interest. This is the sense in which the general will is sometimes equal to individual will and sometimes a regulator of it. Hlail Gildin points out that citizens "want others to continue obeying the law that they violate."[66] The general will continues to guide individual conscience even when it is usurped by self-interest in particular cases. This is why it is possible both to define the general will in opposition to particular will and to make the general will the will of all. For Rousseau, particular will is both destructive of social unity and stubbornly entrenched in all societies. It cannot be transcended or even subordinated;[67] rather, it must be made consistent with the general will.

In the absence of a reconciliation of the will of all and the general will, societies will have to settle for an impoverished political sphere that leaves members divided between public and private. Exceptional individuals can take solace in a solitary life, but the flourishing of politics depends on the extent to which "public affairs dominate private ones in the minds of the citizen" (III, xv, 102). Rousseau shared the view of the ancients that politics inevitably creates essentially irresolvable tensions between public and private life. He rejected the notion that individual interests naturally harmonize in politics. Only the active cultivation of republican citizenship can begin to reconcile the tension between public and private, between popular will and rational will. Even the wise man, who makes the greatest happiness of all paramount, always puts his private interest first.[68] So, Rousseau's exaltations of perfect political unity must be understood as utopian metaphors for human happiness.[69] In actually existing societies, citizens are unfortunately fated to live on the uncertain line that divides public from private.

CONCLUSION

Rather than offer a prescription for political action, Rousseau creates an image of perfect political unity to show us the price we pay for the societies we have chosen. Rousseau understood that the will of all would subvert the general will most of the time and that even relatively successful societies would be illegitimate if judged by his standards. At the very least, it is certain that the sovereignty of a robust, Rousseauean general will is incompatible with large, pluralistic societies. Among other things, Rousseau's ideal requires a small community, direct democracy, homogeneity, decentralized power, simplicity of mores, and an agrarian economy—none of which characterize either contemporary Western democracies or eighteenth-century France. Indeed, in most societies, implementation of Rousseau's social contract could easily slide into the totalitarianism Rousseau's critics attach to him. However, Rousseau's *Social Contract* was not intended for most societies. It resembles Cicero's or Plato's *Republic,* in that it presents a picture of the best regime while simultaneously doubting its plausibility. This is why Shklar called Rousseau the "last of the classical utopists."[70]

Except in cases where Rousseau makes explicit empirical recommendations, such as in *Letters Written from the Mountain,* or in *Project for Corsica,* Rousseau's utopian model of political life must be read as a critique of modern society. Rousseau knew that actual sovereign bodies could never match the perfection of the sovereign he described. His portrayals of natural man and Spartan society were self-consciously idealized, more to illustrate the failures of modernity than to celebrate the vibrancy of antiquity. One can read the entirety of Rousseau's corpus (including the autobiographies) as an effort to transcend the divisions produced by modern life, but then one must read it as tragedy, because each of Rousseau's pictures of unity ultimately fail in one way or another. Émile falters without his tutor;[71] history makes both the simplicity of the Clarens estate and the parochialism of Sparta anachronistic; natural man, though inherently good, is a kind of pre-moral beast unsuited to the modern age; and Rousseau's solitary reveries are dominated by his desire to be part of a community. Human beings are destined to live on thin lines and slippery slopes, to remain divided even in the pursuit of unity. Rousseau says that "one must choose between making a man or a citizen, for one cannot make both at the same time."[72] Both his writings and his life belie this possibility—the truth is that one cannot make either and must settle instead for imperfect versions of both. The modern age necessitates politics, and politics necessarily divides man. Rousseau's general will conjures an image of perfect political unity—of what it would mean to completely reconcile popular will and rational will in republican citizenship—but the image must always be bittersweet, because our circumstances make it impossible to realize.

Nonetheless, even if Rousseau's blueprint for political freedom under modern conditions does not suit most societies, his essential political teaching does. Rousseau considered it necessary to think both about abstract principles of justice and legitimacy as well as about the social and cultural prerequisites to the flourishing of those principles. His great political idea, the general will, was an attempt to address both questions at the same time. Indeed, Rousseau's general will incorporates both a set of procedures and an account of their viability. The result is an account of politics that is too demanding and too homogeneous for contemporary circumstances. However, it is not Rousseau's answers so much as his method of inquiry that should provoke our interest. Rousseau inhabits the tension between voluntarism and virtue, between popular will and rational will. He does not posit a faculty, as Kant does, that permits a reconciliation of these forces; nor does he rely on some notion of natural rights or divine authority to overcome the problem. Instead, he struggles within the predicament that characterizes modern politics. Out of a desire to synthesize popular will and rational will, Rousseau generates a set of contradictions and paradoxes. Ironically, it is precisely these paradoxes that can help us find a way within the context of our skepticism toward universal, non-contingent sources of political authority. Rousseau's general will does not reconcile the inexorable tension between popular will and rational will, but it does offer an approach to political theory that makes it possible to thrive within that tension.

NOTES

1. Diderot's entry is translated as "Natural Right," in *Political Writings*, ed. John Hope Mason and Robert Wokler (Cambridge: Cambridge University Press, 1992), 17–21.

2. Diderot, "Natural Right." See also, Judith Shklar, "General Will," in *Dictionary of the History of Ideas*, ed. Philip Wiener (New York: Charles Scribner's Sons, 1973), 2:276 (hereafter cited as "General Will").

3. Diderot, "Natural Right," 20–21.

4. Rousseau, *Geneva Manuscript*, 162.

5. Rousseau, *Geneva Manuscript*, 158.

6. Patrick Riley, preface to *The General Will Before Rousseau* (Princeton, N.J.: Princeton University Press, 1986), xii. Though Rousseau's general will is more modest than Diderot's in this sense, there is another sense in which Rousseau's general will is bolder than most conceptions of a universal will. Whereas those who postulate a general will of all humankind typically assume that the consensus will be quite limited or thin, Rousseau's general will seeks a fuller, thicker consensus.

7. Rousseau, *The First and Second Discourses*, 15.

8. Rousseau, *Reveries of a Solitary Walker* (London: Penguin, 1979), 85.

9. Rousseau, *The Confessions*, 243.

10. Tracy B. Strong invokes the idea of "the common" as a unifying theme in Rousseau's work: *Jean-Jacques Rousseau: The Politics of the Ordinary* (Thousand Oaks, Calif.: Sage Publications, 1994). Jean Starobinski organizes Rousseau's thought around the goal of "transparency" in *Jean-Jacques Rousseau: Transparency and Obstruction* (Chicago: University of Chicago Press, 1971). Ernst Cassirer believed that Rousseau's proto-Kantian account of moral agency held his thought together. See Cassirer, *The Question of Jean-Jacques Rousseau* (Bloomington: Indiana University Press, 1963). Arthur Melzer makes unity the centerpiece of Rousseau's philosophy in *The Natural Goodness of Man: On the System of Rousseau's Thought* (Chicago: University of Chicago Press, 1990).

11. Benjamin Barber, *Superman and Common Men: Freedom Anarchy, and the Revolution* (New York: Praeger, 1971), 39.

12. Riley, *Will and Political Legitimacy*, 100.

13. Allan Bloom, "Jean-Jacques Rousseau," in *History of Political Philosophy*, eds. Leo Strauss and Joseph Cropsey (Chicago: University of Chicago Press, 1987), 559.

14. Allan Bloom, "Jean-Jacques Rousseau," 559.

15. Gildin, *Rousseau's Social Contract*, 155. In *Political Economy*, for example, Rousseau writes, "the most general will is also the most just." See Rousseau, *Political Economy*, 213.

16. Shklar, *Men and Citizens*, 184.

17. Bloom, "Jean-Jacques Rousseau," 569. This undoubtedly begins to explain why Rousseau has an almost religious devotion to the general will.

18. Riley, *Will and Political Legitimacy*, 114.

19. *Émile*, 586.

20. Riley, "Rousseau's General Will: Freedom of a Particular Kind," in *Rousseau and Liberty*, ed. Robert Wokler (Manchester, U.K.: Manchester University Press, 1995), 1.

21. Tzvetan Todorov, *Frêle bonheur* (Paris: Hachette, 1985), 30.

22. Rousseau himself does not use the word autonomy, however I believe it clarifies his meaning. Autonomy is sometimes invoked with normative connotations, as I have used the word "freedom." In this section, I use autonomy to denote the idea of open-ended, formal self-governing, as is captured by Isaiah Berlin's notion of negative liberty. Berlin, "Two Concepts of Liberty," in *Four Essays on Liberty* (Oxford, U.K.: Oxford University Press, 1969). In chapter 8, I argue for a more substantive, less open-ended understanding of autonomy.

23. Frederick Neuhouser, "Freedom, Dependence, and the General Will," *The Philosophical Review* 102 (July 1993): 363.

24. Barth, "Volonté générale et Volonté particulière," 43.

25. Shklar, "General Will," 276.

26. Riley, *Will and Political Legitimacy*, 100.

27. As I noted in chapter 2, Rousseau's argument gets off the ground with the assumption that there is a set of interests, shared by all citizens, that gives content to the general will. This assumption, which we may wish to dispute, strengthens Rousseau's claim that individuals who vote in the minority are mistaken about the general will. Voting in the minority could be the result of two things—either a preference for one's private interest over the general interest or an honest disagreement with regard to the constitutive elements of the "general interest." Rousseau's assumption with regard to the existence of a set of shared interests allows him to ignore the second possibility and to equate political dissent with selfishness.

28. Shklar, *Men and Citizens,* 201.

29. For a discussion of this problem, see Trachtenberg, *Making Citizens.*

30. Rousseau, *Geneva Manuscript*, 182.

31. Rousseau, *Political Economy,* 216.

32. Allan Bloom, trans., *Introduction to Émile or On Education* (New York: Basic, 1979), 40; Rousseau, *Social Contract*, 68.

33. Rousseau, *Political Economy*, 218.

34. Rousseau, *Political Economy*, 223.

35. Rousseau, *The Government of Poland*, ed. Willmoore Kendall (New York: Bobbs-Merrill, 1972), 115.

36. Rousseau, *Geneva Manuscript*, 171; *Political Economy*, 218.

37. Rousseau, *Politics and the Arts*, trans. Allan Bloom (Ithaca N.Y.: Cornell University Press, 1960), 126.

38. Jean Starobinski, *Jean-Jacques Rousseau: Transparency and Obstruction* (Chicago: University of Chicago Press), 80.

39. See Arthur Melzer, "The Origin of the Counter-Enlightenment: Rousseau and the New Religion of Sincerity," *American Political Science Review* 90 (June 1996): 344–60. Melzer shows further how Rousseau's charges against the *philosophes* mirror those he levels against Christianity. For Rousseau, the cosmopolitan, universal foundations of both Enlightenment reason and Christianity threaten the unity of the state.

40. Rousseau, *Geneva Manuscript*, 198.

41. Rousseau, *Letters Written from the Mountain,* in *Oeuvres* (Paris: Seuil, 1971), 404 (Rousseau's italics).

42. Rousseau, *Geneva Manuscript*, 160–61.

43. Rousseau, *Letters Written from the Mountain,* 409.

44. For an example, see Lester Crocker, "Rousseau et la voie du totalitarisme," in *An-nales de philosophie politique* (Paris: Presses Universitaires de France, 1965), 5:121 (here-after cited as *Rousseau et la voie*).

45. Starobinski, "The Accuser and the Accused," in *Jean-Jacques Rousseau*, ed. Harold Bloom (New York: Chelsea House, 1988), 179.

46. Trachtenberg, *Making Citizens*, 245.

47. Crocker, "Rousseau et la voie," 103.

48. Rousseau, *Geneva Manuscript*, 199.

49. Rousseau, "La Nouvelle Héloïse," in *Oeuvres complètes*, 2:45.

50. Hampsher-Monk, "Rousseau and Totalitarianism," 278.

51. Arthur Melzer, *The Natural Goodness of Man*, 98.

52. Charles William Hendel, *Jean-Jacques Rousseau, Moralist* (Oxford, U.K.: Oxford University Press, 1934), 1:118.

53. Crocker, "Rousseau et la voie," 113.

54. Shklar, *Men and Citizens*, 51.

55. Rousseau, *Letters Written from the Mountain*, 90.

56. Rousseau, *Geneva Manuscript*, 163.

57. Alfred Cobban, *Rousseau and the Modern State* (Hamden, Conn.: Archon Books, 1961), 76.

58. This partially explains why Rousseau was not optimistic about the power of repub-lican regimes to endure. See *The Social Contract*, 96–97.

59. Crocker, "Rousseau's *soi-disant* liberty," in *Rousseau and Liberty*, 250.

60. Jacob Talmon, *The Origins of Totalitarian Democracy* (Boulder, Colo.: Westview, 1985), 47.

61. See *Letters Written from the Mountain*, 482, and 497–98.

62. Bloom, *Émile*, 295.

63. Rousseau, preface to *Narcissus*, in *The First and Second Discourses*, 106.

64. Rousseau, *Letter to Monseigneur de Beaumont*, in *Oeuvres*, 359. It should be noted that Rousseau's "civil religion," in contrast to the "religion" he discusses here, does exer-cise influence over the political sphere. Indeed, it would be a contradiction in terms if the civil religion were relegated to the private sphere.

65. Rousseau, *Letter to Mirabeau*, in *The Political Writings of Jean-Jacques Rousseau*, ed. C. E. Vaughn (Cambridge, U.K.: Cambridge University Press, 1915), 160–61.

66. Gildin, *Rousseau's Social Contract*, 152.

67. This directly contradicts the formulation Rousseau gives in *Reveries*, where he says "virtue consists in subordinating your inclinations to the call of duty," see Rousseau, *Reveries of a Solitary Walker*, 96. However it is consistent with the language Rousseau usually uses in *The Social Contract* and *Political Economy*, where he says "virtue is only [the] conformity of the private will to the general"; see Rousseau, *The Social Contract*, 218.

68. Bloom, *Émile*, 253.

69. In *Political Economy*, Rousseau goes so far as to say, "The body politic, taken in-dividually, can be considered to be like a body that is organized, living, and similar to that of a man"; see Rousseau, *Political Economy*, 211.

70. Shklar, *Men and Citizens*, 1. As Bertrand de Jouvenel puts it, "Rousseau the social scientist predicts the destruction of what Rousseau the moralist wills." See de Jouvenal,

"Rousseau's Theory of the Forms of Government," in *Hobbes and Rousseau*, eds. Maurice Cranston and Richard S. Peters (Garden City, N.Y.: Anchor Books, 1972), 496. In *The Geneva Manuscript*, Rousseau insists that a perfect realization of his principles is impossible: "The works of men—always less perfect than nature's—never move so directly toward their goal." See Rousseau, *Geneva Manuscript*, 168.

71. Rousseau, *Émile and Sophie*.
72. Bloom, *Émile*, 39.

Chapter 4

The General Will
in the French Revolution:
Principles of Political Right

> Your example is before me. . . . I want to follow in your venerable footsteps . . .
> and will be happy if, as I follow the perilous path that an incredible revolution
> has opened before us, I remain constantly loyal to the inspirations that I have
> drawn from your writings.
>
> —Maximilien de Robespierre, *"Dédicace à J.-J. Rousseau"*

La Faute à Rousseau!—such is the declaration of many observers of the French
Revolution, who view the Reign of Terror as a conscious attempt to actualize
Rousseau's dual insistence on popular sovereignty and civic virtue.[1] As we have
seen, Rousseau's general will does indeed include both formal principles of popular rule and an account of the values, dispositions, beliefs, and virtues needed to
ensure that popular rule serves freedom. In other words, the general will incorporates consideration of the two basic questions of political theory—What are the
principles of political right? and How can these principles be put into practice?
The general will offers answers to both of these questions, and, perhaps more significantly, it describes the way in which these two questions interact in political
life. This chapter takes up the first question within the context of the French Revolution, examining the revolutionaries' appropriation of the general will and the
abstract principles of justice and legitimacy that they derive from it. Chapter 5 focuses on the second question, through a description of the kind of citizenship the
revolutionaries tried to foster. The French Revolution demonstrates the necessity
and the danger of attending to both questions. Whereas much of contemporary
political theory tends to neglect the question of viability in favor of an exclusive
emphasis on abstract principles of legitimacy and justice, the revolutionaries became so preoccupied with creating *l'homme régénéré* that they lost sight of the
very principles they hoped to instill in this new French citizen.

In order to consider honestly the merits and drawbacks of Rousseau's republicanism, it will be necessary to disentangle the ideas themselves from the use to

which they were put during the Revolution. Some attribute the Revolution's path to Terror to the internal logic of Rousseauean republicanism. In the following two chapters, I draw a distinction between the revolutionaries' conception of the general will and Rousseau's articulation of it. From this distinction, it becomes clear that the Revolution's pathologïes can be better understood not as manifestations of Rousseauean political theory but as departures from it.

The charge *"la faute à Rousseau"* can be approached in a couple of ways: through a study of the historical causes of the French Revolution or through a theoretical inquiry into the relationship between Rousseau's ideas and those animating the Revolution. Historians have spilled much ink pursuing the first approach, in an attempt to determine the nature and extent of Rousseau's influence on the principal figures of the Revolution. Edgar Quinet argues that "the revolutionaries rejected all other thinkers to attach themselves entirely to Rousseau"[2] —a conclusion that a review of the Revolutionary documents reveals to be only a slight exaggeration. Invocations of Rousseau's name dot the spectrum of political opinion during the years of the Revolution, and it is a commonplace that Robespierre identified with Rousseau, even exalted him, pledging eternal loyalty to Rousseau's principles. On the other hand, scholars like Edmé Champion, Daniel Mornet, Joan McDonald, and Carol Blum have at least partially debunked the myth of Rousseau, father of the French Revolution. They point out that *The Social Contract* did not receive a significant circulation in France until 1790 and was hardly read there between its first appearance in 1762 and the beginning of the Revolution in 1789.[3] With respect to the question of historical causation, these historians are undoubtedly wise to point to the innumerable factors involved in an event as complex as the French Revolution. Champion calls it a *"fâcheuse manie"* to understand the French Revolution as an incarnation of Rousseau's thought.[4] Moreover, *La Nouvelle Héloïse* and Rousseau's autobiographical works sold many more copies than his explicitly political writings, implying that Rousseau's ubiquitous presence in revolutionary discourse may have more to do with an adoration for Rousseau the man, than with an allegiance to his political principles. Of course, the claim can always be made that statistical studies of circulation are unreliable measures of the influence of ideas, which often spread in diffuse and informal ways.

Rather than attempting to enter the seemingly intractable debate over historical causation, this chapter and the next one examine the ideas that dominated the French Revolution from a theoretical perspective. They analyze the ways in which the revolutionaries invoked the general will, in an effort to describe the ideological framework(s) animating the events. In the previous chapter, we evaluated arguments about the relationship between Rousseau's general will and a politics of homogenizing repression. As I pointed out there, the legacy of the French Revolution (the Terror in particular) has had a tremendous influence on the way Rousseau has been read and interpreted.[5] In Heinrich Heine's poetic judgment, "Robespierre is nought but the hand, the bloody, bloody hand of

Rousseau."[6] Moreover, Robespierre understood the Revolution and his role in it as the realization of the sublime principles that Rousseau had only theorized. Despite all of this, it may be worth asking whether Rousseau was Rousseauean, in the same sense that it is often asked whether Niccolò Machiavelli was Machiavellian. Just as the term "Machiavellian" came to describe actions that Machiavelli himself may not have endorsed, the identification of Rousseau with the Terror may be similarly ill conceived. While there is a substantial body of historical material investigating the extent to which Rousseau's writings played a causal role in the Revolution, remarkably little theoretical work has been done that seriously investigates the substance of the revolutionaries' ideas as they relate to Rousseau's earlier formulations.[7]

In all likelihood, this has something to do with the prevalence of structural approaches to revolutionary historiography that had dominated until relatively recently. These approaches tend to view ideas as derivative of broader social forces, with little power to affect the trajectory of history in and of themselves. However, with the widespread acceptance of François Furet's emphasis on the importance of the role of ideas in the Revolution, work has emerged on the nature and characteristics of revolutionary thought itself. If the ideas of the French Revolution are worth studying in their own right, the question as to whether they derive specifically from Rousseau's political theory fades in importance. The relevant questions become how the revolutionaries conceptualized the general will, how this conception relates to the events of the Revolution, and how it compares to Rousseau's account of the general will. Joseph Lakanal said it was not *The Social Contract* that caused the Revolution "but in a sense the Revolution that explained *The Social Contract* to us."[8] I share Lakanal's orientation (if not his conclusion) in that I will not concern myself with whether and to what extent Rousseau's ideas caused the French Revolution. Instead, I will focus on the ideas animating the Revolution and reevaluate the relationship between those ideas and Rousseau's political theory.

Though this chapter and the next one consider the place of the general will in revolutionary discourse as a whole, they focus largely on Robespierre and the Jacobins. The choice seems justified, partially because of the consensus that the Jacobins somehow capture everything we take to be distinctive about the French Revolution, but, more importantly, because as self-acknowledged disciples of Rousseau and perpetrators of the Terror, they compel consideration of the tendency toward repression in Rousseau's political thought.

I. THE UBIQUITY OF THE GENERAL WILL

However unclear their conception of the general will (and some seem to have scarcely understood it), most members of the Estates General realized that it was the source of their legitimacy and, as such, that it demanded lip service at the very least. Consequently, it was deployed in the service of almost all of the competing factions. Everyone, from the *monarchiens* to the radical left talked about the general will in ways that differ dramatically, yet share certain commonalities.

Predictably, Rousseau's influence pervades the Declaration of the Rights of Man and Citizen.[9]

> art. 3. The source of all sovereignty resides essentially in the nation; no group, no individual may exercise authority not emanating expressly therefrom.

> art. 6. Law is the expression of the general will; all citizens have the right to concur personally, or through their representatives, in its formation; it must be the same for all, whether it protects or punishes.[10]

More surprising, perhaps, are the arguments advanced by counterrevolutionary conservatives, who used the general will to argue that the laws of the new republic were illegitimate, because they did not reflect their will and, therefore, could not properly be called general in origin as Rousseau had required.[11] Moderate monarchists also used the general will; in their case, it was to argue for a royal veto based on the premise that the monarch somehow best embodied the general will. Even Louis XVI appeared before the National Assembly in a simple black suit to assure the people that he would "defend and maintain constitutional liberty, whose principles the general will, in accord with my own, has sanctioned."[12] Finally, when birds began preying on the rabbits that were crucial to many citizens' subsistence, one of the *cahiers* of the Île-de-France insisted that it was "the general will of the Nation that game should be destroyed since it carries off a third of the subsistence of citizens and this is the intention of our good King who watches over the common good of his people and who loves them."[13]

Indeed, Joan McDonald, in her study of Rousseau and the French Revolution, reports that it is possible to find practically any and every faction appealing to Rousseau.[14] The general will in particular was constantly on the lips of the revolutionaries, according to McDonald, though she argues that they never explained what they meant by it, using Rousseau in an almost arbitrary manner, to bolster particular arguments and policies.[15] While I agree that the general will was put in the service of arguments across the political spectrum, I mean to challenge McDonald on the claim that the revolutionaries offered no coherent explanation of the general will. Despite the absence of a systematic explanation, the character of Revolutionary discourse reveals the animating role played by a conception of the general will that both appropriated and betrayed Rousseau's earlier formulation.

For Rousseau, the general will is a political solution to the problems of dependence and inequality. It sits comfortably with a variety of political alternatives including conservatism, revolution, authoritarianism, democracy, and socialism. Consequently, it is difficult to identify Rousseauean themes based on a traditional understanding of the political spectrum. Instead, the influence of the general will must be sought out at the theoretical foundations of a political platform—in the manner in which revolution, conservatism, authoritarianism, and so forth are justified. Since the key figures of the Revolution invoked the general will in support of all of these, one must not be discouraged by their simple breadth. There are coherencies that emerge that provide insight into the sometimes consistent, sometimes varying models of citizenship advanced during the Revolution.

Almost every competing faction made use of the general will during the Revolution, and they did so in a variety of ways. After all, the factions were competing. Yet, I believe it is still possible to draw something close to a coherent picture of the general will out of the French Revolution. That is not to suggest that every revolutionary subscribed precisely to the version of the general will I am about to describe. It is to suggest that the general will served more than a simply rhetorical role, as an empty vessel into which anything could be poured. In spite of the differences of interpretation during the Revolution, there is much that held the Revolution together—much that contributed to the creation of a new set of norms for politics. Moreover, to the extent that the Revolution produced a coherent picture of the general will, it did so with unmistakable Rousseauean overtones. Though many of the crucial subtleties and the ambivalent spirit of Rousseau's political thought become obscured, the Revolution's principle tenets—a commitment to absolute, popular sovereignty, a faith in the malleability of human nature, and an insistence on the subordination of the particular to the general—descend from Rousseauean republicanism. What must be decided eventually is whether these principles contain inherently the seeds of terror or whether they might be compatible with a respect for human dignity and diversity. I will look first at competing claims for the location of the general will—in the monarch, in the legislature, and in the people themselves—and then at the different ways in which substantive content was assigned to the general will.

II. THE GENERAL WILL AS A PRINCIPLE OF LEGITIMACY

La Volonté Générale, C'est Moi.

Before it was decided that "Louis must die in order that the nation may live,"[16] the assembly considered the possibility of a royal veto that would either allow the king to kill legislation without further discussion (absolute veto) or send it back to the assembly for further consideration (suspensive veto). Figures like Jean-Joseph Mounier and the Comte de Mirabeau hoped to preserve a significant role for the king in the new regime, arguing in favor of the royal veto. However, rather than frame their argument in the traditional terms of divine right or royal prerogative, they accepted Rousseau's republican emphasis on the will of the people as the source of legitimacy.[17] Their approach was to claim that there is a "natural and necessary alliance between the prince and the people . . . founded on their having the same interests and the same fears," which means that they are bound to have the same goal and, consequently, the same will.[18] These claims use the scourge of privilege and the fear of a resurgent aristocracy to argue for an alliance between monarchy and democracy. For Mirabeau, the monarch is as interested as the people in preventing the establishment of an aristocracy, and should therefore be seen as the protector of the people rather than as their enemy.[19] Based on Rousseauean fears of the development of particular or corporate wills within representative bodies, supporters of the royal veto emphasized the king's ability to unify. He has the obvious advantage of unanimity (key to both Rousseauean and revolutionary republicanism) and, so long as his power were structured properly, he would consult the people and act in their interest.[20]

Louis XVI did not understand France's new constitutionalism along these lines. Whereas the constitution defined the monarch as an agent of the general will, empowered to act only in an executive role, Louis viewed the constitution (to the extent that he accepted it) as something that he himself granted to his people of his own volition.[21] In other words, whereas the assembly had declared itself the voice of the general will, Louis assumed himself to be the source of all political authority. As Norman Hampson puts it, "the nation belonged to him rather than he to it." He accepted his obligation to dedicate himself to the people but as someone set apart from the people and, to be sure, set above them.[22] Whereas the revolutionaries envisioned the monarchy as an institution that could ensure the sovereignty of popular will, Louis had no interest in the will of the people. He claimed to be dedicated to the people's interests, but, as we have seen, this is something altogether different from the will of the people.

If the royal veto had any chance at all, it was doomed by the widespread disgust at this conception of monarchy. Hostility to Louis XVI and the French tradition of monarchy torpedoed Mirabeau's otherwise plausible arguments for the separation of powers. Moreover, the drive toward unity and the revolutionaries' eventual embrace of Manichaeism undermined any and all attempts to articulate the advantages of a division of powers. The Jacobins eliminated all ambiguity about the justice of their principles, which meant that one was either for the Revolution or against it. On these terms, a division of power along the lines of the royal veto could only be understood as an attempt to put the will of one above the will of all.[23]

The prototypical revolutionary activity was to issue a claim to represent the general will, and to make matters more complicated, built in to each of these claims was the imperative that the general will be indivisible.[24] The debates over the royal veto multiplied the asserted sites of an entity that almost required one locus by definition. It is noteworthy, nonetheless, that even among supporters of a legislative role for the monarch, Rousseauean concerns dominate. One finds not only the language of the general will, but also an insistence on unified and indivisible sovereignty and a concern for the tendency toward particularity in government. Ultimately, it was the most fundamental element of Rousseau's general will—popular sovereignty—that doomed the royal veto. To satisfy the newly established norm of political life, sovereign power would have to reside much closer to the people themselves.

"The Right to Participate Personally or through Representatives"

The Abbé Sieyès, a representative in the Third Estate and a key architect of the first phases of the Revolution, opposed any kind of royal veto, arguing that subjecting the decision of the National Assembly to appeal threatened the principle of unity on which the Revolution depended.[25] Whereas many Rousseaueans saw the royal veto as a solution to the defects of representation, Sieyès saw nothing defective in representation that might demand remedy.[26] He, along with Marie-Jean-Antoine Caritat de Condorcet, initiated a debate about the potential of a system of representation to breed unity, preserve popular sovereignty, allow for public participation, and ensure the dominance of the general will. For Sieyès and Condorcet, it is through a representative body that Rousseau's fundamental political problem can be solved—to "find a form of association that defends and protects the person and goods of each associate with all the common force, and by means of which each one, uniting with all, nevertheless obeys only himself and remains as free as before."[27]

For Rousseau, the solution to this problem was the total alienation of oneself and all of one's rights to the general will. Ironically, it was only through total alienation that one would lose nothing, since, by becoming a part of an indivisible whole, all rights could be reclaimed under the general will. Sovereignty must, therefore, both originate in the people and be exercised by the people. Were a part of it to be alienated to a legislative body, freedom would be forfeited through the social contract, specifically the freedom to live under self-legislated laws. "The deputies of the people . . . are not nor can they be its representatives; they are merely its agents. They cannot conclude anything definitively. Any law that the people in person has not ratified is null; it is not a law."[28] There were some attempts (if largely rhetorical) to retain this view of representation during the Revolution—by the Jacobins, as would be expected, but also by more moderate Girondins like Pierre Vergniaud, who paraphrased Rousseau on the assembly floor: "Any act emanating from the representatives of the people is an act of tyranny, a usurpation of sovereignty, unless it is submitted to either the formal or tacit ratification of the people."[29] For Vergniaud, while the members of the Assembly are undeniably the representatives (*mandataires*) of the people, their mandate does not have the character of representation (*représentation*). In other words, they have no individual will to express; they are only the organs of the general will, which has already been expressed by the law.[30]

This quixotic Rousseauism, though consistently present among the radicals, remained at the margins of revolutionary practice. For example, a more moderate view of republican politics was written into the Declaration of the Rights of Man and Citizen (even though it too was motivated by a concern to ensure the sovereignty of the general will). Article 6, followed up the strictly Rousseauean declaration that "the law is the expression of the general will" by backtracking from Rousseau with the addition that "all citizens have the right to participate personally, *or through their representatives*."[31] In an even more significant departure from Rousseau, Article 3 declared that "the *source* of all sovereignty resides essentially in the nation."[32] This is a statement that even an authoritarian thinker like Hobbes could quite easily endorse. What distinguishes Rousseau's political theory is its insistence that sovereignty not only emanates *from* the people but that it must also be exercised *by* the people.

Ultimately, the authors of the declaration opted for the language of Sieyès over Rousseau, which meant a renegotiation of the process by which the general will could be formulated. Sieyès was willing to modify Rousseau's insistence that citizens give themselves laws. He believed that a representative body could be a locus of unity that would give orders to the people yet be an emanation of the people. To sustain this belief, Sieyès leaned on Rousseau's conception of a preexisting national will that necessarily directs law making, and de-emphasized Rousseau's insistence on popular participation. In fact, he argued that only an elite representative body could discern the national will, thereby reversing Rousseau's claim about the relationship between representation and the general will. For Sieyès, politics could not insulate itself from the division of labor that had become essential to modern economics. Given the complexity of modern society, representation was not only consistent with popular sovereignty, but the only way popular sovereignty could be effective. Societies are too large and differentiated for the people themselves to express the general will. Only a body of representatives, which dedicates itself to public service, is capable of discerning the general will: "They have all the powers. Since they alone are the agents of the general will, they have no need to consult their constituents about dissent that does not exist."[33] In small societies, direct democracy may have been possible, but the same conditions responsible for the division of labor make direct democracy impossible and necessitate a body of representatives that can dedicate itself to discerning and implementing the national will.

Nevertheless, although he shed some of Rousseau's insistence on participation, Sieyès, along with Condorcet (the Revolution's other major theorist of representation), retained his emphasis on unity in the sovereign and the dominance of the general over the particular. In the name of unity, both Condorcet and Sieyès explicitly opposed a division of power along the lines of the American system of checks and balances. They also agreed that the legislature must find a way of preventing particular interests from infiltrating its decision-making process, which ought to be driven only by the common good.[34] However, they assign delegates much more power and freedom than Rousseau sanctions—the power to make laws and the freedom to deliberate.

For Sieyès and Condorcet, representatives must have extensive freedom to deliberate, in order to generate the general will, which is somehow inchoate or under-specified until the legislature pronounces it. Sieyèsian representatives resemble Rousseau's Legislator. For Rousseau, a people is only a people when it has a general will, and this will may remain latent until the Legislator finds the terms by which it can be expressed and institutionalized. Similarly, only Sieyès's representatives declare the general will, though they ostensibly do so in a manner that respects popular sovereignty. This is justified by the claim that the will these representatives declare is a will that they perceive, not a will that they create. The general will is something that the people desire but can rarely express.

Sieyès's location of the general will in a representative body jettisons both Rousseau's insistence on the popular exercise of sovereign power and Charles de Montsquieu's arguments on behalf of a separation of powers. Whereas republicans believe that freedom is secured best when power is kept in the hands of the people, and constitutionalists prefer to restrict political power through a system of checks and balances, Sieyès saw no need for either. With both constitutionalism and popular sovereignty undermined, the philosophical justification had been provided for the revolutionary practice of asserting oneself as the sovereign representative of the general will.

The account of representation offered by Condorcet and Sieyès has more in common with Thomas Hobbes's view of representation than with Rousseau's. For Hobbes, a group of men is merely a "multitude" until a representative makes them one.

> A multitude of men, are made *One* Person, when they are by one man, or one Person, Represented; so that it be done with the consent of every one of that Multitude in particular. For it is the *Unity* of the Representer, not the *Unity* of the Represented, that maketh the Person *One*.[35]

Whereas for Rousseau, the people are simultaneously one and many—many in that they are each free and equal individuals and one in that they share common customs, characteristics, interests, and virtues—for Hobbes, the people are a multitude, not one but many. The multitude becomes what Hobbes calls "One" or "One Person" through a representative who becomes absolutely sovereign; "and in him consisteth the Essence of the Common-wealth."[36] This representative is what Hobbes calls an "Actor," and, as such, he may only act based on the orders of "he that owneth his words and actions"—the "Author." The author (in this case, the people) grants the representative "Authority," which is defined as the right to carry out actions on its behalf.[37] While the commonwealth is technically the legislator, it has neither the capacity nor the authority to do anything except through its representative (the sovereign). The will of the representative becomes synonymous with the will of the commonwealth and, though the sovereign will has been authorized by the people, they do not exercise sovereignty. Rather, they find themselves within this representative, which is to say that they become a people through him, that they acquire unity in him.

It is important to distinguish between Hobbes's representative and an elected leader, which Hobbes calls a "minister of the sovereign," since, in an elective system, sovereignty resides in the voting body. By representation, Hobbes means a transfer of sovereignty, a step the revolutionaries resisted to varying degrees, insisting instead on occupying the ground Rousseau resisted between "the most austere democracy and the most complete Hobbism."

Whereas for Hobbes unity clearly comes only through representation, for Rousseau the general will exists prior to political deliberation and can only be distorted, never bolstered, by representation. Sieyès borrowed a bit from Rousseau and a bit from Hobbes, accepting what he preferred to call a "national will" that precedes politics, while arguing that only a representative body can express this will. Ultimately for Sieyès, the general will resides in the representative body and its will ought to be regarded as the will of the people. He distinguishes between a "real communal will" and a "representative communal will,"[38] the second of which becomes a surrogate for the nation. Sieyès believed the nation was the key unit of political analysis, and he famously argued that the Third Estate was the true embodiment of the nation's will. However, despite his exaltations of the Third Estate, Sieyès was profoundly distrustful of the people, arguing not for the Third Estate but for the "representatives of the third estate" as the "source of national will."[39]

Still, Sieyès would not go so far as to transfer sovereignty to the Third Estate. "No public mandatory . . . exercises a power that belongs to him personally; it is the power of all. The latter has only been committed to him."[40] Moreover, nothing beyond the power to maintain order (*le bon ordre*) should be transferred to this representative body. When the nation grows to a certain size, it detaches from the common will "all that is necessary to watch over and provide for public needs; and the exercise of this part of the national will and consequently of power is conferred on some of their members."[41] This power has only been committed to these delegates on a contingent basis; it can never be alienated, because the will of the people can never be alienated. In this sense, Sieyès followed Rousseau, insisting that the common will "does not lie fully and unrestrainedly in the corps of representatives; it is only a portion of the great national common will."[42] While the representative body is empowered to define and implement the general will, the nation remains its source. It is in this way that Sieyès occupies a middle ground between Hobbes's view that sovereignty and the power to exercise sovereignty reside in the representative and Rousseau's claim that both reside in the citizenry. The people are sovereign, on Sieyès's account, but the power to exercise sovereignty can and should be transferred to a representative body.

For Rousseau, the general will is most recognizable in the absence of public deliberation, which produces distortion and subversion of the common good for the sake of particular interests. Sieyès and Condorcet, by contrast, see public deliberation by qualified elites as a way of rationalizing the general will, of filtering it through a body that perfects rather than distorts it. By dissociating citizens from sovereignty, the tension between popular will and rational will could be mitigated, though we may wish to insist on the loss incurred with respect to freedom understood as self-rule. Moreover, we ought to ask what will preclude the tyranny of faction if sovereignty is removed from the people and institutional constraints on the use of power are repudiated—that is, if both the traditional liberal and the traditional republican constraints on the use of power are jettisoned.

"Le Peuple" Alone and Exclusively

As the radical Jacobins vanquished their more moderate rivals in the Revolution's struggle for power, so did they vanquish, for all practical purposes, all arguments on behalf of representation or other institutional constraints on popular sovereignty. The Jacobins viewed any formal constraint on popular will as treasonous, even if that constraint would serve to rationalize it. Pierre Joseph Duhem dramatized the point in front of the Committee on Public Safety: "We are between two evils, treason and ignorance. But between two inevitable evils, it is necessary to choose the least great."[43]

For Robespierre, there was never a need to face this dilemma because of his unique understanding of popular will. He believed, for example, that the evils of society never come from the people; rather they originate always in the government. While the interest of the people is equivalent to the public good, the interest of one man alone is particular.[44] Consequently, "to be good, the people need only prefer itself to those who are not part of the people," while "to be good, it is necessary for the magistrate to sacrifice himself to the people."[45] Because representatives are almost always corrupt, the power to legislate the general will ought to remain seated, as much as possible, in the people (though, of course, the people require agents to declare its will). "Any institution that does not assume the people are good and the magistrate corruptible is vicious."[46] Robespierre never tired of exalting the virtues of the people, who are naturally right and good, who follow the laws of justice and reason, and who possess the response to the vices of the despotism of government. By using Rousseau's language of general and particular, the people become good by definition for Robespierre; once the adjectives of general and particular are mapped onto the people and the government respectively, all that follows from each term can be exploited. Popular will and rational will become equalized by definition, and the organization of government is as easy as unbridling the people's natural goodness. The reconciliation of popular will and rational will, which Condorcet and Sieyès pursued through representation, results spontaneously from the sovereignty of the people. That which emerged (ideally) from deliberation for Sieyès and Condorcet, arises automatically for Robespierre and the Jacobins.[47]

Robespierre's mythical idealization of *le peuple* rested less on what he thought the people were than on what they were not, namely aristocrats or partisans of any other factional group. This pattern of what we might describe as definition through exclusion pervaded discussions of popular will during the Revolution. The shared presupposition that the nation must be united and indivisible sparked a struggle over who would be considered a member of this nation. While a few fading voices within the Third Estate, like Comte Mirabeau's and Pierre-Victor Malouet's, hoped to create an inclusive nation with room for the clergy and nobility, Sieyès and Robespierre equated the Third Estate with the nation and demanded that the other two be treated as foreigners. In their view, the first two estates deserved ostracism, because they had constituted themselves as nations apart from everyone else.

Malouet was equally critical of the first two estates' tendency to isolate themselves from the nation, but he warned that it would be disastrous to reconstitute the Estates General without them. "We cannot renounce the principle of the indivisiblity of the Estates General, but neither can we declare ourselves to be its sole representatives."[48] Malouet's and Mirabeau's exhortations to conciliation between the Estates fell victim to the strategy of mobilization and unification based on exclusion. The Third Estate's exclusive claim to embody the nation was formally consecrated by its assumption of the name "National Assembly" and its claim to speak on behalf of the nation as a whole. Sieyès, who was the driving force behind the Third Estate's assertion of sovereignty, described the other two estates as nations, "no more able to mix in the affairs of the others than the Estates General of Holland or the Council of Venice, for example, could vote in the deliberations of the English Parliament."[49] Sieyès's final claim about the Third Estate in *Qu'est ce que le Tiers État?* is an ironic one—"What does [the Third Estate] ask?—To be something." The Third Estate has the right to be everything, according to Sieyès; its sheer percentage of the population and commonality of interest justifies its speaking on behalf of the nation as a whole. In some sense, the Third Estate becomes the nation as whole: "*Le Tiers État est une nation complète.*"[50]

Robespierre followed Sieyès with respect to the claims of the Third Estate against the other two, initially framing the central conflict of the Revolution in the terms of aristocratic privilege. This allowed the bourgeoisie to unite with the *sans-culottes* against the nobility. As events progressed though—as "intrigue and ambition stopped [the Revolution]"[51]—Robespierre began to define the people in opposition to the bourgeoisie. The source of disunity and factionalism in France, according to the Robespierre of the Committee of Public Safety, was the bourgeois, with its vices of affluence, atheism, and self-interest.[52] For Robespierre, the people now had to be defined not only in opposition to the nobility, but to the bourgeoisie as well because it too had revealed itself to be particular.

The general will must embody the will of every member of society, as Rousseau had explained and the Jacobins had accepted. Consequently the Jacobins' exclusion of ever more segments of the French population from the general will had to be justified by a redefinition of the nation. Initially, the aristocrats were excluded, then the Jacobins went after the clergy and the bourgeoisie, and, ultimately, they declared almost anyone with whom they disagreed an enemy of the republic. These enemies had somehow forfeited their place as part of the French nation. At this point, it is worth noting, Jacobin politics aside, that the imperative to unify associated with the general will need not issue in the strategy of unification through exclusion. Indeed, as we shall see in section IV, Rousseau's insistence that the general will embody the will of every citizen is designed to prevent precisely this type of exclusion. While a system of aristocracy cannot be made compatible with the general will, Rousseau gives reason to believe popular sovereignty can be compatible with a variety of social differences.

III. THE GENERAL WILL IN CONTEXT

Rousseau is often criticized for leaving the substantive content of the general will undefined, allowing different societies to define its content in drastically different (even oppressive) ways. Of course, the general will's formal, open-ended character can be interpreted as either an asset or a liability. This chapter has so far explored three possible loci for the formulation of the general will—the monarch, a representative body, and the people. This section considers the substance of that articulation; in other words, it looks at the ways in which the revolutionaries filled in he content of the general will—what it expressed as opposed to who expressed it.

Equal Participation, Equal Treatment

For all of their differences, the various incarnations of the general will in French politics share Rousseau's basic procedural point that the general will must both emanate from all and apply equally to all. The first half of this requirement bears on the question of civic participation and the second on the question of equal treatment before the law, or what we might now call equal protection. From a Rousseauean perspective, there must be no limitation on popular suffrage (though even Rousseau himself did not remain entirely faithful to this principle).[53] Nonetheless, the revolutionaries introduced limitations on equal participation as soon as they proclaimed the idea itself. Sieyès and most moderate revolutionaries invoked a distinction between active and passive citizens, which they used to exclude the propertyless from suffrage. However, the ascendance of the radicals spelled the end of this distinction, and, in August of 1792, universal suffrage was proclaimed.[54] "Who are truly the active citizens?" Robespierre asked. "Those who have taken the Bastille, those who work the fields; while the *fainéants* of the court and the clergy, despite the immensity of their domains, are merely vegetables."[55] If the general will is truly general and truly sovereign, then all individuals must share the same political rights, regardless of their status as property holders.

The revolutionaries deployed the doctrine of equal rights against those in favor of the old system of privilege; however, they went so far in their attack as to undermine the doctrine itself. In other words, not satisfied with the inclusion of the people into the political process, they proceeded to exclude segments of the population. As we saw in the previous section, Rousseau's insistence that the general will emanate from all and apply equally to all cuts both for and against Jacobin assertions of popular sovereignty.

Sovereignty as Popular, Absolute, Indivisible

The widespread acceptance of popular sovereignty replaced the fundamental principle of the old regime—privilege—with the principle of equality. French republicanism was constructed in opposition to feudalism, and republican equality was opposed to feudal privilege. Consequently, the revolutionaries replaced the class-based language of "Estates" with the egalitarian language of the "nation" or the "people." "Privilege humiliates 25 million people to honor 200,000," Sieyès wrote. "The nation can only be the generality of citizens."[56] Actually, for the revolutionaries, the nation never included everyone. Sieyès himself equated it with the Third Estate, using the nobility as an entity against which he hoped to define the nation. Furthermore, as mentioned above, the principle of equality was violated almost as soon as it was established through the distinction between active and passive citizens, the exclusion of women and blacks, and the marginalizing of anyone taken to be an "enemy" of the republic. Still, the norm of equality and popular sovereignty persisted, and any action seen to be at odds with the principles of republicanism had to be justified within the republican framework. Even apparent abdications of republican values were justified as somehow serving the interests of the people and protecting the integrity of its sovereignty.

In the realm of ideas, at least, the French Revolution spelled the end of hierarchy based on birth and the beginning of the modern individual, understood as equal and autonomous. The will of one fraction of the body politic could no longer be assumed to represent the will of the people as a whole. Because each individual was seen as an equal member of society, each citizen's opinion acquired political significance. This begins to explain the competition among would-be leaders to define themselves as the embodiment of the general will. The people had become the key force in politics, and public opinion had become the source of power. This fact forms the background for the competition of discourses that became one of the Revolution's central activities. The pervasive acceptance of the principle of popular sovereignty set theoretical standards for legitimacy to which all of the major revolutionaries adhered.

The revolutionaries' categorical attachment to equality and repudiation of privilege resulted not only in the radical transfer of sovereignty to the people but also in the preservation of the tradition of *absolute* sovereignty. Fearful that any limitation on the general will could be exploited by particular interests, the revolutionaries refused to institute checks on popular sovereignty. The "monarch," a concept that had previously been coterminous with the "social body," became entirely alienated from it, with the entity called the "nation" replacing it. But the absolute and indivisible nature of the king's sovereignty was preserved—pure democracy replaced absolute monarchy. The notion that sovereignty must be absolute, that the state must be superior to society characterizes French politics both before and after the Revolution. The term "sovereignty" itself is of French origin, and the logic of absolute sovereignty goes back as least as far as Louis XIV's famous *"L'État, c'est moi."* Lucien Jaume reports that Louis XVI fondly repeated, *"Le roi et la nation ne font qu'un.*" The absolute and indivisible nature of royal sovereignty was ap-propriated into the articulation of popular sovereignty during the Revolution.[57] The way the revolutionaries defined the general will was thus radically different from the monarchical tradition and yet identical with respect to the extent and scope of its jurisdiction. The people simply took the place of the king.

Popular Will, Rational Will, General Will

Inevitably, the actual legislation that emerged during the Revolution failed to live up to most expectations for the rectitude of popular will. In response, the revolu-tionaries either questioned the extent to which laws reflected the true general will or distinguished between an unerring, constant general will and the often-mis-guided vicissitudes of popular will. When Louis-Antoine Saint-Just took excep-tion to an early Revolutionary constitution, he argued that it did not reflect the general will, having been drafted by a group of scoundrels, masquerading as deputies of the people.[58] Moreover, it eventually became clear to the Jacobins that the actual will of the people was not always consistent with their ostensible virtue.

As we saw in chapter 2, Rousseau had written,

the general will is always right and always tends toward the public utility. But it does not follow that the people's deliberations always have the same rectitude. One always wants what is good for oneself, but one does not always see it. The people is never corrupted, but it is often fooled, and only then does it appear to want what is bad.[59]

For this reason, many revolutionaries resisted what they took to be Rousseau's general will. They equated the general will with the reign of opinion (as opposed to natural rights or reason) and argued that the general will must coincide with justice to be legitimate.[60] As demonstrated in the previous chapter, Rousseau was acutely aware of this problem. In fact, the passage just cited is followed immedi-ately by Rousseau's famous distinction between the will of all and the general will, through which he tries to distinguish between the simple agglomeration of individual wills (will of all) and a will that is somehow rationalized or general-ized in accordance with the common good (general will). Still, Sieyès, Saint-Just, Jean-Paul Marat, and Robespierre all criticized Rousseau's general will for its lack of attention to justice. They quite facilely interpreted the general will in a manner consistent with a particular, substantive conception of natural rights.

Here again, the revolutionaries modified Rousseau's insistence on popular par-ticipation. For Condorcet, for example, "the right to participate is only the right to participate rationally."[61] A universalist discourse, emphasizing interests and prin-ciples common to humankind as a whole emerged with almost as much force as the discourse of popular sovereignty. Moreover, the two discourses were viewed as complementary. Robespierre asked, "Who among us does not sense the growth of all faculties . . . in thinking that it is not for one people that we fight, but for the universe; not for the men who live today, but for all those who will exist?"[62] This eclectic embrace of both the cosmopolitan and the patriotic provided the revolutionaries with the rhetorical tools to evade the thorny tension between popular sovereignty and universal reason. Instead, they struggled with the tension politically, forced, as Keith Baker puts it, to contain the principle of popular sovereignty that they themselves unleashed.[63] The citizens are sovereign, to be sure, but even a figure as radical as Robespierre noted that there exists something above the people—namely justice. Though early on Robespierre seemed convinced that popular will could not fail to be anything other the general will, he later pointed out that there are eternal truths, "universal maxims of justice, unalterable, imprescriptible, created to be applied to all peoples."[64] These truths must govern the deliberation of citizens deciding on the general will—"Do not forget that your reason must not tyrannize over universal reason."[65] Arguments like these threaten popular sovereignty with supposedly objective claims to an understanding of truth, reason, and the public interest. While democracy cannot entirely escape them, these limitations on popular sovereignty clear the way for usurpations, legitimized by claims to a deeper understanding of the true general will.

This undoubtedly explains why Rousseau trod so lightly over this territory. Nonetheless, as argued above, one does him a disservice by ignoring the attention he paid to the conflict between simple popular will and a higher, rationalized general will. Among the revolutionaries, Condorcet was probably most sensitive to this problem, having attempted to devise a procedure for arriving at a general will that would come closest to the true interests of the people. He favored a constant dialogue between the people and their local representatives, local representatives and national representatives, and back down again, with maximum participation. Applying his expertise as a mathematician, Condorcet concluded that the higher the number of individuals participating in the making of a decision, the greater the likelihood that that decision will coincide with the truth.[66] Having reconciled himself to the fact that rule of the majority cannot be avoided in a democracy, Condorcet committed himself to maximizing the probability that the will of the majority would approximate the public interest.

In this respect, Condorcet's *Essay on the Application of Mathematics to the Theory of Decision-Making* approaches the same problem Rousseau addressed with his distinction between the general will and the will of all, which attempts to distinguish between the simple agglomeration of particular interests (will of all) and the subordination of particular interests to the common good (the general will). Both thinkers viewed simple majoritarianism as a battle of particular interests that produces nothing more than the will of the strongest party. For Condorcet, this problem could be addressed through procedural constraints on the expression of popular will. For the Jacobins, a committee with alleged insight into the true general will could serve as a proxy for the actually existing will of the people. However, for Rousseau neither of these options could be made compatible with popular sovereignty. As discussed in the previous chapter, both the general will and the will of all are comprised of particular wills. In order to respect popular sovereignty, whatever the majority of particular wills declares must be procedurally accepted as the true general will. To ensure that these particular wills are rationalized, Rousseau focuses on the role of government, which must make civic education and civil religion the cornerstone of political life. The Jacobins shared Rousseau's dual commitment to popular sovereignty and the rationalization or generalization of popular will, but they dispensed with all of Rousseau's caveats, warnings, safeguards, and strategies with regard to how popular will might be rationalized without being usurped.

IV. ROUSSEAU, FATHER OF THE REVOLUTION?

Though the general will began the Revolution as the ultimate expression of popular sovereignty and republican politics, it rapidly became nothing more than a justification for minority government. One cannot help but wonder whether a transformation of this kind is the inevitable result of a politics grounded in a conception of the general will. This section attempts to expose the relationship between the ideas animating the important historical developments of the Revolution and the general will as defined both by Rousseau and by the revolutionaries themselves. Through this approach, it will be possible to draw some conclusions about the repressive/emancipatory tendencies of a politics grounded in the general will.

Representation

Since, for Rousseau, law is simply the declaration of the general will and the general will resides by definition in the body of citizens, it cannot be represented in the legislative power.[67] Put differently, no part of the body politic can ever declare the general will (that is, make law) on behalf of the citizenry as a whole. Now, even his staunchest followers were forced to renegotiate Rousseau's bald repudiation of representation. They typically justified their embrace of representation by appealing to the practical contingencies of a large republic and to the capability of a representative assembly to embody the general will. Though important, these arguments ignore the essence of Rousseau's critique of representation, which is anchored in his definition of freedom, in particular his claim that men are free only to the extent that they give themselves laws. While a benevolent monarch or an enlightened representative body may be able to address the needs of a large republic and even resist the dangers of particularity, neither meets Rousseau's strict standards for self-legislation.

Chapter 15 of Book III of *The Social Contract* begins with an account of the evolution of a bourgeoisie concerned more with commerce and the arts than with public affairs. As usual, Sparta and Rome loom large as Rousseau bemoans the declining interest in civic participation. The chapter begins as follows: "As soon as public service ceases to be the main business of the citizens, and they prefer to serve with their pocketbooks rather than with their persons, the State is already close to its ruin."[68] Rousseau's rejection of representation is usually explained as part of his aversion toward corporate interests and the threat of particularity to the general will. While this undoubtedly motivates much of Rousseau's apprehension, there is a simpler, procedural argument that is of equal importance. The general will cannot be represented for the same reason that it cannot be alienated.[69] The "general good" or the "general spirit" could quite straightforwardly be represented, and might plausibly be best discerned by a virtuous, intelligent elite. However, "will" emphasizes the active participation of each citizen—a prerequisite to Rousseau's republican freedom. It is in this context that Rousseau criticizes the English people, who only "thinks it is free." "It greatly deceives itself," writes Rousseau, "it is free only during the election of the members of Parliament. As soon as they are elected it is a slave, it is nothing."[70] For many, it is in living under the law that freedom is enjoyed; for Rousseau, freedom lies in law making.

Rousseau concedes that this conception of freedom can be realized only in very small communities where the people as a whole can convene. Thus, the only truly Rousseauean solution to the problem of representation is precluded by the exigencies of modernity. Some revolutionaries saw the suspensive veto as a possible solution to the problem because it could act as a direct appeal to the people if the legislature ever abdicated its responsibility to the general will.[71] In this way, it could counteract the tendency of the legislature to act out of self-interest—an advantage to be sure, but one that depended on the character of the monarch and did not address Rousseau's procedural insistence on popular participation in the legislative process. Despite these concerns, the Assembly opted (initially) for the suspensive veto to balance competing interests in endowing the legislature with the power to enact the general will and restraining it from mobilizing the public force for particular interests.

Even Rousseau had made some concessions to the need for representation in *The Government of Poland,* but he never accepted the idea that a division of power could be compatible with the sovereignty of the general will. Rousseau's grudging acceptance of representation was simply a response to the empirical constraints of a large republic like Poland. Moreover, when he articulates his theory of representation, he remains loyal to the distinction he laid out in *The Social Contract* between representatives, who make law, and deputies, who merely enact the general will. The establishment of an assembly, for Rousseau, ought to be justified as a way of "giving to the constitution of a large kingdom the stability and vigor of that of a tiny republic."[72] Accomplishing this is impossible but can be most closely approximated through a federal system of dietines (in the case of Poland), each of which would elect deputies to declare their general will in a national assembly. In order to forestall the inevitable corruption of these deputies,

Rousseau advocates frequent elections and rigid monitoring of the deputies' behavior. They should be held strictly to the instructions issued by the people: "In a word, the nation does not send deputies to the Diet to give voice to their own sentiments but to declare the nation's own will."[73] Unlike those who favor a legislative assembly with the power to deliberate, Rousseau is skeptical about the allegiance of an elected elite to the general will. In short, unlike Sieyès and Condorcet who are profoundly distrustful of the people, Rousseau—though not always convinced of the people's virtue himself—fears the corruption of deputies even more.

It is commonly argued that the Jacobins fell prey to their own warnings about individual will and ambition, and that may very well be the case, yet there is also something appealing about their claims to embody popular will—at least for those who accept the right of the people to rule themselves. Representation was rarely justified on its own merits. Instead, the need for representative bodies was typically expressed through an appeal to the great size and population of the French nation, reducing it to barely more than a practical exigency. Given the general embrace of popular sovereignty, it is somehow bizarre that, as Brian Singer puts it, the "state's entire *raison d'être* was reduced to a problem of logistics."[74] For someone like Sieyès, who had tremendous faith in the power of representatives to formulate the general will, this is not a significant concern. However, many revolutionaries, and all of the radicals, distrusted the people's deputies and believed with Rousseau that only the people themselves embody virtue and will the public good. The Jacobins' abuse of power might be viewed as a vindication of Sieyès's skepticism toward popular sovereignty; however, it could equally be explained as a failure to respect the duties of a deputy of the people. While partisans of representation might recommend a system of representation that distances legislators from the vagaries of public opinion, others may advocate binding representatives to the people ever more rigorously. The Jacobins, alas, followed neither course; instead, they both undermined all arguments for representation and declared themselves the sole voice of the people.

Popular Will and Rational Will

In a way, the Jacobin usurpation of the power to declare the general will was inevitable. The actually expressed will of the people could never live up to the standards they had set for popular will. It eventually became clear that the Jacobins had no intention of sharing power with the people. They eschewed referendum, a process they had previously advocated, and began to think of themselves as the sole repositories of the people's will.[75] Eventually, they took the next step, insisting on the political exclusion of certain "enemies of the Revolution" as vehemently as they insisted on the inclusion of the lower classes. This shift lives out the tension between popular sovereignty and virtue that Rousseau theorized so profoundly. It reveals the sense in which a commitment to democracy must always be qualified, either through the conditioning of popular will or by an institutional check. For Rousseau, it was crucial that each individual arrive at the general will on his own, so that he would be obeying laws he gave himself. However, this deliberation must be of a special, generalized, rationalized sort, free of the passions that tend toward particularity. Put simply, citizens must be virtuous. Similarly, the Jacobin commitment to universal suffrage was contingent on its faith in the virtue of the people. "One finds that liberty is a corruption of independence and that it is only estimable inasmuch as it brings the simplicity of virtue."[76] As indicated above, there was a connection between the Jacobins' insistence on absolute popular sovereignty and their faith in the goodness of the people.

Rousseau understood the dangers involved in equating popular will with rational will or political right, but he was far more reluctant to put limitations on the popular exercise of sovereignty. For him, any discrepancy between the unerring general will and transient popular will must be addressed through the cultivation of a political culture, emphasizing unity, patriotism, and virtue. Procedurally, the will of the people must be accepted as right on any given decision, in order to preserve the freedom of obeying laws given to oneself. In contrast, Jacobin practice subordinated all procedural standards of legitimacy to their project of creating *l'homme régénéré*. Patrice Higonnet describes this as the Jacobins' "rejection of constitutional procedure for the sake of some higher truth."[77] Better, perhaps, to say that the Jacobins constrained popular will by replacing the higher truth that is constitutional procedure with their own, particular conception of a higher truth. As we have seen, egalitarian societies inevitably constrain popular will in various ways. The best criticism of the Jacobins is not that they took an interest in the rectitude of popular will, but that they approached the problem in an oppressive manner.

Rousseau's paradox of founding captures the inexorable political tension between rational will and popular will: "For a young people to be able to relish sound principles of political theory and follow the fundamental rules of statecraft, the effect would have to become the cause; the social spirit, which should be created by these institutions, would have to preside over their very foundation."[78] Robespierre understood his theory of revolutionary government as an attempt at resolving Rousseau's paradox. Robespierre came to think of the entire Revolution as a founding. He distinguished between constitutional government, which is concerned primarily with insulating individuals from the abuses of public power, and revolutionary government, which must deploy its power against its enemies. "Under constitutional rule it is almost sufficient to protect individuals from the encroachment of state power: under a revolutionary regime, state power itself must protect itself against all the factions that attack it."[79] Revolutionary government could only be justified as a temporary provision, of course, but a necessary one, nonetheless, required in the case of the French Revolution to fend off the counterrevolution and begin the process of founding a republican government.

Regardless of their circumstances, egalitarian societies strive perpetually for a reconciliation of rational will and popular will. Paradoxically, efforts to rationalize popular will risk undermining it in the process. The very idea of a rational will generally begs the question of where the authority for truth claims originates. Moreover, even if this problem is somehow overcome, there remains the practical challenge of rationalizing will without threatening individual autonomy. For Rousseau, this paradox issued in skepticism with regard to the possibilities for freedom through politics. The revolutionaries had no such ambivalence. If they were to succeed in founding a republic and making citizens, they had to overcome Rousseau's paradox. In doing so, they clearly transgressed elements of Rousseau's conception of the general will; however, their failures put a burden of justification on those who consider themselves republicans—that is, republicans must demonstrate how will can be rationalized consistent with a respect for individual autonomy and social pluralism. We must show how the politicization of citizen's values, beliefs, and characteristics can be defended against attempts to conceptualize politics in purely formal or procedural terms.

Exclusion/Coercion

The French Revolution is often taken as evidence for the charge that the general will justifies the exclusion and/or coercion of dissenters. Procedurally, the general will requires that all citizens participate in its formulation. In some ways, this should be enough to de-legitimize the patterns of exclusion that characterized the French Revolution. However, the general will also had an ideal, transcendent quality that might encourage those with a disposition to look past its procedural constraints. In addition, one might accept the claim that all citizens participate but use that argument to exclude some members of society from citizenship. For the Jacobins, the people—*le peuple*—were citizens, but one's membership in *le peuple* was never certain. The term "the people" often seems more of an ideal than an actuality, a description of political unity that solves the ancient philosophical problem of the one and the many by including only those characterized by a certain set of interests and virtues. Anyone lacking these things is excluded from *le peuple* by definition, whether it be because they are aristocrats, clergymen, or simply corrupted by aristocratic or bourgeois vices. Lucien Jaume calls the people a "collective individual . . . more moral than political."[80] Indeed, "the people," in its various forms seems to be more an image of what the Revolution ought to be than a description resembling anything that it actually was.[81] When Sieyès writes that the Third Estate is "everything," he is making an empirically false statement. The statement must be understood normatively, to imply that the Third Estate embodies everything of political relevance; that the voices of the other two estates have no place in French politics.

While defenders of the Third Estate were skilled at explaining what the people were not, they were less expert at explaining what the people were. Robespierre said "the family of French legislators, the *patrie*, is the whole human race minus the tyrants and their accomplices."[82] This method of definition by exclusion was a popular way of singling out enemies. The term "aristocrat" became an epithet and was used to attack anyone determined to be at odds with the goals of the Revolution, even those who came from the lower classes. The Girondin leader J. P. Brissot had an alternate way of excluding certain people and opinions while remaining loyal to the undivided goodness of the people. He accepted the claim that the people are never wrong, but added that there is a "multitude which is not the people," and it is "often wrong, often misled."[83]

These semantic tricks allow for a tendentious reconciliation of rational will and popular will, but they betray the spirit of Rousseau's approach to the problem. They respect neither Rousseau's procedural account of the formulation of the general will, nor his subtle approach to the rationalization of will. In fact, there is a very definite sense in which this general will is more Sieyèsian than Rousseauean.

Sieyès and the Terror

Political theorists have proposed two principal strategies for avoiding factional tyranny. Liberals advocate limiting political power through the separation of powers, while republicans favor generalized participation and close ties between the people and their deputies. Sieyès rejected the separation of powers as a violation of the nation's united will, while advocating restrictions on popular participation and an insulated body of representatives that would declare the general will. Robespierre repudiated this Sieyèsian position on a philosophical level, returning to Rousseau's distinction between deputies and representatives, insisting, for example, that members of the convention be called *mandataires* and never *représentants*, because will cannot be represented.[84] He demanded that these *mandataires* be tied closely to the people and that they mirror the people's characteristics and wishes. Whereas for Sieyès, representatives required some independence from the people in order to rationally formulate the general will for Robespierre, the source of government corruption was its distance from the people. If possible, the assembly should "deliberate in the presence of the people as a whole. Under the eyes of such a great number of witnesses, neither corruption, nor intrigue, nor perfidy would dare show itself; only the general will would be consulted."[85] Robespierre makes it clear that he has internalized Rousseau's conception of a pre-given general will that need not be debated, only acknowledged, expressed, and implemented.

Despite this philosophical disagreement, in practice, the Jacobins minimized popular participation and usurped all political power in the name of its role as defender of the Revolution. As Alfred Cobban writes, "the right of the purged convention to almost absolute powers of sovereignty is the outstanding feature in the political theory of Robespierre in his final two years."[86] The Jacobins' claim to embody the general will became a justification for almost anything they did, with the convenient addition that deliberation among representatives would only distort or corrupt the pure will of the people. They opposed the empowering of a representative body on the grounds that its tendency toward particularity violates the very reason government is instituted—"to respect the general will." Robespierre told the convention, "The men who govern have an individual will, and all will seeks to dominate."[87] The self-delusion drips off of every word for the modern reader, who sees clearly that the Jacobins were precisely that "individual will" that seeks to dominate in the absence of checks on public power and institutional procedures that ensure popular participation. Though they started out respecting the will of the people, they soon decided that the general will was something that only they could see.

Because the actually existing will of the people could be ignored and all institutional constraints on public power had been undermined, there was no principle by which the Terror could be contained. The logic is profoundly Sieyèsian. As Istvan Hont writes, Sieyès "used the idea of the nation against the mixed constitution tradition and the tradition of direct popular republicanism."[88] Both the traditional liberal and the traditional republican constraints on public power had been eroded by the Sieyèsian doctrine that sovereignty ought to be singular, absolute, and distanced from the people. With the doctrines of popular rule and constitutionalism undermined, French politics became exceedingly vulnerable to factional tyranny.

Hegel, Rousseau, and the Revolution

G. W. F. Hegel, in scattered but important writings on the Revolution, tells a different story.[89] For him, it was Rousseau who served as the ideological forefather of the Terror. Hegel famously described the Terror as the inevitable consequence of a theory (Rousseau's in particular) grounded in the notion that "what is fundamental, substantive, and primary is supposed to be the will of a single person in his own private self-will."[90] Hegel views the general will as arbitrary, because its substance depends on the vagaries of individual will. Without some "higher" will that can limit or direct the general will (what Hegel refers to as the "Idea"), there is nothing to resist the ascendance of a tyrannical faction like the Jacobins. With the account of the general will we now have at our disposal, we can unsettle some of Hegel's assumptions and assess the accuracy of his claim.

Hegel sees terror as the inevitable result of a philosophy grounded in individual will, because individual will intrinsically projects itself as universal—that is, it asserts itself as "universal freedom" and considers anything excluded from it a faction.

> Before the universal can perform a deed it must concentrate itself into the One of individuality and put at the head an individual self-consciousness; for the universal will is only an *actual* will in a self, which is a One. But thereby all other individuals are

excluded from the entirety of this deed and have only a limited share in it. . . . Universal freedom, therefore, can produce neither a positive work nor a deed; there is left for it only *negative* action; it is merely the *fury* of destruction.[91]

The general will, on this account, because it is not a transcendence of individual will but rather constituted by it, inevitably degenerates into factional conflict characterized by competing claims to universality. What comes to be called the government is only the victorious faction and can be nothing more in the absence of a higher will that reconciles competing factions.[92]

Rousseau had conceived of the will, on Hegel's account, only in its individual form and only abstractly, without the concrete comprehension of absolute truth. This combination of the abstract and the individual left popular will indeterminate and arbitrary, which suffices for interactions in civil society but produces a fury of destruction at the level of the state. Because Rousseau's general will remains abstract and posits that every individual rule himself, the government will always be seen as a faction, interposing itself between the people and their true wills.[93] Each individual feels entitled to proclaim one's will the general will, because one does not recognize a higher, universal will.

Hegel connects (what he perceives to be) Rousseau's emphasis on individual will with (what he perceives to be) the abstract nature of the general will. For Hegel, the doctrine of individual rights promotes an abstract conception of the self, stripped of all social and cultural characteristics. This empowers the general will to destroy but not to create, for it wants to remove all constraints on behavior that the individual does not legislate for himself. For Hegel, this explains the brutal oppression by which the Revolution consumed its own children. Once the opposition replaced the government of the *ancien régime*, it immediately had its own opposition of people hoping to tear apart a system of authority that, they felt, did not reflect their will. All existing norms of interaction are called into question by the general will, which views them as barriers to the freedom of each individual to live only according to laws he gives himself.

Hegel seems to have been ignorant of Rousseau's distinction between the general will and the will of all, which addresses the essence of Hegel's criticism. Rousseau does make individual will the center of his political thought, but he has a bifurcated conception of individual will, which he divides into private will and general will. He does not go as far as positing a higher will, originating from somewhere other than individual human beings, for he did not believe it humanly possible to conceptualize anything other than a personal will. However, like Hegel, he understands that politics requires something more than the agglomeration of private wills, and that popular will must be constrained by something resembling Hegel's higher will, or Idea.

Hegel's description of subjective freedom's tendency to universalize itself accurately captures the battle for legitimacy that characterized the competition between factions in the French Revolution. In doing so, he makes a compelling case for some limitation on the expression of the general will. However, his notion of a higher will, of an "Idea" driving history toward a reconciliation of particular wills, suffers from its own problems. Though I cannot rehearse these concerns here, there is broad agreement that it presumes a dubious teleology of human history and subjectivity as progressing inexorably toward transcendence of the dichotomies characteristic of political life. Moreover, it is not at all clear how Hegel's metaphysical conception of the Idea contributes anything to democratic theory, which must consider how to rationalize will within the constraints of democratic procedure.

Hegel criticizes Rousseau for describing only a procedure by which laws might be made as opposed to the substance of those laws. Rousseau, of course, has his reasons for avoiding grand pronouncements of a higher will or "Idea" that might fill in the substance of legislation. Whereas Hegel believed that the general will did not pay enough attention to the particularities of a given context, Rousseau leaves the substance of the general will undetermined as a way of respecting those very particularities. In refusing to assign substance to the general will, Rousseau strives to respect the tendency of popular will to vary over space and time. He places some constraints on popular will and recognizes the need for a variety of resources to rationalize or generalize popular will, but he resists offering an account of the substance of the general will, which he understands as contingent on a variety of circumstances. This, I believe, accurately captures the predicament of egalitarian societies—namely that they require transcendent principles with which they can never feel totally secure. Rousseau theorizes from within this tension rather than positing a magical solution to it, and this is the great virtue of his political theory.

CONCLUSION

Constantly invoked during the Revolution, it is no surprise that Rousseau's name has come to be associated with that event, in all its dimensions. Indeed, Rousseau's abstract principles of political right do resemble those of the revolutionaries—popular sovereignty, equality, and freedom as self-rule. However, revolutionary practice often departed from Rousseau's conception of these terms. For Rousseau, the procedure for determining the general will required popular participation and lacked the resources for a total reconciliation of popular will and rational will. To the extent that this reconciliation could be achieved, it would have to occur through the cultivation of citizenship. The revolutionaries, on the other hand, abandoned both popular participation and Rousseau's skepticism about the chances for a reconciliation of rational will and popular will. They defined popular will in whatever tendentious manner suited them at the time, rarely respecting the constitutional procedures designed to ascertain it. With all institutional restrictions on the use of public power eviscerated and the refusal to share power with the people, nothing could contain the Jacobins' factional tyranny.

96   *Chapter 4*

NOTES

1. Jacques Julliard's book on the consequences of popular sovereignty is titled *La Faute à Rousseau* (Paris: Seuil, 1985). Jacob Talmon writes: "Rousseau's 'general will,' an ambiguous concept, sometimes conceived as valid *a priori*, sometimes as immanent in the will of man, exclusive and implying unanimity, became the driving force of totalitarian democracy and the source of all its contradictions and antinomies," in *The Origins of Totalitarian Democracy*, 6.

2. Edmé Champion, *J. J. Rousseau et la Révolution Française* (Paris: Librairie Armand Colin, 1909), 9.

3. See, for example, Daniel Mornet, *Les Origines intellectuelles de la Revolution française* (Paris: Librairie Armand Colin, 1954), 96; Joan McDonald, *Rousseau and the French Revolution, 1762–1791* (London: Althone Press, 1965), 44; Champion, *J. J. Rousseau et la Révolution Française*; and Carol Blum, *Rousseau and the Republic of Virtue* (Ithaca, N.Y.: Cornell University Press, 1986).

4. Champion, preface to *J. J. Rousseau et la Révolution Française*, vii.

5. See McDonald, *Rousseau and the French Revolution*.

6. Quoted in Barber, *Superman and Common Men*, 37.

7. Pierre Rosanvallon's *Le Sacre du Citoyen: Histoire du Suffrage Universel en France* (Paris: Gallimard, 1992), and Lucien Jaume's *Le discours Jacobin et la démocratie* (Paris: Éditions Fayard, 1989) are notable exceptions (hereafter cited as *Discours Jacobin*). Chapter 6 of James Miller's *Rousseau: Dreamer of Democracy* (New Haven, Conn.: Yale University Press, 1984), though largely historical, provides some theoretical insights as well. Talmon takes a theoretical approach in *The Origins of Totalitarian Democracy*. He traces the excesses of the French Revolution to Rousseau and claims to have established close to a one-to-one connection between Rousseau's political thought and totalitarianism. Though I share Talmon's orientation toward the political theory animating the French Revolution, I draw more moderate conclusions. Talmon's one-dimensional picture of both the Jacobins and Rousseau produce all too easy conclusions about their totalitarian tendencies. Moreover, they implicitly point toward an ostensibly non-problematic alternative of a safe and secure liberalism. If the complexity of Rousseau's thought is appreciated and the Revolution is seen as more than the Terror, Talmon's conclusions become unreasonable, and one is compelled to be more ambivalent, both about republicanism and liberalism.

8. Bernard Manin, "Rousseau," in *A Critical Dictionary of the French Revolution*, ed. François Furet and Mona Ozouf (Cambridge, Mass.: Harvard University Press, 1989), 841. Joan McDonald adds, "it wasn't the influence of Rousseau's principles that created the Revolution; rather the Revolution created their influence." See McDonald, *Rousseau and the French Revolution*, 10.

9. Bernard Gagnebin charts Rousseau's influence on the Declaration of Rights and Man in "L'Influence de Rousseau sur la Déclaration des droits de l'homme et du citoyen," in *Reappraisals of Rousseau*, ed. Simon Harvey, Marian Hobson, David Kelley, and Samuel S. B. Taylor (Manchester, U.K.: Manchester University Press, 1980).

10. "Declaration of the Rights of Man and Citizen, 27 August, 1789," in *A Documentary Survey of the French Revolution*, ed. John Hall Stewart (New York: Macmillan, 1951), 114.

11. McDonald, *Rousseau and the French Revolution*, 137. It is notable that though the Declaration of the Rights of Man and Citizen included Rousseau's claim that the general will be general in object, it left out the equally important requirement that it be general in origin as well. In the following, I will explore the ways in which sacrifices like this one become inevitable when practical prescriptions are taken from a theory that has embraced paradox.

12. Quoted in Simon Schama, *Citizens: A Chronicle of the French Revolution* (New York: Vintage, 1989), 502 (hereafter cited as *Citizens*).

13. Schama, *Citizens*, 323.

14. McDonald, *Rousseau and the French Revolution*, 172.

15. McDonald, *Rousseau and the French Revolution*, 89, 116. McDonald's study must be understood within the context of the previously popular belief that the French Revolution was in some way an actualization of Rousseau's political theory. She argues convincingly that the revolutionaries' use of the general will bears little resemblance to Rousseau's formulation of it. This, however, is quite different from the claim that they offer no coherent versions of the general will themselves. This chapter is intended to articulate the theory animating these versions of the general will.

16. Robespierre, *Oeuvres* (Paris: Leroux, 1958), 9:130.

17. "It is for the advantage of the people and not at all for his own particular advantage that the monarch intervenes in legislation; and it is in this sense that one can and that one must say that the royal veto is in no way the royal prerogative, but the property and the domain of the nation." Mirabeau, "On the Right of Veto," 1 September 1789, in *Orateurs de la Révolution Française*, ed. François Furet and Ran Halévi (Paris: Gallimard, 1989), 1:676.

18. Mirabeau, "On the Right of Veto." Mirabeau added, "The prince is the perpetual representative of the people, just as the deputies are their elected representative for certain time periods," 677.

19. Mirabeau, "On the Right of Veto," 678, 674.

20. Stanislas-Marie-Adélaïde, comte de Clermont-Tonnerre, "Discours sur le Projet de Loi Relatif à la Régence," 23 March 1791, in *Orateurs de la Révolution Française*, 267.

21. Norman Hampson, "The Idea of the Nation in Revolutionary France," in *Reshaping France: Town, Country, and Region during the French Revolution*, ed. Alan Forrest and Peter Jones (Manchester, U.K.: Manchester University Press, 1991), 16.

22. Hampson, "The Idea of the Nation in Revolutionary France," 16.

23. Jean Massin, *Robespierre* (Paris: Alinéa, 1988), 28.

24. See François Furet, *Interpreting the French Revolution* (London: Cambridge University Press, 1981).

25. Keith Michael Baker, *Inventing the French Revolution* (London: Cambridge University Press, 1990), 298.

26. Baker, *Inventing the French Revolution*, 298.

27. Rousseau, *The Social Contract*, 53.

28. Rousseau, *The Social Contract*, 102.

29. Pierre Vergniaud, "On the Appeal to the People," 31 December 1792, in *Orators of the French Revolution*, ed. H. Morse Stephens (Oxford, U.K.: Clarendon, 1892), 1:328.

30. Vergniaud, "On the Appeal to the People," 329.

31. Baker, *Inventing the French Revolution*, 271 (italics added).

32. Italics added.

33. Emmanuel Sieyès, "Qu'est ce que le tiers état?" in *Écrits politiques*, ed. Roberto Zapperi (Paris: Éditions des Archives Contemporaines, 1985), 178.

34. Sieyès writes, "in a national Assembly, particular interests must remain isolated, and the wishes of the plurality must always conform to the general good." Sieyès, "Qu'est ce que le tiers état?" 180. Likewise, Condorcet writes, "the wishes of every assembly must, by the very form through which they are collected, truly express the general will." Quoted in Rolf Reichardt, *Reform und Revolution bei Condorcet* (Bonn: Ludwig Röhrscheid Verlag, 1973), 244.

35. Thomas Hobbes, *Leviathan*, ed. C. B. MacPherson (London, Penguin, 1968), 220 (italics in original).

36. Hobbes, *Leviathan*, 228.

37. Hobbes, *Leviathan*, 218.

38. Sieyès, "Qu'est ce que le tiers état?" 159.

39. Sieyès, "Qu'est ce que le tiers état?" 201.

40. Quoted in Murray Forsyth, *Reason and Revolution: The Political Thought of the Abbé Sieyès* (New York: Holmes & Meier, 1987), 119.

41. Forsyth, *Reason and Revolution*, 76.

42. Forsyth, *Reason and Revolution*, 76.

43. Quoted in Rosanvallon, *Le Sacre du Citoyen*, 178.

44. Robespierre, 10 May 1793, *Oeuvres*, 10:496.

45. Robespierre, 10 May 1793, *Oeuvres*, 10:496

46. Robespierre, 10 May 1793, *Oeuvres*, 10:495.

47. Rosanvallon, *Le Sacre du Citoyen*, 192.

48. Malouet, 17 June 1789, in *Orateurs de la Révolution Française*, 447.

49. Forsyth, *Reason and Revolution*, 71.

50. Sieyès, "Qu'est ce que le tiers état?" 118. Sieyès adds on p. 203, "The Third estate is the equivalent of the general will."

51. Robespierre, *Discours et Rapports* (Paris: Charpertier et Fasquelle, 1908), 174.

52. François Furet and Denis Richet, *The French Revolution* (London: Weidenfeld & Nicholson, 1970), 199.

53. See the counsel Rousseau offers to Geneva in his *Letters Written from the Mountain*.

54. "Universal suffrage" is a bit of a misnomer in this context because, though the Jacobins favored suffrage for blacks and Jews, they never considered enfranchising women. Joan Landes has shown how the Jacobin conception of citizenship depended on the exclusion of women from public life. See her *Women in the Public Sphere* (Ithaca, N.Y.: Cornell University Press, 1988).

55. Quoted in Schama, *Citizens*, 498.

56. Emmanuel Sieyès, "Essai sur les Privilèges," in *Écrits Politiques*, 95.

57. Jaume, *Discours Jacobin*, 172.

58. Louis-Antoine Saint-Just, *Théorie Politique* (Paris: Seuil, 1976), 132.

59. Rousseau, *The Social Contract*, 61.

60. This was the argument put forth by Achille Nicolas Isnard in a pamphlet issued in October of 1789 called *Observations sur le Principe qui a produit les Révolutions de France, de Genève et d'Amérique*. Isnard claimed that allowing the general will to dictate the laws makes them arbitrary. He arrives at this conclusion by equating the general will

with popular will, which, he argues, is not always enlightened. To make the general will sovereign is to confound the end of politics with the means. The end of politics is to be ruled by supreme reason and, though it is the wish of all to live by the laws of reason, the general will does not always reflect that wish. This interpretation of Rousseau's general will appears to have been shared by revolutionaries across the political spectrum.

61. Keith Michael Baker, *Condorcet: From Natural Philosophy to Social Mathematics* (Chicago: University of Chicago Press, 1975), 253.

62. Quoted in Massin, *Robespierre*, 230.

63. "Constitution," in *Orateurs de la Révolution Française*, 491.

64. Cobban, *Rousseau and the Modern State*, 137.

65. Cobban, *Rousseau and the Modern State*, 137.

66. See Condorcet, "Essay on the Application of Mathematics to the Theory of Decision-Making," in *Condorcet: Selected Writings*, ed. Keith Michael Baker (Indianapolis: Bobbs-Merrill, 1976).

67. Rousseau, *The Social Contract*, 103.

68. Rousseau, *The Social Contract*, 101.

69. Rousseau, *The Social Contract*, 102.

70. Rousseau, *The Social Contract*, 102.

71. Mirabeau says, "the monarch could be forced to turn the public force against the people (if their intervention had not been required to complete the acts of legislation) and declare legislation to be in conformity with the general will." See Mirabeau, *Orateurs de la Révolution Française*, 675. Malouet adds, "because their [the representatives'] will, their personal interest, may be in conflict with the general will and general interest, it makes sense for the nation to demand a guarantee from the only one above all private interests, the man who has an eminent interest in the maintenance of the Constitution by which he exists as monarch, and without which he cannot be anything. . . . It follows from this, *Messieurs*, that the royal veto is a national right and prerogative, conferred to the leader of the nation by the nation, to declare and guarantee that a resolution of the representatives is or is not the expression of the general will." "On the Royal Veto," 1 September 1789, *Orateurs de La Révolution Française*, 458.

72. Rousseau, *The Government of Poland* (Indianapolis: Hackett, 1985), 25.

73. Rousseau, *The Government of Poland*, 37.

74. Brian Singer, *Society, Theory and the French Revolution* (Houndmills, Basingstoke, Hampshire, U.K.: Macmillan, 1986), 130.

75. Patrice Higonnet, *Goodness beyond Virtue: Jacobins during the French Revolution* (Cambridge, Mass.: Harvard University Press, 1998), 41, 54.

76. Saint-Just, *Théorie Politique*, 92.

77. Higonnet, *Goodness beyond Virtue*, 23.

78. Rousseau, *The Social Contract*, 69.

79. Robespierre, 25 December 1793, *Oeuvres*, 10:99.

80. Jaume, *Discours Jacobin*, 153, 154.

81. Danton illustrates this strange use of "the people": "I demand of you citizens that you . . . be the people; every man with a spark of patriotism in his breast, every man who wishes to show himself a Frenchman, must stand by the people; it is the people that brought us forth; we are not its fathers, we are its children." *Speeches of Georges Jacques Danton* (New York: International Publishers, 1928). Danton seems to be asking the people to be the people; actually he is asking the human beings before him to live up to an ideal of The People.

82. Robespierre, 5 November 1792, in *Oeuvres*, 9:58.

83. Quoted in Norman Hampson, *Will and Circumstance: Montesquieu, Rousseau, and the French Revolution* (London: Gerald Duckworth, 1983), 182.

84. See Cobban, *Aspects of the French Revolution* (New York: George Braziller, 1968), 148.

85. Robespierre, 10 May 1793, "Sur la Constitution," in *Oeuvres*, 10:500–1.

86. Cobban, *Aspects of the French Revolution*, 162.

87. Robespierre, 10 May 1793, *Oeuvres*, 10:496.

88. Istvan Hont, "The Permanent Crisis of a Divided Mankind: 'Contemporary Crisis of the Nation State' in Historical Perspective," in *The Crisis of the Nation State*, ed. John Dunn (Oxford, U.K.: Blackwell Publishers, 1995), 191.

89. G. W. F. Hegel, *The Philosophy of History* (New York: Dover, 1958), 438–57; Hegel, *Philosophy of Right* (Oxford, U.K., Oxford University Press, 1967), 33; and *Hegel's Phenomenology of Spirit* (Oxford, U.K., Oxford University Press, 1977), 355–64.

90. Hegel, *Philosophy of Right*, 33.

91. Hegel, *Hegel's Phenomenology of Spirit*, 359.

92. Hegel, *Hegel's Phenomenology of Spirit*, 360.

93. Steven B. Smith, *Hegel's Critique of Liberalism* (Chicago: University of Chicago Press, 1989), 90.

Chapter 5

The General Will in the French Revolution: Creating Citizens

One of the few things for which the Jacobins could never be criticized would be a failure to recognize the importance of civic virtue. On the contrary, they were dedicated to the project of creating *l'homme régénéré*, so much so that they transgressed most of the principles of political right that they had articulated. Most students of the Revolution have interpreted this abdication of basic principles as a warning against the politicization of citizens' beliefs, values, characteristics, and virtues. As I have argued up to this point, this kind of politicization is both inevitable and, when properly conceived, desirable. In this chapter, as in the last, I will distinguish between the political practice of the Revolution and theoretical approaches to the problem of citizenship, both Rousseau's and those favored by the revolutionaries themselves. Once these distinctions are made, it should be possible to consider the possibility of a politics, grounded in the general will, that understands freedom as self-rule and pursues a shared identity while also respecting difference and individual rights.

Before dismissing Jacobinism as simple zealotry, it is worth considering the social context in which the revolutionaries found themselves. One way of explaining Jacobinism is as "an effort to establish citizenship as the dominant identity of every Frenchman—against the alternative identities of religion, estate, family, and region."[1] The Revolution had overthrown traditional corporatism; it revolutionized political conduct in just a few years, replacing the norm of privilege with the norm of equality as the French regime's dominant principle. Though the Jacobins' totalizing conception of citizenship is hardly defensible, one might quite easily be persuaded by the notion that citizenship ought to replace religion, estate, family, and region as the dominant identity in a free society. Pursuing this goal in the context of the legacies of the *ancien régime* ought not be equated with a concern for citizens' values, beliefs, and virtues in a more stable context. The lesson to be learned from the French Revolution as regards citizenship may have less to do with *whether or not* to build citizens, and more to do with *how*.

I. CIVIC VIRTUE IN THE FRENCH REVOLUTION

Building Citizens

Their jettisoning of Rousseau's insistence on unmediated popular sovereignty in no way dissuaded the revolutionaries from a Rousseauean emphasis on the cultivation of patriotism and virtue. This produced a combination of an unchecked, unaccountable faction of rulers with the power and motivation to involve itself in the care of the souls of its constituents. As we saw in the previous chapter, if republican goals are to be pursued, it is crucial that republicanism's first principle—popular sovereignty—be respected. By straying from this principle, the Jacobins became arbitrary and tyrannical in their effort to cultivate citizenship.

The Jacobins' basic understanding of citizenship is grounded in Rousseau's distinction between men who pursue their self-interest without regard for the public interest, and citizens who relate everything to the public interest. They called this willingness to dedicate oneself to the public interest "virtue" and believed the fate of the French republic to be dependent on it. To ensure civic virtue, the Jacobins encouraged citizens to replace their old religious icons with a "republican Ten Commandments" and altars of Jean-Pierre Marat or Louis Michel Le Peletier.[2] They held festivals of celebration in honor of the republic and cultivated precisely what Enlightenment *philosophes* like Condorcet had proscribed—"a blind enthusiasm" for the constitution, the "creation of a kind of political religion."[3]

Whereas Condorcet thought politics ought to be exclusively a matter of reason, the Revolution made use of sentiment as well, combining both to produce an ostensibly rationalized general will. It was Condorcet who had written that "In every law it is necessary to ask first what is just, and then what is the best means of ensuring that the just is observed."[4] This latter claim is simply a restatement of what I have called the second fundamental question of political theory, the question of viability. However, whereas for Condorcet the free exercise of reason was the key both to understanding the nature of justice and to ensuring that it is observed, the Jacobins adopted Rousseau's emphasis on sentiment to cultivate desirable dispositions.

As such, Saint-Just used the language of "family" to describe the bond citizens would feel for each other once they had renounced their pride.[5] In this way, the sentiment involved in love of oneself (*amour-propre*) can be broadened to include all compatriots. Even for Rousseau, the great enemy of *amour-propre,* love of the fatherland could transform *amour-propre* into virtue. It remains self-love, vanity even, but it ascends by becoming general, by becoming a passion that we control rather than one that controls us. It becomes disciplined and channeled in a manner conducive to the flourishing of freedom and virtue.

This was the ancient picture of virtue, transposed onto French society via the writings of Montesquieu and Rousseau, and it is a picture that goes largely unchallenged. As François Furet writes, "French thought, by and large, eschewed the recourse to the notion that there is a final harmony of interests, and that particular conflicts will benefit the common good."[6] For the revolutionaries, difference bordered on treason, because its divisiveness inhibited the formulation of the general will. Identifying with a particular group automatically meant a subversion of the general will, reminiscent of the *privilèges* that had initially provided the very impetus for the Revolution. Having begun as an uprising against all inequalities and class distinctions, it is not surprising that the Revolution renounced difference altogether.

The festivals of the Revolution centered around the theme of unity and consensus. All national differences were supposedly transcended into the generality of the new French republic. Indeed, this is the dominant theme of Jules Michelet's famous history/celebration of the Revolution—all Frenchmen walking as one, under the flag of fraternity. The old regime had artificially imposed division on a people naturally destined for unity, and, through the ascendance of the nation, all of these old allegiances were supposed to evaporate. In many ways they did. The *patrie* became divine, as society demanded a religious loyalty previously reserved for the Church, and division became heresy.

Jacobin calls for a *volonté une* highlight the group's drive to unity and reveal the sense in which the project was doomed from the beginning. Outlawing difference inevitably leads to disaster and, more importantly, is by no means the best way to cultivate unity. Unity can be cultivated either through the elimination of difference or through its integration. Individuals might adapt themselves to a given political identity, but that identity might itself adapt and evolve. For all of the monarchy's deficiencies, it did support the peaceful coexistence of *corps*, communities and provinces, and generally respected the laws through which particularism expressed itself.[7] The fundamental rupture with the past meant that these old particularities could no longer be tolerated. However, the displacement of the norm of privilege with the norm of equality cannot be blamed for the Jacobins' totalizing approach to citizenship. Citizenship, if it is to support freedom and respect difference, cannot be an exhaustive identity. It must, as Sieyès hoped, impose unity on diversity, and it must be cultivated within the confines of the institutions of popular sovereignty.

"Our Revolution Calls for Character"

"Other revolutions called only for ambition," said Robespierre; "ours calls for character."[8] It is not especially unusual to call for limitations on the self-interested pursuit of power. Classical liberal writers such as Montesquieu and Locke, who ground politics in an understanding of self-interest, nevertheless offer accounts of the virtues needed to sustain a republic and the boundaries within which reason must operate. Robespierre goes much further. Though he believed that the Revolution clearly served the interest of the majority of French people, Robespierre rejected the idea that self-interest alone, however rationalized or enlightened, could sustain the French republic. Instead, the Jacobins sought "an order where all base and cruel passions are locked up, where every beneficent and generous passion is awakened."[9] They appropriated Rousseau's glorification of man's natural goodness and the corresponding embrace of a politics designed to reconstitute it. Whereas early-Enlightenment theorists of human nature had taken man as he is in civilized society—ambitious, vain, and decadent—and transposed those characteristics back onto natural man, the revolutionaries followed Rousseau in attributing those characteristics to the societies of modern Europe rather than to human nature. This produced a concern for moral as well as political reform. Individuals were not addressed with respect to the characteristics that they had but with respect to the characteristics they could have had; they were measured against an ideal of natural goodness and its political cousin, virtue.

Since Alexis de Tocqueville, students of the Revolution have been mitigating its radicalness through an emphasis on the ways in which the new regime resembled the old one and even perpetuated many aspects of it. The Jacobin concern for character appropriates a Christian focus on the goodness of the soul as well as an old regime-style emphasis on the differentiated social status of each member of society over and above their shared status as citizens. Whereas rational deliberation and organized participation are typically considered the hallmark of a robust republican regime, the key word for the French was *sensibilité;* "to possess *un coeur sensible* [a feeling heart] was the precondition for morality," while tears were valued as a mark of authenticity and the "saboteur of polite disguise."[10] Antirevolutionary forces had to be not only defeated, according to the Jacobins, but "unmasked." More than their beliefs or actions, it was an individual's essence that mattered to the Jacobins; their status as citizens was tied to their moral integrity, or what Saint-Just often referred to as "probity." Those painted as opponents never merely undermined the public good—rather they "slandered" (*calumné*) the people. The battle for legitimacy went beyond practical political questions to questions of character: Robespierre, for example, accused the Girondins not of wrongheadedness, but of having "slandered Paris." Here, Robespierre makes a moral accusation as opposed to a political one, by framing his remarks in the context of an assault on character rather than as a dispute over policy. The Jacobins believed that their enemies had done more than simply undermine the interests of the people; they had betrayed the people; as Crane Brinton puts it, "they had sinned."[11]

Robespierre approached politics through morality; for him, the French Revolution provided a modern forum for the classic battle between good and evil. More than simply misguided, opponents were, for Robespierre, "*fripons*" (rascals), worlds apart from those "few and generous men" who are "desirous of the people's happiness."[12] Robespierre did not stop at unmasking the "*fripons*" and "*scélérats*" (scoundrels) who opposed him; he attempted to make himself transparent as well; that is, he kept nothing private, striving to purge himself of all hypocrisy, to pour everything into his public self. When twenty-first century ears hear Robespierre described by his pseudonym—the Incorruptible—we cannot help but interpret it with a smirk, but Robespierre's belief that moral regeneration must precede political reform was not seen by his constituents as self-serving or hypocritical. We must resist the tendency to interpret "Robespierre, the Incorruptible" the way we interpret "Michael Jackson, the King of Pop," as nothing but a propagandistic attempt at self-aggrandizement. Robespierre's incorruptibility was taken seriously; as Patrice Gueniffey writes, Robespierre "eliminated in himself all distinction between public and private."[13] Perhaps I go too far, but there is an important historical reality that supports this position. The Jacobins, as political leaders, acted in opposition to their "objective" interests as members of civil society. As Brinton claims, they are one of history's few examples of men acting without regard for their material interests.[14]

Not much hangs on whether I have exaggerated Robespierre's moral purity (and I almost certainly have). The more important point is to be clear about the standard to which he hoped to elevate politics. Even if it were the case that a few exceptional men had succeeded in making themselves transparent and in sacrificing everything to their understanding of the public good, the Jacobins' conception of citizenship sets up impossible standards and is governed by a self-defeating logic. The Jacobins reversed the presumption of citizenship, by which I mean individuals were not entirely worthy of respect prima facie, but had to first prove their "quality as citizens."[15] A person was not suspect based on class as in the old regime, but now he had to prove himself—to show himself to be virtuous, perhaps even transparent. Men were not entitled to political rights a priori; first they had to become citizens. In this way, the Revolution constructed its own pattern of exclusion, one that was defined in opposition to that of the old regime but that perpetuated the pathology of social division.

II. ROUSSEAU, FATHER OF THE REVOLUTION?

The revolutionaries invoked Rousseau's name more in conjunction with his *Confessions* and *La Nouvelle Héloïse* than with his explicitly political writings. In these writings, one finds Rousseau's account of man's most sublime sentiments and virtues, but one does not find the skepticism he expressed about the political possibilities of cultivating these qualities. Nonetheless, in emphasizing citizenship, the Revolution does pick up on a theme that Rousseau makes primary.

For Rousseau, republics demand virtuous citizens, willing to subordinate their private interest to the public good. Unfortunately, the sacrifice of private interest required of the virtuous citizen is a sacrifice antithetical to modern political life. Consequently, useful passions must be evoked. Rousseau wrote, "All the sentiments we dominate are legitimate; all those which dominate us are criminal."[16] The supremacy of the general will depends on reason, to be certain, but it also requires, according to Robespierre, that the individual "take pleasure and pride in the prosperity and the glory of the *patrie*."[17] Reason is necessary to know the general will, but one must also be capable of subordinating one's private interest to it, and that sacrifice requires passion or sentiment.[18]

Liberté and *égalité* make up much of the substance of the general will, but *fraternité* (the third of the revolutionary triumvirate conspicuously missing from the celebrated documents of the American Revolution) ensures that it predominates. Rousseau advises the Poles to see to it that "the most numerous part of the nation shall be tied to [the] fatherland . . . by bonds of affection."[19] The revolutionaries invoked fraternity as a way of cultivating an instinct toward the common good that would reconcile individual and general, such that, as Rousseau prescribed, citizens would see the common interest as their private interest. Rousseau counseled in *Émile*, "it is important in every age to clothe reason in forms where it will be loved."[20] Cultivating fraternal bonds through education, public festivals, and civil religion contributes to certain sentiments, even prejudices, conducive to virtue and, consequently, to freedom.

In chapter 3, I argued that Rousseau's paradoxical, dual commitment to voluntarism and virtue provides the key to understanding the fundamental lessons of his political thought. Rousseau's prodigy expresses the paradox near the end of *Émile*: "'What course have I chosen! To remain what you have made me.'"[21] Does anyone doubt that Rousseau was aware of the irony in this statement? It can be dismissed as incoherent or understood as an expression of the tension between the respect due to the decisions of autonomous individuals and the need to ensure that those decisions be reasonable. Rousseauean democracy shares similarities with liberal democracy, but it is distinguished by its emphasis on the need for civic education—the imperative to teach people what they want, to use Rousseauean language. Democracy in particular precludes strict liberalism, because it is democracy that requires virtue more than any other regime. These competing imperatives produce citizens who, like Émile, become free only when they are "obligated"—that is, "obligated to make their wills conform to reason."[22]

The tragic irony present in Rousseau's proposals for the formation of citizens is absent from the revolutionaries' aspirations to remake human nature. They were hardly impeded by the obvious theoretical tension between paternalism and freedom, seizing on Rousseau's counsel to change human nature without appreciating the spirit in which he uttered it.[23] There seems to have been a prevailing acceptance among the revolutionaries that the sovereignty of the general will required a level of enlightenment and/or virtue that was lacking among their French compatriots. They perceived themselves to be surrounded by the Frenchmen Rousseau had described in *The Discourses* and, as such, they used the language of "regeneration" in the hopes that they could reconstitute man's original goodness.[24] So much had been lost in the process of producing the *messieurs* of the *ancien régime,* and it could only be reclaimed through the making of citizens with a single-minded devotion to the *patrie*.[25]

But the revolutionaries went further than Rousseau, and the project of regeneration came to be an end in itself, superseding fidelity to the principles and institutions of constitutional government. It turns out that, along with their cynicism regarding the virtue of the French, the revolutionaries held the conviction that citizens could be made, that human nature could be transformed to conform to the laws of reason and to the dictates of virtue. This implies a social obligation to educate the public, to "create an instinct to do good and avoid bad," as Rousseau put it.[26] To simply accept the will of each citizen without filtering it through the process of civic education would be sheer laziness. Therefore, Saint-Just insists on preserving the "difference between being free and declaring oneself independent to do bad."[27]

If we put aside the important questions about the philosophical possibilities of claims to true knowledge of good and bad, we see the logic of Saint-Just's position. Democracies must certainly be concerned with the substance and not only the procedure of the general will. However, they cannot be exclusively concerned with substance either, if that focus comes at the expense of procedural safeguards to autonomous willing. However problematic, Rousseau insisted on both virtuous and autonomous willing. He theorized within the tension between popular will and rational will, searching for ways to rationalize the results of popular decision making while respecting popular sovereignty.

Rationalizing Will

Just as Rousseau can be called both an Enlightenment and an anti-Enlightenment figure, there is a similar ambivalence about the French Revolution. While it did replace certain myths with the ideas of the Enlightenment, it went on to mythologize those ideas. In other words, although the Revolution appropriated Enlightenment ideas, it did not fully accept its method—specifically the use of reason alone to emancipate men. The formal language of the general will had to be supplemented with an exaltation of the "people" or the "nation" that could recuperate the symbolism and grace of Christian life. As François Furet puts it "the French had come to re-invent society under the name of the 'people' or the 'nation', and . . . they came to set it up as the new god of a fictitious community."[28] Though the sovereign body was (even at its most democratic) simply the sum of the citizens, it had something of a spiritual character, manufactured by the leaders of the Revolution. Reliance on rationality alone could never serve to rationalize popular will; ironically, it was thought that only nonrational means could rationalize popular will.

In a way, Rousseau necessitates this kind of mythologizing when he sets up the paradox of instituting a society that must be united even before it is instituted.

> For a young people to be able to relish sound principles of political theory and follow the fundamental rules of statecraft, the effect would have to become the cause; the social spirit, which should be created by these institutions, would have to preside over their very foundation; and men would have to be before law what they should become by means of law.[29]

Laws transform human nature; they turn men into citizens, but these laws cannot arise unless there are already citizens to agree to them. As explained in chapter 3, the general will is both the embodiment of freedom and a precondition for it. To escape/illustrate this paradox, Rousseau invokes the Legislator, himself a mythical figure, an outsider possessing the godly power to know human passions without experiencing them. He performs what Rousseau calls a "miracle" by bestowing upon a people a body of laws that they "might obey freely, and bear with docility the yoke of public happiness."[30] The Legislator must possess a "superior intelligence," conducive to discerning the laws that will lead to future glory. In short, "it would take gods to give men laws."[31]

With the gods unavailable, leaders, must play the role of the gods, or at least the role of their vicars. Only through an appeal to the authority of the gods, can the paradox of founding a free republic be overcome. This is what Rousseau means when he advises statesmen to speak "the language of the common people" and to "persuade without convincing."[32] For Rousseau, democracies must have recourse to a nondemocratic strategy at the moment of their founding. Absent a robust, republican political culture, the sovereignty of the general will cannot be presupposed and the regime's legitimacy is placed in doubt. In fact, this dilemma transcends the particular moment of founding. The process of founding and re-founding, of returning to the origins of the regime, continues through the steady cultivation of binding myths. As Leo Strauss put it in his essay on *The First Discourse*, "society stands or falls by a specific obfuscation against which philosophy necessarily revolts."[33] The Enlightenment ideal of emancipation through reason alone breaks down when applied to the problem of transforming men governed by particular interest into citizens devoted to the common good. The Legislator does not speak what Rousseau calls "his own language" to the people (that is, reason); rather, he produces myths that persuade citizens to obey, without convincing them through logical argumentation. In this way, they "become before the law what they should become by means of law."

This discussion should help explain why Rousseau dismisses the possibility of the actual appearance of a statesman in the mold of his Legislator.[34] The Legislator plays an allegorical role in Rousseau's argument by illustrating a paradox inherent in democracy. To address the paradox, societies must turn to the methods discussed in chapter 3—civic education, public festivals, and civil religion. They must cultivate the social conditions that unify a citizen body, and that is a process that inevitably involves the production of myths. It is for this reason that Rousseau describes the "talent of leaders" as the ability to "disguise their power to make it less odious."[35]

Though the general will is ideally composed of the will of every individual, in reality, the will of some part of the citizenry acquires the status of unanimous will. During the Revolution, most decisions were made in oligarchic fashion, and the notion of the will of the people was used principally as a way of legitimizing those decisions. As opposed to originating in public deliberation, the general will was largely manufactured by the revolutionary clubs. As Augustin Cochin put it "the true people, in 1789, only existed . . . in the consciousness or imagination . . . of a small number of the initiated, seized young, trained endlessly, brought up since birth in philosophical societies."[36] Of course, there was a kind of accountability, because the fate of the Revolution's leaders often depended on public opinion, which had acquired power for the first time by virtue of its status as the origin of political legitimacy. Nonetheless, as Furet has shown, the fundamental story of the period from 1789 to the ninth of Thermidor 1794 was the struggle for the dominant symbolic position of "the people."[37] The revolutionaries confronted the Rousseauean problem of founding a free society; Frenchmen had to already be what they would become in a democracy.

The term "general will" itself acquired a mythical status, somehow legitimizing absolute power so long as it was justified as serving the nation. This is, of course, the danger of a politics that resorts to myths. While mythmaking may be the only solution to the paradox of a democratic founding, in the process it romanticizes politics, expanding its bounds such that the sphere of politics wins control over the spirit as well as the mind, the soul as well as the body, the private as well as the public. This expansion of the general will to matters spiritual, to questions of character, took the Revolution down the path of coercion, exclusion, repression, and homogenizing terror. The remainder of this chapter follows the course of this progression and concludes with a discussion of its bearing on the way we think of Rousseau and the general will.

Jacobinism and the Division between Public and Private

Having laid out the Jacobins' understanding of citizenship, we can make sense of Robespierre's claim that terror is "less a particular principle than a consequence of the general principle of democracy."[38] Once the world is seen as inevitably divided into good and evil, no measure can be too extreme. Moreover, by equating evil with hypocrisy and hypocrisy with a preference for the particular over the general, the Jacobins ensured an endless cycle of purging. As R. R. Palmer says, "the hunt for hypocrites is boundless."[39] Better, perhaps, to accept the inevitability of tension between the particular and the general, as Rousseau's political theory suggests. Whereas the drive toward transparency makes hypocrisy a crime, the preservation of a private sphere neutralizes hypocrisy, allowing it to exist within the confines of a democratic system. The Jacobins viewed this logic as subversive, based on the belief that private vices would always undermine popular sovereignty. Mona Ozouf writes, "Gone was the possibility of retreating into privacy; as Robespierre said in his last, dramatic speech, the minute the people returned to its private abodes, 'intriguers reemerged, and charlatans resumed their roles.'"[40] Having made character a matter of public concern, the subsuming of the private into the public inevitably followed. "The manner of public greeting, the wearing of the cockade, dress, use of the familiar *tu*, the way to choose friends, and, at Saint-Just's insistence, to end friendships: all these were matters for legislation."[41]

The creation of *l'homme régénéré*, a favorite project of the Revolution, meant the elimination of the distinction between public and private. The distinction between civic virtue and private virtue was not operative in Robespierre's mind; for him, public virtues were composed of the private virtues. Robespierre epitomized the prototypical Jacobin—transparent, incorruptible—a man who's private virtue guaranteed his civic virtue. In contrast, Georges Jacques Danton, who differentiated between his private behavior and his public commitment came to be singled out as corrupt. Danton protested the assimilation of the private into the public and insisted on his devotion to the *patrie:* "when I consider myself relative to the common good I feel elevated; my son does not belong to me, he belongs to the Republic; it is the Republic that must dictate his duties to him so that he might serve it well."[42] Nonetheless, he went to the guillotine, and his pleas for moderation were sacrificed to the perceived need for a perfectly united single will, or *volonté une*.

Commonly, Rousseau's political theory is seen as a justification for the Jacobin evisceration of the public/private divide. Jacob Talmon writes, Rousseau "was unaware that total and highly emotional absorption in the collective political endeavour is calculated to kill all privacy."[43] However, unlike Robespierre, Rousseau distinguished between different wills of the people, specifically a private will, a corporate will, and a general will. As explained in chapter 2, though Rousseau's ideal involves a perfectly united society, which would have no need for a strict public/private divide, he restricts the sphere of politics to that which pertains to the common good or to that which the citizens share in common. Rousseau's general will is imperialistic in that it attains perfection when the citizenry becomes perfectly united, but he puts limits on the scope of politics. Whereas Rousseau's general will is limited to defined (if not rigidly defined) matters of public concern, Robespierre's single will recognizes no distinction between public and private matters. In Rousseau's conception of citizenship each member of society remains engaged in a struggle against oneself, against the tendency to prefer one's private will over the general will. Though a reconciliation of the two is held up as the ideal, Rousseau concedes that, in practice, the private will is never totally transcended. Political life comes to be epitomized not by the transcendence of the public/private divide but by a never-ending struggle to subordinate the private to the public. By contrast, Robespierre's single will is a will to an all-encompassing homogeneity that wants to skip over the intractable struggle between private and general will. It insists on one people, united, regardless of the obstacles in its way. Robespierre asked rhetorically, "Do we have the right to have a will contrary to the general will and a wisdom different from universal reason?"[44] Whereas Rousseau reserved an extra-political space for the private will, Robespierre rejected the very notion of a space that might be extra-political and denied the very right to a private will.

The Search for Enemies

Once a position of this rigidity is assumed, a politics of terror must inevitably follow: first, because disagreement becomes the equivalent of subverting the general will; second, because disagreement becomes a matter of good and evil, and the evil must be treated as enemies rather than mere political opponents. "Enemies are vicious men and the rich; their methods are calumny and hypocrisy. There are only two parties in France: the people and its enemies, and these are distinguished by character."[45] Those who disagreed were not simply wrong but "vicious"; they were cancers on the republic and could not simply be punished, but rather had to be annihilated. Not surprisingly, Robespierre's speeches feature heavily the word "*anéantir*" (annihilate)—the natural policy outcome of the Jacobins' Manichean creed. It was not enough to subdue enemies and co-opting them was certainly out of the question because the Jacobins perceived their enemies to be corrupt in their very essence, as products of the society of the old regime.

Saint-Just does not advocate regicide for Louis XVI as a response to any crimes he committed as a king, "but simply for being a king which is never justified."[46] When one's crime becomes synonymous with one's being, as in this case, the only logical punishment is death or annihilation. There is no space for a politics of compromise or transaction when politics penetrates to the core of one's character. The execution of the king without trial was justified on two grounds: (1) A trial would inevitably call the legitimacy of the Revolution itself into question (as Saint-Just put it, "if the King is innocent, the people are guilty"[47]), and (2) "One cannot judge a king as one would judge a citizen; to judge is to apply the law and a law is a relationship to justice; what relationship is there between a king and justice?"[48] The first argument makes sense strategically, but it does not bear on the Jacobin conception of citizenship or the general will. The second argument follows the typical Jacobin logic of establishing conditions on who will be respected as a rights-bearing citizen, and, while it may have some plausibility when applied to the king, the Jacobins used it to justify a general pattern of exclusion.

The Revolution was anti-classist and anti-feudal—against any division—which is to say that it was anti-pluralist. It did not value deliberation or even consent, at least to the extent that they implied discussion, compromise, and eventual agreement. It valued will, and a special kind of will at that. It valued a unanimous, pre-political will, comprised of the ingredients for legitimacy and justice. This value structure has the disadvantage of excluding all those who do not conform to its a priori standards, as the events of the Revolution bear out. When the legitimacy of popular sovereignty is made to depend on unanimity, a division inevitably emerges between those considered part of the people and those who become enemies of the people by the simple fact of their exclusion. The critic can only see this as a chicken-and-egg problem. Is the myth of a perfectly united nation created as a way of marginalizing ostensible enemies of the people, or are there certain natural enemies of the reunion of particular wills in the sovereign body? In the case of the

French Revolution, the answer is probably yes on both counts. The aristocratic resistance and the counterrevolution were obstinately opposed to popular sovereignty and could not be incorporated into the general will. However, most likely due to the success of the alliance built against these reactionaries, the Revolution turned the strategy of unification through exclusion back on itself.

At first it seems impossible to reconcile the Revolution's unanimist ideal with the factional in-fighting that dominated much of the period. How could the revolutionaries insist on unity at the same time they insisted on the difference between Jacobin and Girondin, for example? What becomes clear through a study of the Revolution is that the quest for unity depended on exclusion from the beginning. As Cochin wrote, "Patriotism, which is entirely negative in this sense, has more to do with killing off the small *patries* than with giving life to the large one."[49] Since there was such a consensus both about the need for virtue and about the definition of virtue as the relinquishing of the particular, the myth of popular unity could be quite effectively deployed against anyone who could be described as an aristocrat, foreigner, a member of a faction, even bourgeois, self-interested, ambitious, or simply different. The entity called "*le peuple*," which was originally understood broadly and ideologically to include all Frenchmen except those opposed to popular sovereignty, gradually came to exclude more and more people, climaxing with the Terror, where it seemed to denote only those who agreed with Robespierre.

As Bernard Manin writes, the Jacobins justified government "not by reference to the complex and extravagant theory of total alienation (Rousseau) but in a far simpler way: by painting a picture, with all its train of images and passions, of the enemies with whom France was at war."[50] Having disposed of the king, the Jacobins turned to their adversaries in the National Convention of 1792–1795, ultimately targeting any organized minority. It turned out that the Jacobin strategy of unification fed off of a process of marginalization. It was the process of purging enemies that sustained the Jacobins, not progress toward eliminating them. Describing Marat, Mona Ozouf writes that he "displayed a kind of indifference toward those whom he cast as conspirators. They served mainly to prove that he was not one of them and to guarantee the purity and integrity of his words."[51] The pure were only pure in contrast to the corrupt and, therefore, they needed the corrupt or at least some image of corruption against which they could cast themselves. Saint-Just said that the republic consists in the extermination of everything that opposes it,[52] but were this possible, the republic he had intended to establish would probably have perished along with its opponents. From the beginning, the Revolution relied on enemies against which it could cultivate its own unity. The Revolution needed to be betrayed, because it was through the identification of betrayers that unity was nourished. Moreover, when the unity of the Revolution seemed most in doubt, the distinction between the people and its enemies was asserted with even greater rigidity.[53] Unable to construct a substantive definition of the general will, the Jacobins resorted to singling out enemies, a strategy that produced a cycle of violence and sacrificed individual liberty to a particular conception of the collective project.

Initially, the idea of the French nation was seen as a unifying concept, an identity that would bring Frenchmen together. Sieyès, for example, did not think the abolition of privilege meant the political exclusion and physical destruction of aristocrats; rather he assumed it meant no more than that the Estates General would be transformed into the National Assembly and operate according to the norm of equality.[54] However, the Jacobins opted against deploying the idea of the nation or the people as a means of integrating a divided, atomized French population. They opted instead to build unity within one segment of the population through vilification and exclusion of others.

Individual Rights

The general will implies first and foremost a transfer of sovereignty to the people, both in Rousseau and in the French Revolution. However, for Rousseau, to the extent that popular sovereignty was an end in itself, it was only as a procedural requirement for legitimacy. Rousseau ultimately justified popular sovereignty as a necessary means to individual freedom. For all of Rousseau's emphasis on unity, he continued to view individual freedom as the ultimate goal of politics. Fraternity and patriotism were of the utmost importance but they were fundamentally instrumental—the means to the goal of individual freedom. The Jacobins took exception to Rousseau's use of the individual as the fundamental unit of political analysis. This implied nothing less than a rejection of the basis of the social contract, to the extent that it was understood as the joining of previously isolated individuals. Saint-Just insisted that man is sociable by nature and accused Rousseau of arming proponents of tyranny by emphasizing the importance of the individual.[55] For the Jacobins, the formula was quite straightforward: individualism is a threat to unity. Of course, Rousseau shared this sentiment, but he was careful to distinguish between the end of politics and the means to that end. This is the source of what ends up becoming an incoherence in the Jacobin position. Consider the following statements from Saint-Just and Robespierre, respectively:

The path of fate is good only in the republic, where individual liberty reigns.[56]

There is oppression against the social body when even one of its members is oppressed.[57]

Despite this rhetoric, the Jacobins supported censorship and purged dissenters regularly. Now, it is always possible to claim consistency based on the need to protect the general will from the enemies of freedom. But, in actuality, the Jacobins were much more preoccupied with virtue than they were with individual freedom. Where Rousseau tried to respect both voluntarism and virtue, the Jacobins were quite willing to sacrifice the former to the latter. The means became the end for the Jacobins; revolutionary government, initially justified as necessary to the establishment of a constitutional regime, took on a legitimacy of its own, one which sacrificed individual autonomy.

Robespierre invoked the general will as a symbolic description of the transfer of sovereignty to the people. He ignored Rousseau's institutional safeguards, in a manner that installed revolutionary radicalism within the framework of the French absolutist political tradition. Though we typically understand the French Revolution to have been primarily about rights, the Jacobins did little more than pay lip service to rights, emphasizing instead the absolute power conferred onto the people's representatives by the transfer of sovereignty to the general will. Whereas resistance to the regime had been a right, even an obligation, under the old regime, "once the regime of liberty had been established . . . the claim to resist 'oppression' by the new order was mockery . . . defiant of the general good."[58] Moreover, Robespierre distinguished between terror perpetrated by the monarchy, and the "salutary terror of the justice of the people."[59] Whereas Rousseau believed that freedom could never be consistent with terror,[60] Robespierre felt that the Revolution could best be preserved by purging it. There would be harmony in the new order because only patriots would remain. This regime was a dictatorship, to be sure, but Robespierre believed in the possibility of a dictatorship of liberty.

By rejecting what they considered to be the vulgar liberty of formal individual rights, the Jacobins believed themselves to be carrying out Rousseau's legacy and, in a way, they were. It is certainly one of the dangers of Rousseau's political theory that people must be made to will in accordance with the general will. And the Jacobins followed Rousseau in distinguishing between simple free will and enlightened will, a distinction that requires leaders to form citizens and lead the people toward their true will. Yet, the Jacobins held a largely anti-Rousseauean set of priorities and violated the procedural constraints on power Rousseau had deemed essential to political legitimacy.

Rousseau distinguished between the authoritarian power governments require to build social unity on a cultural level and illegitimate violation of the procedural constraints on the exercise of institutional power. While the former is necessary to cultivate civic virtue and ensure the flourishing of freedom, the latter is an unjustifiable assaulton something Roussean viewed as a prerequisite to freedom itself. As explained in chapter 2, Rousseau modified the traditional liberal conception of the public/private divide but he did not abandon it. While he believed in an expansive public role, he insisted as well on preserving a space for difference, not because difference deserved respect, but because its direct repression could not be made consistent with freedom. Difference had to be attacked subtly, through the cultivation of common norms and traditions. Purges and forceful coercion would be considered not only illegitimate but ineffectual, because virtue demands a transformation of actual will as opposed to fearful conformity.

Rousseau thought politics demanded equal fidelity to the rights of the nation and the rights of the individual, even that each required the other. However it is impossible to ignore the tension between the two in Rousseau's definition of freedom—willing what is best for oneself without any external constraint. There is both a Jacobin and an anti-Jacobin view of freedom in this definition. In one sense, freedom for Rousseau consists less in doing one's will than in not being submitted to that of other people. Understood this way, freedom becomes a will against dependence. However, freedom requires not only independence or autonomy but rationalized or generalized willing as well—doing what is best for oneself. Recall that the social contract involved making oneself dependent on all (as a means to avoid being dependent on the will of any part thereof), and this required the subordination of the individual to the whole. This is the element of Rousseauean freedom seized upon by the Jacobins at the expense of its provisions for individual rights and autonomy.

For the Jacobins, it was only the People in the sense of "*le peuple*" that mattered and not the people as individuals. The rights to liberty and property were not absolute. Only equality was absolute (and the Jacobins were willing to sacrifice almost everything to approximate their ideal of it); the other rights were empty formalisms in and of themselves and could only be exercised properly in conjunction with strong republican values. Moreover, equality referred not to individual rights but to the social whole; as Ozouf has noted, it was not so much equality as identity.[61] Arguments in favor of absolute protection for individual rights gave way to the claim that enemies of the Revolution must be discovered and purged. Despite rhetoric condemning the oppression or sacrifice of even one member of society, Robespierre was in reality a utilitarian.[62] Almost anything could be justified as long as it contributed to the supreme good—the *salut public*. In this most important of ways, the Jacobins parted from Rousseau. Furet writes, "at the very moment when the Revolution believed it was implementing Jean-Jacques' ideas, it demonstrated the validity of Rousseau's pessimism."[63] For Rousseau, politics must somehow find a way of flourishing within the tension between individual rights and the collective good; it must simultaneously build citizens and respect citizens' autonomy. In the Revolution, the former imperative overwhelmed the latter, as Rousseau had feared it could.

Politics without Limits

The disjunction between Rousseau's articulation of the general will and the Jacobins' actualization of it is most apparent in the Revolution's disposition toward French customs and tradition. Rousseau counseled forcefully against disrupting the social peace at almost any cost, advising the Poles, for example, to work within their feudal framework, a system implicitly repudiated in Rousseau's *Social Contract,* but nonetheless one that could not be dismantled without great cost. For Rousseau, reason, virtue, patriotism, and tradition were all important

factors for ensuring the dominion of the general will. However, almost by definition, the version of the general will that emerged during the Revolution could not
include a respect for French customs and tradition. With the network of feudal relations dismantled and previous norms of social interaction discredited, power
"lay on the ground" to use Hippolyte Taine's language, waiting to be picked up
by the most opportunistic—"this was not a revolution, but a *dissolution*," Taine
wrote.[64] Indeed, it certainly was a far cry from Rousseau's advice to the Poles:
"never permit one of your laws to fall into desuetude, not even a law that does not
matter one way or the other; not even if it is downright bad."[65]

Traditions and customs provide a locus around which a national character can
be cultivated. Given what Rousseau had to say about legitimacy in *The Social
Contract*, one would have expected him to condemn the government of Poland
and urge a revolution. Instead, he urges the Poles to "never lose sight of the important maxim: 'do not change anything, add nothing, subtract nothing, unless
you have to.'"[66] Rousseau prefigures Edmund Burke's criticisms of the Revolution
as well as some of the arguments made by French conservatives during the Revolutionary years. In a way, conservatives were more faithful to Rousseau's general will than the radicals, because of their emphasis on the relationship between
social unity and respect for tradition. None of this is to imply that the general will
is antirevolutionary. It is neither intrinsically revolutionary nor antirevolutionary,
reactionary, or radical. In takes no clear stance on these questions, focusing instead on questions of legitimacy, unity, and virtue.

Robespierre could not abide a compromise of the kind Rousseau laid out for
Poland: "Either you do everything for freedom or nothing; either you are fully
free or you are a slave."[67] As is widely noted but perhaps not fully appreciated,
the French Revolution was really The Revolution. It involved not only a transfer
of sovereignty, as all revolutions do, but the destruction of an entire way of social
and political interaction. Though Rousseau is rarely associated with moderation,
the contrast with the Jacobin incarnation of the general will brings out the moderation in Rousseau—the Montesquieu in him.

The Jacobins had no use for limits. The good—justice, the people, and the general will—must be exalted without limit, and the bad—hypocrisy, the nobility,
and private interests—must be annihilated. Robespierre wore fanaticism as a
badge of honor: "the only fanaticism we have to fear is immorality."[68] In this context, pleas for moderation were interpreted as attacks on the Revolution's aspirations to the regeneration of man's pure, natural goodness. Mirabeau's proposals
to construct institutional checks on power, for example—to balance power with
power as the Americans had done—were rejected based on a repudiation of their
theoretical foundation in a conception of human nature as ambitious and self-
interested. "There is no middle point," Saint-Just wrote, by which he meant there
could be no compromise between the people and Louis XVI. "Louis must reign
or die; by engaging in discussion with him you indict yourselves in order to accuse him."[69] In its will to overturn society, the Revolution succeeded. Though it

has become conventional wisdom that the Revolution preserved certain significant characteristics of the old regime, the existing apparatus of control was entirely dismantled—privilege, nobility, and the independence of the Church. Whereas Rousseau advised the Poles to begin by loving everything that belonged to them, the French, as Edmund Burke put it, "began by despising everything that belonged to [them]."[70]

Considerations of this kind call into question the common conception that Rousseau was a theorist of revolution. However, it is clear that Rousseau was The Theorist of The Revolution. As George Rudé writes, Rousseau inspired Robespierre's relating of political to ethical ends, his definition of utility in terms of morality, his faith in the natural goodness of the people, his distrust of representation, his emphasis on equality, his assertion of the sovereignty of the people, and his invocation of the general will.[71] It is, of course, a matter for debate whether this inspiration was grounded in a fair and accurate understanding of Rousseau's political thought. To balance Rudé's list, one could produce a list of elements in Rousseau's political thought ignored or transgressed by Robespierre. This list would include things like a respect for autonomy, an insistence on procedural safeguards on the legislative process, attention to the distinction between public and private, and a tragic sensibility about the paradoxes of politics.

It has often been said that the French Revolution was really two revolutions, one culminating in 1789, driven by the ideas of Montesquieu and the *philosophes,* and the other epitomized by 1793 and inspired by Rousseau. On this account, 1789 is associated with limited government and individual rights, and 1793 with absolute sovereignty and an emphasis on virtue or the subordination of the private. What my reading of Rousseau suggests is that both sides of this distinction simplify and, therefore, distort Rousseau's complex political thought. While the Jacobins were the most zealous in their embrace of Rousseau, one could argue Rousseauean principles pervade 1789 as much as they do 1793. Edmé Champion, writes that "if someone told Rousseau he triumphed with the Mountain he would have replied that neither Grimm or Diderot slandered me as cruelly."[72] After all, in 1793, the Revolution formally and officially abandoned the project of establishing a republic of laws. If the general will meant anything for Rousseau it meant replacing the arbitrary power of a particular individual or group with the generalized power of the people as a whole, and this transition was described by Rousseau as the rule of law.

This probably explains why the Jacobins, self-described disciples of Rousseau, began to distance themselves, not only from Rousseau, but from the whole of previous political thought around the time of the formation of the Committee on Public Safety. As we have seen, Rousseau explicitly condemned organizations on the model of the revolutionary clubs. More than this though, the Jacobins recognized that they had abandoned (temporarily) the institutions of democratic rule. Georges Couthon argued, for example, "As long as the revolutionary machine is still running, you would hurt the people by giving them the task of electing public functionaries, or the people might name men who would betray them."[73] Robespierre believed that the special principles of revolutionary government had yet to be described in any work of political philosophy. He certainly did not find them in Rousseau's *Social Contract,* a copy of which he kept on his desk at all times: "The theory of revolutionary government is as new as the revolution that originated it. One should not look for it in the works of political writers."[74]

CONCLUSION

In appropriating the general will as a model of citizenship, the French Revolution followed both Rousseau's method and the substance of his arguments. With regard to method, the revolutionaries always advocated both an abstract set of principles and a specific ideal of citizenship; they thought simultaneously about the principles of political right and about the prerequisites for putting those principles into practice. Substantively, they appropriated Rousseau's commitment to popular sovereignty, equality, and, above all, virtue. However, they pursued these ideals in contradictory ways that undermined their own principles and transgressed essential aspects of Rousseau's political thought. In their attempts to rationalize will, they subverted popular sovereignty; in their effort to build unity, they violated basic liberties; and, in fighting to eliminate privilege, they destroyed sources of stability.

Nonetheless, while these differences between Rousseau's ideas and those animating the Revolution are important, it would be unwise to push aside the very real challenge the French Revolution poses to the legacy of Rousseau's political thought. Though I believe I have made the case that the resources exist within Rousseau's work to absolve him from the charge of proto-totalitarianism, the dangers of a robust republican conception of the general will continue to loom large. It may not be possible to preserve Rousseau's strong procedural constraints on politics if one takes seriously his emphasis on virtue, unity, and social engineering. The Anglo-American response to the tension between voluntarism and virtue, between popular will and rational will, has been some version of liberalism. This approach has the advantage of placing a formal boundary on the scope of political power. In contrast, Robespierre's virtue knew no limits, no formal constraints on power, and his attempt at actualizing it verified Montesquieu's claim that "even virtue has need of limits."[75] However, as we saw in chapter 1, liberalism, as it is typically conceived, leans too heavily on formal constraints without paying sufficient attention to the problem of cultivating citizenship. Rousseau, on the other hand, wants both the institutional advantages of constitutional limits and avenues for the cultivation of a republican political culture. And he is at his most profound when he writes within the inexorable tension between the two.

The story I have told in this chapter has been about the absence and/or destruction of institutional limitations on political power in the name of forming republican citizens. It has been a story about the destructive tendencies of a politics that embraces too much. By making citizens' moral goodness a matter of political concern, the Revolution transformed political conflict into a moral battle between good and evil. This meant purges of those who disagreed and an evisceration of the public/private divide, which came to be seen as nothing more than a cloak for the fomentation of anti-republican factions. And, with demands for a single, republican will, individualism came to be viewed as another form of faction, threatening the unity of the Revolution.

As noted in chapter 4, Hegel believes himself to have answered the challenge posed by the Terror with his transcendental account of freedom concretized in an ethical community or *Sittlichkeit*. Likewise, liberalism understands itself as a response to the Revolution's slide into Terror and to what liberals see as Rousseau's authoritarianism. However, Rousseau's work itself suggests a strategy for cultivating republican citizenship while safeguarding freedom and avoiding the homogenizing repression that became characteristic of the Revolution. Rousseau distinguishes (though perhaps not forcefully enough) between democratic institutions and democratic political culture. While he embraced a broad array of strategies for making citizens, for cultivating a strong republican sensibility, he also insisted on certain procedural requirements—specifically the free and equal participation of every citizen in the legislative process. Though this participation dwindles to practically nothing in Rousseau's ideal, that occurs only because citizens are so united that they always already agree. In most actually existing societies, there will be no such consensus, and, as argued in chapter 2, the scope of politics must contract accordingly. What must be emphasized here is that this procedural requirement of free and equal participation can never be sacrificed or even pushed aside temporarily. This is because the free and equal participation of all citizens is the essence of the general will, and it is for this reason that Rousseau insisted that no individual could be sacrificed for the whole and why he would have said "you slander me worse than Grimm" if he had heard his name associated with the Jacobins.

Yet, for Rousseau, democratic institutions were only the scaffolding for a robust politics. True freedom in politics is possible only through the cultivation, perhaps even indoctrination, of a strong republican spirit. Paradoxically, freedom or "willing what is best for oneself without any external constraint" depends on one of the things that imperils it. Like Rousseau, the Revolution wanted to affirm both the rights of the individual and the rights of the nation together, or, more accurately, like Rousseau, it wanted to eliminate the gap between the individual and the social. In chapter 3, we considered Rousseau's doubts about the possibilities of such a project. The Jacobins vindicate those doubts, illustrating the contradictions involved in a constitution that tries to affirm both the individual and the nation, both liberal individualism and a unitary conception of popular sovereignty. One could equally imagine a society that neglected social obligations and the character of its citizenry in favor of untrammeled individualism and legalism.

(One may even be living in one.) Rousseau wants to avoid either through the founding of a regime that combines both.

As indicated previously, it was the spirit of the early phases of the Revolution to jointly affirm the rights of the individual and the rights of the nation. Though the Jacobins proved incapable of achieving this synthesis, we should not assume that a politics grounded in the general will lacks the resources to do so. While the Bolsheviks are typically considered latter-day Jacobins, Patrice Higonnet points out that we might equally think of the Third Republic as an heir to the Jacobin legacy.[76] It too espoused national and individual goals and managed to do so without resorting to Terror.[77] Once the proper distinctions are drawn between Jacobin practice and republican theory, the foundation can be laid for an integrative, inclusive account of citizenship.

NOTES

1. Walzer, "Citizenship," 211.

2. Crane Brinton, *A Decade of Revolution: 1789–1799* (New York: Harper and Row, 1934), 157.

3. Condorcet, "The Nature and Purpose of Public Instruction," in *Condorcet: Selected Writings*, 131.

4. Condorcet, "Essay on the Constitution and Functions of the Provisional Assemblies," in *Selected Writings*, 84.

5. Saint-Just, *Théorie Politique*, 258.

6. Furet, *Interpreting the French Revolution*, 30.

7. Daniel Roche, *France in the Enlightenment* (Cambridge, Mass.: Harvard University Press, 1998), 277.

8. Robespierre, July 26, 1794, *Oeuvres*, 10:544.

9. Robespierre, "Sur les principes de morale politique que doivent guider la convention nationale dans l'administration intérieure de la république," in *Textes choisis* (Paris: Éditions Sociales, 1958), 3:112.

10. Schama, *Citizens*, 149, 50.

11. Brinton, *The Jacobins: An Essay in the New History* (New York: Russell & Russell, 1961), 148 (hereafter cited as *The Jacobins*). The Jacobins became so preoccupied with the character of citizens that they lost all sense of equity and proportion. Saint-Just, speaking before the National Convention, argued that it was insufficient to punish only those who bore the republic ill will. "You should punish not only traitors but the indifferent as well; you should punish whoever is passive and does nothing for the Republic." Quoted in Hampson, "The Idea of the Nation in Revolutionary France," in *Reshaping France:Town, Country, and Region during the French Revolution*, ed. Alan Forrest and Peter Jones (Manchester, U.K.: Manchester University Press, 1991), 19. Moreover, punishment became more a matter of judgment than of fact, since individuals were suspect not for an act they had committed but for the kind of persons that they were. See Hampson, "The Idea of the Nation in Revolutionary France," 20. As Hampson writes, "The trial itself was a matter of conviction in more ways than one: what the jury was doing was deciding whether the accused looked like a member of the nation or not. In the latter case, it was logical to ordain

that the only penalty available to the court should be death, irrespective of the seriousness of the offence, since it involved a breach of the social contract."

12. Talmon, *The Origins of Totalitarian Democracy*, 135.

13. Patrice Gueniffey, "Robespierre," in *A Critical Dictionary of the French Revolution*, ed. François Furet and Mona Ozouf (Cambridge, Mass.: Harvard University Press), 299.

14. Brinton, *The Jacobins*, 152.

15. Robespierre, 8 May 1793, *Oeuvres*, 9:489.

16. Bloom, ed., *Émile*, 445.

17. Robespierre, 5 February 1794, *Oeuvres*, 10:112.

18. "Furthermore, since the art of generalizing ideas in this way is one of the most difficult and belated exercises of human understanding, will the average man ever be capable of deriving his rules of conduct from this manner of reasoning?" See *Geneva Manuscript*, 161. In *The Government of Poland*, Rousseau writes, "a sound constitution is one that holds sway over the hearts of citizens," and "a man who had no passions would surely be a very bad citizen." See *The Government of Poland*, ed. Wilmoore Kendall (Indianapolis: Hackett, 1985), 4. Saint-Just used this logic to refute Condorcet's rationalist conception of the general will, arguing that the general will is sensed more by the heart than by reason. See Jaume, *Discours Jacobin*, 318–23.

19. Rousseau, *The Government of Poland*, 94.

20. Bloom, ed., *Émile*, 325.

21. Bloom, ed., *Émile*, 471.

22. Rousseau, *The Social Contract*, 67.

23. Even a rationalist like Condorcet accepted the rhetoric of the formative project, though he was much more moderate than the radicals (and, it should be added, generally ignored in his moderation). Condorcet writes, "Society also has an obligation to provide public instruction as a means of perfecting the human race," in "The Nature and Purpose of Public Instruction," in *Condorcet: Selected Writings*, 111.

24. See Mona Ozouf's "La Révolution française et l'idée et l'image du régicide," in *L'homme régénéré* (Paris: Gallimard, 1989), 116–57.

25. Bertrand Barère, one of the leaders of the Committee of Public Safety, described the obstacles to French republicanism: "The Republic lasted for seven centuries on the banks of the Tiber; it has lasted for seven years on the banks of the Seine. It suited grave patriots like the Romans; it is not at all suited to fickle cosmopolitans like the French. Rome had political customs; Paris has effeminate ways. The Capitol was both the temple of Mars and of Jupiter; the Exchange is the temple of Fortune as well as the temple of Power. The Romans loved liberty in their very nature, they possessed its principles and habits; the French have habits and governmental traditions that are opposed to the liberty and energy of a republic." See Barère, *Memoirs of Bertrand Barère* (London: H. S. Nichols, 1896), 47. Robespierre recognized the same problem: "We have raised the temple of liberty with hands still withered by the irons of despotism." Quoted in Cobban, *Aspects of the French Revolution*, 172.

26. Robespierre, *Textes Choisis*, 3:168.

27. Saint-Just, *Oeuvres complètes* (Paris: G. Lebovici, 1984), 820.

28. Furet, *Interpreting the French Revolution*, 193.

29. Rousseau, *The Social Contract*, 69.

30. Rousseau, *The Social Contract*, 70.

31. Rousseau, *The Social Contract*, 68.

32. Rousseau, *The Social Contract*, 69.

33. Leo Strauss, "On the Intention of Rousseau," in *Hobbes and Rousseau*, eds. Maurice Cranston and Richard S. Peters (Garden City, N.Y.: Anchor, 1972), 284.

34. Rousseau, *Geneva Manuscript*, 171.

35. Rousseau, *Political Economy*, 215.

36. Augustin Cochin, *L'Esprit du Jacobinisme: Une Interprétation Sociologique de la Révolution Française* (Paris: Presses Universitaires de France, 1979), 96 (hereafter cited as *L'Esprit du Jacobinisme*).

37. Furet, *Interpreting the French Revolution*, 50.

38. Robespierre, *Textes choisis*, 3:119.

39. R. R. Palmer, *Twelve Who Ruled* (Princeton, N.J.: Princeton University Press, 1941), 163.

40. Ozouf, "Liberty," in *A Critical Dictionary of the French Revolution*, 724.

41. Ozouf, "Liberty," 724.

42. Georges Jacques Danton, "On National Education," 13 August 1793, in *Orators of the French Revolution*, 2:259.

43. Talmon, *The Origins of Totalitarian Democracy*, 47.

44. Robespierre, "Le procès du roi," in *Textes choisis*, 2:78.

45. Quoted in Norman Hampson, *The Life and Opinions of Maximilien Robespierre* (London: Gerald Duckworth, 1974), 146.

46. Saint-Just, *Oeuvres complètes*, 380.

47. Saint-Just, *Oeuvres complètes*, 399.

48. Saint-Just, *Oeuvres complètes*, 379.

49. Cochin, *L'esprit du Jacobinisme*, 182.

50. Bernard Manin, "Rousseau," in *A Critical Dictionary of the French Revolution*, 837.

51. Ozouf, "Marat," in *A Critical Dictionary of the French Revolution*, 249.

52. Schama, *Citizens*, 787.

53. See Singer, *Society, Theory, and the French Revolution*, 196.

54. Pasquale Pasquino, "Citoyenneté, égalité et liberté chez J.-J. Rousseau et E. Sieyès," *Cahiers Bernard Lazare*, no. 121–22 (1988), 54.

55. Jaume, "Le Jacobinisme de Jean-Jacques Rousseau: Influence ou mode de légitimation?" in *Jean-Jacques Rousseau and the Revolution*, ed. Jean Roy (Ottawa: North American Association for the Study of Jean-Jacques Rousseau, 1991), 69.

56. Saint-Just, *Théorie Politique*, 58.

57. Robespierre, 24 April 1793, in *Textes Choisis*, 2:140.

58. Talmon, *The Origins of Totalitarian Democracy*, 113.

59. Robespierre, "Le procès du roi," in *Textes choisis*, 2:81.

60. In his "Discourse on Political Economy," Rousseau writes, "if one means that a government is permitted to sacrifice one innocent person for the benefit of the multitude, I understand this maxim as one of the most abominable that tyranny has ever invented." See Rousseau, "Discourse of Political Economy, in *Oeuvres complètes*, 3:256.

61. Ozouf, "Equality," in *A Critical Dictionary of the French Revolution*, 681.

62. Cobban, *Rousseau and the Modern State*, 137.

63. Furet, *Interpreting the French Revolution*, 31.

64. Hippolyte Taine, *The Origins of Contemporary France* (Chicago: The University of Chicago Press, 1974), 75 (italics in original).

65. Rousseau, *The Government of Poland*, 66. He adds, "things must not necessarily be left as they are; but it is to say that you must lay hands on them only with extreme caution." *The Government of Poland*, 3.

66. Rousseau, *The Government of Poland*, 43.

67. Rousseau, *Oeuvres*, 7:164.

68. Robespierre, "Contre le philosophisme et pour la liberté des cultes," in *Textes choisis*, 3:85.

69. Saint-Just, *Oeuvres complètes*, 378.

70. Burke, *Reflections on the Revolution in France* (Indianapolis: Hackett Publishing Co., 1987), 31.

71. George Rudé, *Robespierre, Portrait of a Revolutionary Democrat* (London; Collins, 1975), 97.

72. Champion, *J. J. Rousseau et la Révolution Française*, 264.

73. Georges Couthon, as quoted in Anne Sa'adah, *The Shaping of Liberal Politics on Revolutionary France* (Princeton, N.J.: Princeton University Press, 1990), 189.

74. Robespierre, "Sur les principes du gouvernement révolutionnaire," in *Textes choisis*, 3:99. Bernard Manin reports that the Jacobins never invoked Rousseau to justify the Committee of Public Safety. See Furet and Ozouf, *Critical Dictionary of the French Revolution*, 836.

75. Charles de Secondat de Montesquieu, *The Spirit of the Laws* (New York: Cambridge University Press, 1989), 155.

76. Higonnet, *Goodness beyond Virtue: Jacobins during the French Revolution*, 329–30.

77. I do not mean to minimize the injustices perpetrated by the Third Republic in the name of cultivating unit. I invoke the Third Republic not to unqualifiedly extol it, but to add some texture to our catalog of the possible outcomes of attending politically to the character of citizens.

Chapter 6

Limiting Sovereign Power: Benjamin Constant and Nineteenth-Century French Liberalism

This chapter evaluates the liberal response to absolute, popular sovereignty in nineteenth-century France through an analysis of Benjamin Constant's appropriation and revision of Jean-Jacques Rousseau's general will. I argue that while the liberals of Restoration France adumbrated a compelling argument against absolute sovereignty, their alternative—the sovereignty of reason—is ultimately unsatisfying. Constant's revamped general will fails to escape the tensions captured so well by the general will in its Rousseauean incarnation—tensions between popular will and rational will, between voluntarism and virtue, between, in Rousseauean terms, the will of all and the general will. Contemporary liberal theory is also implicated in the chapter: first, by the critique of Constant and of the sovereignty of reason and, second, through a juxtaposition with the more historically minded liberalism of Restoration France.

I. NINETEENTH-CENTURY FRENCH LIBERALISM

The Reign of Terror and Napoleon's ensuing dictatorship provide the historical backdrop and intellectual focus for the liberalism prevalent in nineteenth-century France—often called "historical" liberalism. Though various disagreements divided liberal thinkers like François Guizot, Pierre Paul Royer-Collard, Germaine de Stael, Benjamin Constant, and Alexis de Tocqueville, they were all historians to various degrees and they all adopted a historical perspective toward normative issues. This French brand of liberalism has recently experienced a renaissance as a result of the resurgence of liberal thought in contemporary France. It has been toward the writings of Constant, Tocqueville, and the Doctrinaires that new French liberals have turned, rather than toward the more analytic brand of liberalism that has dominated Anglo-American thought over the last few decades.[1]

The depth of insight available in these nineteenth-century texts may come as something of a surprise, given French society's limited experience with liberal politics at the time of their appearance. Perhaps we should have more confidence in contemporary political theorists, who write with the benefit of years of historical experience with liberal regimes. On the other hand, it may be the case that theorists perched on the cusp of great political change are uniquely able to discern the advantages and disadvantages, the patterns and pathologies characteristic of the regimes that are on the way in and those on the way out. One advantage these historically minded thinkers have for this project is that they consciously developed their liberalism, first, as a response to the events of the Revolution and Empire and, second, in dialogue with Rousseau.[2] Consequently, they offer us the opportunity to assess our differences with Rousseau and our response to the Revolution from the perspective of a political theory that is quite similar to the one that dominates our era.

For the most part, nineteenth-century French liberals neither repudiated nor embraced the Revolution; rather, they were torn, much as we were in chapters 4 and 5, between sympathy for the Revolution's principles and disdain for the oppression it generated. They condemned the Revolution for having removed the obstacles that mitigated tyranny but did not go as far as siding with conservatives like Louis de Bonald and Joseph de Maistre, who insisted that only the political institutions and social hierarchies of the *ancien régime* could restore stability. Rather than take a side in favor of popular versus monarchical sovereignty, the liberals targeted sovereign power itself, specifically the French proclivity to understand that power as absolute. From this perspective, they came to view Jacobinism and Bonapartism as two heads of the same monster—absolute, unlimited sovereignty. For these thinkers, the most important legacy of the Revolution was the sense in which it was not revolutionary at all—its adherence to the doctrine of absolute sovereignty, established by Richelieu and Louis XIV. The Revolution's attack on the social hierarchies of the old regime removed the last checks on tyranny. Napoleon, like Robespierre before him, could say that he alone spoke in the name of the people and, therefore, that he alone spoke for France. Napoleon himself emphasized the continuity between Louis XIV, the Jacobins, and the Empire; from his perspective, they all defended the state against the power of the factions within France.[3] Constant perceived the same continuity but described it differently; for him, liberty had been destroyed by two different forces applying the same principle—arbitrariness. For Constant, as for the other liberals, *jacobinisme d'en bas* [Robespierre] and *jacobinisme d'en haut* [Napoleon] were different strands of the same political pathology.[4]

This pathology was never far from the thought of nineteenth-century French liberals, and the political theory they devised was more of a pragmatic response to a particular set of circumstances than an abstract, rationalist account of rights. Conservative in spirit, French liberalism sought a set of institutions that could safeguard liberty and security without sliding back into revolutionary tyranny or even further back into royal despotism. In contrast to the popular tendency to think of liberalism and democracy as natural allies, this period in French history offers an example of liberalism originating as a response to democracy, or at least a particular kind of democracy. The relationship between liberalism and democracy thus became a central question for these thinkers. This, in a sense, is the central question for this book as well, in that it attempts to negotiate the tension between rational will and popular will.

Liberalism meant many things in Restoration France, from a mild republicanism to a mild Bonapartism, and there were many disagreements among a group of thinkers we somewhat imprecisely call "liberals." However, they all repudiated the principle of absolute sovereignty and they all demanded a limitation on popular will. The sovereignty of the general will must be limited; of that they were convinced. Of course, the inevitable and difficult question is: limited by what? The characteristic answer of Restoration liberals was that reason must limit popular sovereignty. This answer failed to satisfy in 1848 just as it fails to satisfy today in its more palatable, though fundamentally similar, articulations. Robespierre and Napoleon showed why sovereignty ought not to be absolute, but liberals (past and present) are at pains to show how it can be limited legitimately.

II. CONSTANT'S CRITIQUE OF ROUSSEAU

The significance of Rousseau's political theory did not escape any of the nineteenth-century French liberals (though some of his subtlety did elude them).[5] Constant seemed unable to make up his mind about Rousseau, writing in the same sentence that Rousseau "cherished all theories of liberty" while offering "pretexts for every claim that tyranny makes."[6] At times, Constant argued that Rousseau's principles themselves naturally produce tyranny,[7] but he typically moderated that strong claim with the clarification that it was not Rousseau's principles themselves that were at fault as much as the language of justification he provided potential tyrants. In *The Spirit of Conquest and Usurpation,* he footnoted the claim that Rousseau furnished "weapons and pretexts to all kinds of tyranny," with the insistence that he did "not wish to join Rousseau's detractors."[8] It is probably safe to assume that a writer is about to do some detracting after a caveat like this. Still, although Constant did attack Rousseau on many points, he usually conveyed unease about doing so.

Constant begins his most important work of political writing with a nod to Rousseau: "Our present constitution formally recognizes the principle of the sovereignty of the people, that is the supremacy of the general will over any particular will. Indeed this principle cannot be contested."[9] Constant could not jettison the general will without alienating large portions of his audience; instead, he accepted it and reappropriated it to serve what he took to be the ultimate goal of politics—individual (as opposed to republican) liberty. From the first chapter of

Principles of Politics, Constant incorporates his conception of limited sovereignty into the ostensibly incontestable principle of the supremacy of the general will. He begins by making allusion to Robespierre and Napoleon, who, despite their assertions to the contrary, did not respect the sovereignty of the general will; rather they perpetrated "evils" and "crimes," committed on the "*pretext* of enforcing the general will (italics added)."[10] In so doing, according to Constant, they violated the sovereignty of the people, defined as the supremacy of the general will over any particular will. "The law must be either the expression of the will of all, or that of the will of some,"[11] and the Revolution and Empire were examples of the latter. As for the actual power of implementing the general will,

> it will be equally legitimate whoever sets his hands on it. . . . If you suppose that the power of a small number is sanctioned by the assent of all, then that power becomes the general will. This principle applies to all institutions. Theocracy, royalty, aristocracy, whenever they rule men's minds, are simply the general will. When, on the other hand, they fail to rule them, they are nothing but force. In short there are only two sorts of power in the world: one, illegitimate, is force; and the other, legitimate, is the general will.[12]

Already, in the first few paragraphs of *Principles of Politics*, we have Constant's fundamental theory of sovereignty along with the ambiguity that characterizes it. Whereas, for Rousseau, the general will designated (among other things) a procedure by which laws could be described as legitimate, Constant implies that there exists an independent criterion for determining legitimacy. In so doing, Constant exposes himself to the most common criticism of Rousseau's general will, namely that it is never the people's actual will but rather some rationalized version of popular will, inevitably dictated from on high.

However, Constant does not share this common criticism of Rousseau. He does not worry that the general will might be dictated by something outside public deliberation; rather, he is concerned that the general will might be dictated by potential tyrants rather than by a particular conception of reason. Constant tries to shift the debate over sovereignty away from the question of who holds sovereign power to the nature of that power itself. He pledges allegiance to the principle of popular sovereignty, to be sure, but he redefines it to mean something other than the rule of the people. Popular sovereignty, which for Rousseau was an indisputable prerequisite for political legitimacy, becomes one of several legitimate possibilities for Constant. Power is legitimate, whoever holds it, so long as they rule according to the "will of all." However, the question for Constant—and for contemporary liberals—is how the will of all can be known if not through the participation of all, which is to say, through popular sovereignty? Constant's answer will be that reason prescribes certain principles that no democratic majority can legitimately contradict.

Neither Rousseau, nor the *ancien régime,* nor the Revolution, nor the Empire ever considered limiting state power; the individual was thought to be free only through the sovereignty of the state. Constant's principal political goal was to call into question the legitimacy of unlimited sovereignty. He disputed Rousseau's belief that individuals could maximize their freedom by alienating all of their rights to the community as a whole; he denied the claim that when "each gives himself to all, he gives himself to no one."[13] Constant writes, "it happens that, in giving oneself to all, one does not give oneself to nobody, on the contrary one submits oneself to those who act in the name of all."[14] As we have seen, the revolutionaries did not alter the scope and extent of sovereignty; they simply transferred absolute sovereignty from the monarch to the people. This, Constant claimed, was the great error of French civilization—that it failed to acknowledge the existence of a sphere of human activity outside the jurisdiction of the state.

In a letter to his aunt, Anne-Paulina-Adrienne de Nassau, Constant became defensive,

> Why, I ask you, am I accused of having a weak character? This is an accusation to which all enlightened people are exposed, because they see both sides, or, better said, the thousand sides of things. Because it is impossible for them to make up their minds, they have the appearance of staggering from one side to the other.[15]

Here, Constant responds to the French prejudice against diversity in politics. Prior to the liberalism of the early nineteenth century, the French had viewed difference as a threat to unity, and absolute sovereignty as the most effective way to preserve it. Constant insisted on dividing human life into two spheres, which we might call the public and the private. The public is the domain over which the sovereign power had authority, whereas the private designates the realm of human activity that is "outside any social competence," as Constant puts it.[16] The state has jurisdiction over questions pertaining to the people as a whole (which remain undifferentiated for Constant), but it must abstain from involvement in matters of individual liberty, which may have a thousand sides and must be left up to the discretion of the individual.[17]

Rousseau, too, distinguished between that which is "of the essence of the social compact" and that which can be "set aside" from it.[18] Constant either ignored or missed this, but that is not of particular importance, because his real disagreement with Rousseau is over the "exact nature" and "precise extent" of the general will. Without a precise and exact definition of the general will, the triumph of the theory of the sovereignty of the general will "could become a calamity in its application."[19] Whereas Rousseau made only occasional allusions to the distinction between the public and the private, Constant made it the essence of the general will.

For Rousseau and the revolutionaries, the general will referred only to matters of common concern. For Constant, it expressed the shared human desire for political institutions that would respect equally matters of common concern and matters of individual discretion. His general will did not stand in opposition to particular will; rather it sought to safeguard a sphere of particularity, which it also identified as the sphere of freedom. Whereas Rousseau left it to the sovereign body to decide the scope of the general will, Constant insisted that there is a part of the human being that remains independent, regardless of how the sovereign body is constructed and regardless of how it arrives at its decisions. What part of the human being is this? Constant writes that "citizens have individual rights, independent from all social authority, and . . . these rights are personal liberty, religious liberty, liberty of opinion, a guarantee against arbitrary power and the enjoyment of property."[20] There must be a means of protecting individuals from government infringement in these matters. Constant accuses Rousseau of having underestimated the risks posed by a government wielding the power of absolute sovereignty. Governments cannot be trusted to implement the general will under these circumstances; some conception of limited sovereignty must itself become part of the general will if despotism is to be avoided.

III. WHAT IS FREEDOM?

It will have become clear by now that this liberal response to Rousseau's republican view of sovereignty can be traced to a disagreement about the nature of freedom. For liberals, freedom is primarily noninterference or the absence of external obstacles, whereas, for Rousseau, freedom is largely defined as self-rule or non-domination. As James I. MacAdam puts it, "Rousseau has in mind *freedom for* political power; Constant, *freedom from* political power."[21] Like any strict distinction, this one distorts (as we will soon see) as well as illuminates, but it does convey something important about the contrast between the way liberal and republican thinkers conceptualize the sovereignty of the general will.[22]

Constant famously undermines freedom as self-rule, not through a critique of the concept itself, but by situating it historically, such that it comes to seem anachronistic.

That liberty consisted in active participation in collective power rather than in the peaceful enjoyment of individual independence. And to ensure that participation, it was necessary for the citizens to sacrifice a large part of this enjoyment; but that sacrifice is absurd to ask, and impossible to exact, at the state the people have reached.[23]

By picturing this passage in *Émile* or *The Second Discourse*, we can come to an understanding of the difference between Constant and Rousseau. It would actually suit Rousseau quite well—as a lament, of course, which is not how Constant intends it. Constant uses it as an ostensibly value-free sociological claim, a response to the growing size, diversity, and differentiation of modern societies. By making a sociological, as opposed to a normative claim, Constant cleverly avoids criticizing the kind of freedom Rousseau had described so compellingly. Freedom as the active participation in public power becomes inappropriate to the times rather than inherently despotic. Constant is even able to acknowledge in

Rousseau "a love for the most pure liberty," which allows him to avoid alienating Rousseau's many admirers. Rousseau is somewhat absolved, guilty only of confusing two types of liberty. The Jacobins too escape the charge of despotism; they are criticized instead for the far less vicious sin of failing to acknowledge the exigencies of the time. "Things are possible in one age, but not in another; this is a truth that is often neglected."[24]

For us moderns, Constant writes, freedom includes "individual liberty, free press, absence of arbitrary power," and "respect for the rights of all."[25] Constant, of course, means arbitrary public power, whereas Rousseau worried more about the relationships of domination that develop within the private sphere. Constant clearly views the threats to freedom as primarily political: "For forty years I have defended the same principle: liberty in everything: in religion, in philosophy, in literature, in industry, in politics; and by liberty I mean the triumph of individuality, as much over the masses who claim the right to enslave the minority to the majority as over any authority that wishes to govern by despotism."[26] Rousseau would be quick to point out that Constant forgets the chief threat to freedom—self-interested individuals or factions who oppress segments of the citizenry through social rather than explicitly political means. Constant's response is that the French have overestimated the dangers of individualism and underestimated the risks associated with centralized power; that they have placed too much importance on collective liberty and not enough on individual liberty. Whereas for Rousseau, freedom is embodied in popular sovereignty understood as self-rule, for Constant, "the abstract recognition of the sovereignty of the people does not in the least increase the amount of liberty given to individuals."[27]

Constant presents us with two kinds of liberty—one noble but antiquated, the other pragmatic and suited to our time—and leads us to believe that he prefers the latter. However, things are not this simple; there is the matter of the "surprise ending" to his famous essay, "The Liberty of the Ancients Compared with that of the Moderns."[28] He writes, "far from renouncing either of the two sorts of freedom which I have described to you, it is necessary, as I have shown, to learn to combine the two together."[29] Constant's ambivalence shows how politics demands simultaneous concern for both the liberty of the ancients and that of the moderns or (to use Isaiah Berlin's terms) for positive and negative liberty. While political (positive) liberty was essential to Rousseauean freedom, Constant instrumentalizes it, deploying it as a means to safeguard civil (negative) liberty, rather than valorizing it as an end in itself. "The axiom of the sovereignty of the people has been considered as a principle of liberty," but "it is a principle of guarantee" because it is designed "to prevent one individual from seizing the authority, which only belongs to the entire association."[30] Republican freedom is not neglected by Constant and the other French liberals, but it is subordinated to the only political goal that is an end in itself—individual freedom. This subordination of republican freedom to individual freedom provides the theoretical framework for limiting sovereign power.

Chapter 6

IV. THE LIBERAL ACCOUNT OF LIMITED SOVEREIGNTY

Constant believed that sovereign power always ends up in the hands of the few, regardless of where it is believed to originate and even to reside. These power holders possess no special wisdom, nothing that necessarily distinguishes their political judgment from that of ordinary citizens; their opinions are as fallible as anyone else's. Rousseau's *Social Contract,* according to Constant, threatens liberty because, "the government manages all the forces of society and determines all of the particular tendencies, such that they are combined with the tendency of the whole."[31] Constant's argument about the dangers of concentrating all the forces of society is a compelling response to Rousseau, but his claim that the government controls everything is a misreading that should be clarified. In fact, Rousseau might defend his scheme of political institutions as the most effective way of protecting society against the sovereignty of the few. He was acutely sensitive to the risks of usurpation by representatives or government officials, which is why he insisted that the power of deputies be severely restricted.[32] Constant frequently ignores the distinction between government and sovereign, a distinction that Rousseau always insisted upon. Where Constant truly disagrees with Rousseau is not over the tendency of governments to become despotic, but over the most effective strategy for ensuring that they do not. Whereas for Rousseau, absolute, popular sovereignty was the only way to ensure that deputies of the people would not subordinate the general will to their own particular wills, Constant believed that absolute sovereignty of any kind would inevitably be invoked as a justification for despotism. While Rousseau believed the question of who possessed power mattered most, for Constant, what mattered was the power itself and not who possessed it.

Constant goes so far as to claim that the "abstract recognition of the sovereignty of the people does not *in the least* increase the amount of liberty given to individuals [italics added]."[33] Rousseau disagrees on two counts. First, he believed that self-rule itself was a crucial element of human liberty and, second, he believed that popular sovereignty was the only way to secure the kind of individual liberty Constant favored. However, for Constant and other nineteenth-century liberals looking back on the events of the Revolution and Empire, the transfer of sovereignty to the people, in and of itself, simply paved the way for a new kind of despotism (popular)—one that we should understand as more similar than different from the old despotism (monarchical). Sovereignty, according to Constant, exists only in a limited manner, regardless of whether or not it represents the people as a whole.

> As soon as the general will becomes all powerful, the representatives of this general will will become all the more formidable in that they call themselves only docile instruments of this pretended will. . . . What no tyrant would dare do in his own name, they legitimize through the limitless social authority.[34]

At this point in his argument, Constant stops using the "general will" to designate the collective preference for the principles of limited government and individual rights. Here he uses it as a contrast to individual will and contradicts the claim he made at the outset of *Principles of Politics*—that the general will is the source of legitimacy. He now claims that "the general will is by no means due more respect than the individual will, whenever it strays from its own sphere."[35] Constant has equated the general will with popular will, or what Rousseau might call the will of all. This invocation of the general will stands in contrast to his earlier use of it to designate a particular set of political principles—a contrast that reminds one of the distinction Rousseau tries to make between the actual will of the people (which might be the will of all) and the true will of the people (which is always the general will).[36]

By using the general will to denote the popular will—by which he means whatever the people will at a given time—Constant means to suggest that oppression depends on the degree of force and not on who is exercising it. People criticize regimes—monarchy, aristocracy, democracy—without comprehending that the real culprit is the degree of power and not its holders.[37] The arbitrary will of the people can be better, as bad, or worse than the arbitrary will of a monarch; for Constant it is arbitrariness itself that must be targeted.

What prevents arbitrary power, according to Constant?—"the observance of procedures."[38] Procedures act as limits on sovereign power; indeed, they can be understood as the practical application of the idea of limited sovereignty. The procedures Constant had in mind were the election of representatives and the monarchical veto. Constant viewed these institutional constraints on popular sovereignty as necessary to the functioning of modern societies. As we have seen, in responding to Rousseau, Constant's broad claim was that Rousseau overlooked the dangers of unlimited sovereignty. It should be noted that he was equally vociferous about a more specific claim, namely that, by declaring that sovereignty could not be represented, Rousseau ensured that it could not be exercised. These arguments are connected in a way that becomes particularly clear if we understand them within the context of Constant's distinction between the liberty of the ancients and the liberty of the moderns. Neither direct nor absolute sovereignty posed a threat to the freedom of the ancients, according to Constant, because the ancient polis had a relatively small, homogeneous citizen body. Under these conditions, liberty could be a direct, collective exercise of sovereign power.[39] In large, differentiated, modern societies, two main changes must occur: participation in sovereign power must become indirect through representation, and liberty must become a matter of individual independence as opposed to collective participation in a Rousseauean general will.

For Constant, procedures like representation were the solution to the problem nineteenth-century French liberals set for themselves—how to remain loyal to the ideas of the Revolution without degenerating into despotism. In this way, the power of both the people and the monarch could be tamed, moderated, and balanced. By embracing these procedures, liberals positioned themselves between the Jacobins and the *ancien régime* or, less anachronistically, between the republicans and the *ultraroyalistes*. Jacobins and monarchists both understood sovereignty as a moral question, which meant that neither was willing to compromise. The liberals, on the other hand, took a pragmatic approach to the question of the locus of sovereignty, an approach they could afford to take because, for them, this issue was of no moral relevance. The moral issue for liberals is not who holds power, but toward what ends that power is deployed. Republicans, on the other hand, attach moral relevance to the question of who is sovereign, which raises the question as to whether republican freedom is compatible with representation. In *The Social Contract,* Rousseau said it was not, however, he later reconciled himself to the necessity of representation in large, diverse societies.[40] We may, nevertheless, wish to ask if giving up on this aspect of the general will requires one to abandon the republican conception of freedom that goes along with it. In other words, if we accept that the size and diversity of modern societies necessitate representation, we might also need to accept that the collective identity and sentiment needed to form a Rousseauean general will are lacking as well. I deal with the question of the compatibility of diversity and generality in chapters 7 and 8. For now, I want to focus specifically on the idea of absolute sovereignty itself and on the nineteenth-century, liberal alternative to it—the sovereignty of reason.

V. SHORTCOMINGS OF THE
LIBERAL CRITIQUE OF SOVEREIGNTY

A thinker like Constant could accept the principles of either popular or monarchical sovereignty and, in actuality, he accepted both, forging a "practical compromise," to use Stephen Holmes's phrase.[41] He defended the royal veto as a check on the power of the representatives and accepted popular sovereignty as a means of taming the power of the monarch. Holmes argues that most readers overestimate Constant's opposition to democracy, noting that Constant omitted *Conquête et usurpation* when he collected his pamphlets on representative government in 1818, due to, in Holmes's words, "the disconcertingly Legitimist flavor of the work."[42] Moreover, though Constant opposed all proponents of absolute sovereignty, left and right, the *ultras* eventually displaced the Jacobins as his main target. Finally, there is the fact that, as Holmes puts it, "Constant unambiguously affirmed the sovereignty of the people."[43] Well, we may want to rethink just how unambiguous Constant's affirmation of popular sovereignty was. As I've tried to suggest up to this point, one must be wary of placing too much significance on Constant's formal acceptance of the principle of popular sovereignty; in actuality, Constant reinterprets the concept of absolute sovereignty, such that it comes to mean the sovereignty of reason and can be perfectly compatible with severe restrictions on democratic participation. Holmes wants to distinguish between Constant and the Doctrinaires, who never embraced popular sovereignty, insisting always on the sovereignty of reason. These thinkers are closer than Holmes suggests. While it is true that Constant formally accepted popular sovereignty and never opposed it in and of itself, he always subordinated it to something more or less comparable to what the Doctrinaires call the "sovereignty of reason."

Until now, we have focused on the way in which, juxtaposed to the liberals, the *ultras* and the revolutionaries appear as two sides of the same coin. In this section, we will see how, juxtaposed to Rousseau, it is the liberals and the *ultras* who share a philosophical principle. This principle—a source of legitimacy beyond politics itself—provides liberalism with its great force but also accounts for many of its shortcomings, both in nineteenth-century France and (as I suggest in the conclusion to this chapter) in our own liberal democracy.

For both Louis de Bonald (a prominent *ultra*) and Constant (a prototypical liberal), something other than the deliberation of the people themselves defines the general will. Consider the following passages:

> Thus, the general will of the society or the social body, of the social man, the nature of social beings or of the society, the social will, even the will of God are synonymous expressions in this work. . . . The general will of the society became exterior or manifested itself by fixed and fundamental laws. We shall see, in what follows in this work, how the general will produces the laws, or, what is the same thing, is produced by the laws.[44]

> Some define the laws as the expression of the general will. This is a false definition. The laws are the declaration of the relations of men among themselves. . . . They are not the cause of these relations, which, on the contrary, are anterior to them. They declare that these relations exist. They are the declaration of a fact. They do not create, determine or institute anything, except forms that guarantee that which exists before their institution. It follows that no man, no fraction of society, and not even the society as a whole can appropriately and absolutely attribute the right to make laws to itself. Because the laws are nothing other than the expression of relations that exist between men, and because these relations are determined by the nature of men, making a law is only the new declaration of that which existed previously. The legislator is to the social order what the physicist is to nature. Newton himself could only observe and not declare the laws he recognized, or believed he recognized.[45]

Rousseau has been attacked over and over again for distinguishing between the true, as opposed to the overtly expressed, will of the people. Here, we see how neither the liberal Constant nor the monarchist Bonald are able to wriggle free of this distinction. For Rousseau, the paradox was how to reconcile what the people actually will with what they ought to will. On the liberal account, the people do not hold responsibility for exercising sovereignty, at least not with respect to the basic principles of political legitimacy. Therefore, there will be no discrepancy between what the people actually will and what they ought to will. It is not nec-

essary that the people actually will anything, with respect to these basic principles.[46] Ideal and actual will can be reconciled through basic liberal values and institutions, which must embody the will of all human beings since they are
grounded in eternal precepts of reason. Though the eternal source of authority is
different for the *ultras* (God) than it is for the liberals (reason), both schools arrive at the force of their argument through an appeal to a pre-political authority.

For the *ultras*, this pre-political authority issues in a very specifically defined
sovereign authority—the hereditary or divine monarch. For liberals, the question
of the locus of sovereignty remains open. Not explicitly antidemocratic, Restoration liberals left open the possibility that sovereignty could be popularly exercised, though they were, by and large, skeptical about the rectitude of the will of
the people. But if the liberal view of sovereignty does not designate any specific
individual or group of individuals as sovereign, how are political questions to be
adjudicated? In Royer-Collard's words,

> there are those who attribute sovereignty as a right belonging exclusively to individ-
> uals, whether one, many, or all those composing a society; and these are, in principle
> the founders of despotism. . . . The second class of governments is founded on the
> truth that sovereignty belongs as a right to no individual whatever, since the perfect
> and continued apprehension, the fixed and inviolable application of justice and rea-
> son do not belong to our imperfect nature.[47]

As a reaction to Robespierre and Napoleon Bonaparte, Royer-Collard's recon-
figuration of the discourse on sovereignty has a certain appeal. Of course, the
use of "justice" and "reason" is somewhat unsatisfying—it is still not clear how
these abstractions will be concretized. Restoration liberals embraced representation, as noted earlier, but, as Constant points out, "the representatives of a nation do not have the right to do what the nation itself does not have the right to
do."[48] The liberal view of the exercise of sovereignty can be summarized co-
herently as the representation of interests and rights as opposed to the representation of will. Guizot goes so far as to label ignorant those who view popular election and democratic deliberation as the keys to good government. What
is necessary, Guizot writes, "is to commit the interests of activity and progress
to the care of their natural and willing protectors."[49] For Guizot, the natural protector of the public interest was the bourgeois middle class, for which he was
the leading spokesman.[50]

But was the sovereignty of reason nothing more than bourgeois ideology? Constant certainly did not think so. He believed there were certain basic principles
that are universal and accessible by all—if only they have reason, as Kant would
say. "If everyone understood each other well, everyone would agree about liberty;
because everyone wants it thoroughly. There is no one who would not like tran-
quility, security, the use of his possessions, personal safety; in sum, all the advantages that liberty gives."[51] Constant may be right in saying that we all want
safety, security, and the enjoyment of our possessions, but he is surely presump-
tuous in assuming that we share the same understanding of these goods and of the

best way to procure them. Though Constant often accuses Rousseau of over-whelming particular will with the general will, here, it is he who ignores the am-biguity in the way people interpret the dictates of reason.

The profundity of nineteenth-century French political philosophy pales in comparison to French philosophy in the eighteenth century, but, as Roger Soltau has noted, the nineteenth century did have one advantage over the eighteenth—it was free to test its principles in practice.[52] Should it count against liberal theory that nineteenth-century liberal practice produced an oligarchy that ruled in the in-terest of bankers and merchants? Perhaps not, but as was the case with the Rev-olution and Rousseau, the July Monarchy serves to illustrate some of the inher-ent tendencies of liberal theory. In the case of Rousseau and the Revolution, we were able to draw a reasonably clear line between Rousseau's political theory and the theory and events of the Revolution. With regard to liberal political theory and the political practice of the July Monarchy, I do not believe as clear a distinction can be made. Fortunately, attributing the events of the July Monarchy to liberal theory will not be nearly as catastrophic to liberalism as a link between the Ter-ror and Rousseauean republicanism would be to Rousseau.

When a set of truths is defined as transcendent or beyond the scope of human deliberation, it is only a matter of time before certain views, and possibly certain people, are excluded from the political process. In the case of nineteenth-century French liberalism, the idea of the sovereignty of reason, truth, and justice produced the actual sovereignty of the middle class, what Soltau calls a "financial aristoc-racy."[53] Guizot, who essentially directed the July Monarchy, accused of despotism those "who attribute sovereignty as a right belonging exclusively to individuals, whether one, many, or all those composing a society."[54] His fellow Doctrinaire, Charles de Rémusat, added that political power should be held by those "most ca-pable of making the collective law of the society prevail—knowledge, justice, rea-son, truth."[55] Most contemporary liberals would have no problem dismissing the Doctrinaires' antidemocratic excesses as non-intrinsic to liberalism at the very least, and perhaps even in violation of a genuine acceptance of liberal equality. Sure enough, liberalism can be compatible with far more popular participation than that which characterized the July Monarchy. Nonetheless, all liberals accept the nineteenth-century French liberals' basic claim—namely, that sovereign power, to be legitimate, must be limited by some conception of justice or reason. Reason, truth, and justice do not reside anywhere completely, Guizot writes, but there is the implication in his political thought that the principles articulated in his own writings come pretty close.[56] Any doctrine that places certain principles be-yond the scope of public deliberation must accept this authoritarian consequence. This does not undermine the many advantages of liberalism; however it does com-pel us to reevaluate the ground from which we dismiss republican citizenship as authoritarian, as I do in the conclusion to this chapter.

By 1848, the policies of Guizot and French king Louis-Philippe had been dis-credited as self-serving. André Jardin, in his history of French liberalism, notes that nineteenth-century republicans never quite accepted the liberal idea that there

are rights and duties anterior to positive laws.[57] This posture of insecurity or un-
easiness (though somewhat vague) may be preferable to the dogmatic (though
more coherent) insistence on a set of principles that transcend all political circumstances. As Constant's critique of Robespierre and Napoleon shows, some
conception of limited sovereignty is an indispensable safeguard against tyranny.
But, as the actions of the liberal republic of 1830–1848 demonstrate, abstract
principles can be deployed to disenfranchise certain groups and to serve the exclusive interests of others. Royer-Collard writes that the legitimate imposition of
will occurs when "such will manifests itself in conformity to law; when it has for
its object the protection of the legitimate interests which have their origin in
law."[58] What are these legitimate interests and who will discern them? According
to Rousseau, the people as a whole decide (at least theoretically). Restoration liberals thought that their idea of the sovereignty of reason resolved the question of
the place of power. At best, though, it merely displaces it; at worst, it smuggles
in an answer, as in the case of the oligarchy that controlled the July Monarchy.
Jean-Claude Lamberti writes,

> The idea, cherished by liberals, of the rule of law is in the final analysis rather am-
> biguous: the question is, what law will rule? If it is natural law, the reflection of tran-
> scendental justice or reason, its rule is assured in a vague and uncertain way, only by
> a people's adherence to a set of religious and moral beliefs constituting its idea of
> what is right.[59]

Liberalism cannot escape the paradox Rousseau's general will illustrates so
clearly. Just as Rousseau problematically advocated both autonomy and socialization, most liberals advocate both consent and limitations on popular will.
Nineteenth-century French liberalism illustrates how this dual commitment is
also problematic. For these liberals, the general will, rather than expressing the
actual will of each citizen, expresses their broad interest in individual freedom
and limited government. For individuals to recognize this version of the general
will and to consent to it, they must be properly socialized. This point does not undermine the doctrine of liberalism but rather forces it to confront an inherent tension. Liberals cannot escape the paradox, characteristic of all political theory that
strives to respect the interests of all citizens. Just as was the case with Rousseau,
nineteenth-century French liberalism reveals how government in the interest *of*
the people may require government somewhat removed *from* the people. Once
this problem is recognized, all of the questions return with regard to who or what
governs the substance of individual and collective interests.

VI. ADVANTAGES OF HISTORICAL LIBERALISM

Constant did not lack entirely Rousseau's sense of paradox. Consequently, his political thought offers some resources for dealing with the tensions that character-

ize egalitarian politics. For example, though Constant emphasized private rights above all else, he recognized that "private rights could be endangered by excessive privatization."[60] Constant understood that isolated, depoliticized citizens would be vulnerable to a usurpation of their rights. The conclusion to "The Liberty of the Ancients Compared with that of the Moderns" communicates Constant's preference for an uneasy synthesis of ancient and modern liberty, as opposed to a renunciation of the former in favor of the latter. Citizens must be formed such that they pursue "something more than mere self-interest: they need real beliefs; they need morality. Self-interest tends to isolate [citizens]."[61] Constant's liberalism is thus not dogmatic about remaining purely formal—about creating a sphere of activity that is totally insulated from political considerations. For example, according to Constant, "it is important that people occupy themselves politically with their interests"; otherwise, Constant argued, liberty is endangered.[62] All of the liberal thinkers in Restoration France were concerned about the cultural prerequisites to the flourishing of freedom, which is to say they were concerned about the viability of a liberal regime. They worried that the dissolution of traditional social bonds would produce a *societé en poussière,* in which depoliticized citizens would be vulnerable to the forces of despotism.

This type of judgment, with respect to the activity and characteristics of citizens, sits somewhat uneasily alongside the liberal respect for a sphere of individual autonomy. Yet, Constant's acceptance of this tension is laudable and offers an interesting contrast to the now common valorization of liberalism's formality. Larry Siedentop distinguishes between "English liberal thought," which he describes as decontextualized, analytical, and ahistorical, and "French liberal thought," which founded a sociology to complement its political science.[63] Rather than postulate a pre-social, isolated individual as the starting point of their theorizing, the French situated citizens in their sociohistorical context. French liberal thought, according to Siedentop,

> rejected a wholly normative approach to political theory, developing models which made possible the analysis of social and economic change, and, a fortiori, the limits of political choice. . . . French liberal thought has since the early nineteenth century accepted that questions of political theory cannot be divorced from questions about social structure. The result has been a more historical, less a priori mode of argument . . . with less attention paid to fine logical points and definitions, it is true, but with more concern to show how concepts are joined together in points of view or ideologies, and how these in turn spring out of particular social conditions and help to transform them.[64]

Siedentop suggests that the current debates about the social and cultural prerequisites of liberalism would be vastly different had the history of ideas favored French (as opposed to English) liberalism. Nineteenth-century French liberals would not be especially vulnerable, for example, to Michael Sandel's critique of the "unencumbered self," which he shows to be a fundamental, if implicit, sociological as-

sumption of Anglo-American liberalism.[65] Though we have some exceptions
(John Stuart Mill's "Coleridge" and T. H. Green's "Lecture on Liberal Legislation
and Freedom of Contract, for example") much of Anglo-American liberalism of
the past two centuries has rested on what Siedentop calls a "hidden sociological
premise."[66] Through the assumption of the isolated, unencumbered individual, this
brand of liberalism abstracts away from the tension between autonomy and paternalism, a tension that Rousseau reveals to be at the center of all egalitarian politics. When human beings are understood in their sociological context, it becomes
impossible to understand liberalism as purely formal, and unconvincing to view
liberty as purely political and not moral. A concern for the capacities, character,
and virtues required for the flourishing of freedom cannot be reasonably abandoned if political theory is undertaken within a sociological framework.

Correspondingly, we find in nineteenth-century French liberalism tremendous
attention paid to customs, religion, and patriotism, which are understood as gen-
erators of the solidaristic bonds that resist despotism. While French liberals
stopped short of turning Frenchness into a religion, as may have suited Sparta or
Rome, they did embrace the idea of something along the lines of Rousseau's civil
religion. For Constant and the Doctrinaires, the solidarity that religion provides
acts as an indispensable check on despotism. Constant writes, in almost
Rousseauean language, "Multiply, multiply the bonds which unite men. Make the
fatherland a part of everything, reflected in your local institutions as in so many
faithful mirrors."[67] Constant's liberalism differs from today's analytic liberalism
in that it is less preoccupied with the fine details of legislation—that is, whether
or not a specific policy conforms precisely to liberal values. Constant goes so far
as to write, "The inherent merit of the laws is, let us dare assert, far less important than the spirit with which a nation subjects itself to its laws and obeys
them."[68] This probably overstates Constant's views regarding the importance of
civic virtue and public spirit; he would certainly disapprove of public enthusiasm
for illiberal legislation, for example. Nonetheless, Constant's words convey the
extent to which nineteenth-century French liberals worried about the viability of
a regime, as well as its legitimacy.[69]

CONCLUSION

Nineteenth-century French liberals attended to questions of viability, but their
insistence on limiting sovereign power raises the question as to whether the procedural constraints they favor allow them the discretion to condition popular will
in the ways they view as necessary. This is the mirror image of the problem
Rousseau had—namely how the virtues and public spirit he favors can be cultivated, consistent with a respect for individual rights and autonomy. Liberals are
generally willing to concede that the flourishing of liberal principles requires a
certain set of virtues and some level of citizen solidarity. However, they are at

pains to describe how these qualities of character can be cultivated, consistent with the liberal commitment to individual autonomy.

Rousseau effectively described the multifarious ways human beings oppress each other. However, he underestimated the threat to liberty posed by public power, which he viewed almost exclusively as a path to emancipation. The Revolution and the Empire compelled political thinkers to consider the ways in which sovereign power could be oppressive as well as emancipatory and the French liberals' fundamental teaching on sovereign power serves as a useful corrective to Rousseau's faith in absolute sovereignty.

> When sovereignty is not limited, there is no way to place individuals under the shelter of governments. It is in vain that you pretend to submit governments to the general will. It is always the governments that dictate this will, and all precautions become illusory.[70]

Even if sovereignty is defined as the expression of a Rousseauean general will with its strict insistence on the participation of all citizens, there is always the danger that governments will abuse the power they are delegated. Without limitations on the exercise of power, liberty, however defined, is put at risk; the only conceivable solution to this problem is the liberal notion that any unchecked power is illegitimate.

Still, even if we accept this as the only reasonable solution to excesses of sovereign power, we still face the problem of determining, postulating, and/or discovering the authority by which sovereign power will be limited. Constant writes, "not even the will of an entire people can make just what is unjust. The representatives of a nation do not have the right to do what the nation itself has not the right to do. . . . the consent of a people cannot make legitimate what is illegitimate."[71] This position, while coherent, is somehow unsatisfying.[72] Perhaps Rousseau's less coherent paradoxes of sovereign power suit a post-metaphysical era, skeptical toward abstract appeals to the dictates of reason. If the liberal position is coherent but unsatisfying, Rousseau's might be described ironically as incoherent yet satisfying. The notion of a transcendent authority standing above the autonomy of the will has always been problematic. Now, when even reason itself is viewed as plural, this kind of universal abstraction becomes even less credible.

For liberals, some transcendental authority recognizes rights, whereas for Rousseau it is the democratic sovereign. As Guizot points out, "the paramount interests of social peace and political liberty are placed in danger by the democratic public."[73] Guizot's fear is not altogether unfounded; however, the liberal strategy for securing rights has problems of its own. Liberal constraints on sovereignty depend on dubious abstractions that are, at best, vague formalisms and, at worst, ideological justifications for oligarchy. When Constant writes that "the jurisdiction of . . . sovereignty stops at the point where the independence of individual life starts," he repeats a platitude that could describe Rousseauean republicanism just as accurately as it describes nineteenth-century French liberalism. The question, of course, is where that line ought to be drawn. Rousseau makes this ambiguity the center of his political thought, which may be how he manages to be incoherent yet satisfying, or at least more satisfying than a strictly doctrinal liberalism.[74]

During of the French Restoration, the limits on popular will that followed from the sovereignty of reason seemed a small price to pay, or even no price to pay, for security against the resurgence of despotic power. After 1848, French liberalism withdrew to the margins of French political life until after 1945 when it enjoyed something of a resurgence. It should come as no shock that the liberal notion of limited sovereignty found an audience in the wake of unconscionable abuses of public power. In the aftermath of German fascism and Stalin's purges, Constant's warnings about sovereign power would be as attractive as they were in 1815. "It is easy for an authority to oppress the people like a subject, to force them to manifest as sovereign the will that it prescribes for them. No political organization can evade this danger."[75] Nineteenth-century French liberalism was historical—a response to a particular set of political circumstances. These liberals confronted the very real possibility that small imbalances in the power of the Charter of 1814 liberal institutions could seriously threaten basic liberties. Similarly, postwar liberalism has oriented itself around the perils of twentieth-century totalitarianism.

On the liberal account, Rousseau misidentified the chief threat to freedom in political life. Perhaps, in an era of stable liberal democracy, it would be useful to adopt French liberalism's sociological method and ask ourselves where exactly the chief threat to freedom currently lies. Undoubtedly, we will find use for political institutions that check sovereign power. After all, it was a sociological insight about large, diverse societies that formed the basis for Constant's arguments on behalf of representation and limited sovereignty. On the other hand, upon evaluating the chief threats to freedom in our own societies, we might find reasons to democratize sovereign power—reasons, perhaps, to deploy it against sources of oppression in civil society.

If one believes that citizens are threatened primarily by expansive state power, liberalism's emphasis on limited sovereignty is appealing. If, on the other hand, one believes as Rousseau did that the great threats to individual freedom and social integration come from civil society, Rousseauean republicanism may have more of an appeal. If social, economic, and cultural trends are the most relevant causes of inequality, subordination, and marginalization, a discussion of liberal political principles may not be productive. Instead, public intervention on behalf of a substantive conception of republican citizenship may be warranted. Where the liberal state typically abjures proactive government action aimed at incorporating citizens into the political process, Rousseauean republicanism advocates the equal, active participation of all citizens. Where the liberal state, in the name of individual autonomy, is likely to take a *laissez-faire* approach to the problems of apathy, anomie, corruption, alienation, and disengagement, Rousseauean republicanism will proactively attack these pathologies, out of the conviction that they pose grave threats to personal freedom.

The regimes of Robespierre and Napoleon should be enough to convince anyone that liberty requires institutions that limit sovereign power, similar to the "procedures" Constant describes. However, we ought to be wary of overzealous attempts to limit popular will in the name of abstractions like "reason" or "justice." Proponents of these positions distance themselves from Rousseau's distinction between ideal will and actual will (what Rousseau might call the general will and the will of all). However, they cannot escape the tension between these concepts—a tension that Rousseau reveals to be intrinsic to egalitarian politics. Moreover, limits on popular sovereignty privilege civil or individual liberty at the expense of political or republican liberty.

Ideally, republicans and liberals alike will give up trying to reconcile the tension between rational will and popular will, between the sovereignty of reason and popular sovereignty, between (in Rousseauean terms) the general will and the will of all. Both camps might take a lesson from nineteenth-century French liberals and consider the social and cultural context for which they theorize. In some circumstances, procedural constraints on sovereign power will be justified by the dangers of state despotism, and the civil liberties secured by these constraints will be greater than the political liberty that is surrendered. In other circumstances, expanding sovereign power might be the most effective way to maximize personal freedom, despite the threats broad sovereign power can pose to individual liberty. Most importantly, both liberals and republicans must recognize the inexorable tensions of egalitarian politics. Neither exaltations of democracy, nor appeals to the sovereignty of reason resolve the tension between rational and popular will. Egalitarian politics requires a pragmatic synthesis of civil and political liberty; it demands a respect for autonomy and the cultivation of citizenship—which is to repeat what I have argued throughout the book: Any theory committed to egalitarian politics must both articulate a set of formal principles and address the question of their viability.

NOTES

1. Several works by new French liberals have recently appeared in translation through the New French Thought series, edited by Mark Lilla and Thomas Pavel, and published by Princeton University Press.

2. Roger Soltau, author of a survey of nineteenth-century French political thought, writes, "no thinker has made any really original contribution to nineteenth-century theory who did not first shake off the spell of Jean-Jacques." See Soltau, introduction to *French Political Thought in the Nineteenth Century* (New York: Russell & Russell, 1959), xxxi (hereafter cited as *French Political Thought*).

3. François Bourricaud, "The Rights of the Individual and the General Will in Revolutionary Thought," in *Liberty/Liberté: The American and French Experiences*, ed. Joseph Klaits and Michael H. Haltzel (Washington, D.C.: Woodrow Wilson Center Press, 1991), 22 (hereafter cited as *Liberty/Liberté*).

4. The terms come from George Armstrong Kelly, "The Jacobin and Liberal Contributions to the Founding of the Second and Third French Republics (with an Epilogue on America)," in *Liberty/Liberté*, 133.

5. Soltau writes, "If the Revolution dominates the nineteenth century as an event, so does Rousseau as a thinker, so that virtually every other thinker has to be classed as favourable or hostile to him." See Soltau, introduction to *French Political Thought in the Nineteenth Century*, xxx.

6. Benjamin Constant, "Principles of Politics Applicable to All Representative Governments," in *Benjamin Constant: Political Writings*, ed. Biancamaria Fontana (New York: Cambridge University Press, 1988), 275 (hereafter cited as "Principles of Politics").

7. Constant, in *Cours de Politique Constitutionnelle*, ed. Édouard Laboulaye (Paris: Librairie de Guillaumin, 1872), 1:280.

8. Constant, "The Spirit of Conquest and Usurpation and their Relation to European Civilization," in *Benjamin Constant: Political Writings*, 106.

9. Constant, "Principles of Politics," 175.

10. Constant, "Principles of Politics," 175.

11. Constant, "Principles of Politics." Constant ignores Rousseau's distinction between the general will and the will of all. More importantly, as well shall see, he begs the question as to who or what will determine the general will.

12. Constant, "Principles of Politics," 175.

13. Rousseau, *The Social Contract*, 53.

14. Constant, "Principles of Politics," 178.

15. The letter is quoted by Fontana in *Benjamin Constant: Political Writings*, x.

16. Constant, "Principles of Politics," 177.

17. Rousseau says something similar about matters of individual liberty: "But in addition to the public person, we have to consider the private persons who compose it and whose life and freedom are naturally independent of it. It is a matter, then, of making a clear distinction between the respective rights of the citizens and the sovereign, and between the duties that the former have to fulfill as subjects and the natural rights to which they are entitled as men." Rousseau, *The Social Contract*, 62. As we will see later, this formula is vague and, in and of itself, does not accomplish what Constant assumes it accomplishes. The interesting question becomes how we define what pertains to the people as a whole and what is left to individual discretion. In other words, the issue is where to draw the line between the public and the private.

18. Rousseau, *The Social Contract*, 53.

19. Constant, "Principles of Politics," 175.

20. Constant, "Principles of Politics," 261.

21. James I. MacAdam, "Rousseau and the Friends of Despotism," *Ethics* 71, no. 1 (October 1963): 41.

22. It should be noted that, in this respect, Tocqueville constitutes something of an exception. His brand of liberalism shares as much with Rousseau as it does with Constant. Tocqueville appropriated the doctrine of the sovereignty of reason but also insisted that self-government is an intrinsic component of freedom. Wilhelm Hennis allies Rousseau and Tocqueville in a way that contrasts well with the way Constant and the Doctrinaires understood freedom: To the extent that Rousseau and Tocqueville are liberals, "they are liberals of a very special kind. . . . Certainly the individual needs freedom and guarantees of this freedom, too. But this freedom is active, oriented to the social and political order, and its services are constantly laid claim to by the social and political order—the freedom of the *citoyen,* not of the bourgeois [italics in original]." See Hennis, "In Search of the 'New Science of Politics,' " in *Interpreting Tocqueville's* Democracy in America, ed. Ken Masugi (Lanham, Md.: Rowman & Littlefield, 1991), 44.

23. Constant, "Conquest and Usurpation," in *Benjamin Constant: Political Writings*, 102.

24. Constant, "Conquest and Usurpation," 48.

25. Constant, "Principles of Politics," 172.

26. Quoted by Édouard Laboulaye in his introduction to *Cours de Politique Constitutionelle*, viii.

27. Constant, "Principles of Politics," 175.

28. Stephen Holmes, *Benjamin Constant and the Making of Modern Liberalism* (New Haven, Conn.: Yale University Press, 1984), 154.

29. Constant, *Political Writings*, 327.

30. Quoted in Guy Dodge, *Benjamin Constant's Philosophy of Liberalism* (Chapel Hill, N.C.: The University of North Carolina Press, 1980), 55.

31. Quoted in Paul Hoffmann, "Benjamin Constant: Critique de Jean-Jacques Rousseau," *Revue d'Histoire Littéraire de la France* 82, no. 1 (January–February 1982): 27.

32. See Rousseau, *The Social Contract*, bk. III, chap. xv, and *The Government of Poland*, chap. 7. See also Hoffmann, "Benjamin Constant: Critique de Jean-Jacques Rousseau," 24–30.

33. Constant, "Principles of Politics," 175.

34. Quoted in Dodge, *Bejamin Constant's Philosophy of Liberalism*, 60.

35. Constant, "Principles of Politics," 251. Note that the question continues to be begged as to how one might define the sphere of the general will.

36. Rousseau writes, "The general will is always right, but the judgment that guides it is not always enlightened. . . . Private individuals see the good they reject; the public wants the good it does not see. All are equally in need of guides." *The Social Contract*, 67.

37. See Constant, "Principles of Politics," 176.

38. See Constant, "Principles of Politics," 292.

39. See Constant, "The Liberty of the Ancients Compared with That of the Moderns," in *Political Writings*, 311.

40. See Rousseau, *The Government of Poland*.

41. Stephen Holmes, "Two Concepts of Legitimacy: France After the Revolution," *Political Theory* 10, no. 2 (May 1982): 165–83.

42. Holmes, *Benjamin Constant and the Making of Modern Liberalism*, 2.

43. Holmes, *Benjamin Constant and the Making of Modern Liberalism*, 150.

44. Louis de Bonald, *Oeuvres complètes* (Paris: L. Migne, 1859), 1:147–48.

45. Quoted by Marcel Gauchet, in his preface in Constant, *De la liberté chez les modernes* (Paris: Librairie Générale Française, 1980), 57–58.

46. Liberals may wish to emphasize the centrality of consent to liberal theory. Fair enough, but most liberals are content to settle for tacit consent and they rarely, if ever, make political legitimacy depend on the actual, expressed consent of the citizenry.

47. Quoted in Dodge, *Benjamin Constant's Philosophy of Liberalism*, 72.

48. Constant, *Cours de Politique Constitutionnelle*, 1:283.

49. François Guizot, *Democracy in France* (New York: D. Appleton, 1849), 61.

50. The liberal might reply that Constant was not nearly so hostile to popular sovereignty. She might also reply that what we have come to call liberal democracy successfully resolves the tension nineteenth-century liberals perceived between liberalism and democracy. I take this question up in the conclusion to this chapter but will say here that I do not believe either Constant's liberalism or contemporary liberalism can escape this problem. Constant and contemporary liberals cannot eat their cake and have it too. If we insist on

146 *Chapter 6*

limiting sovereignty through an abstract appeal to reason, we must face the antidemocratic implications of this choice.

51. Constant, *Cours de Politique Constitutionnnelle*, 2:315.

52. See Soltau, *French Political Thought*, xix–xxx.

53. Soltau, *French Political Thought*, 48.

54. Cited by Dodge, *Benjamin Constant's Philosophy of Liberalism*, 72.

55. Quoted in Pierre Rosanvallon, *Le Moment Guizot* (Paris: Gallimard, 1985), 93.

56. See Rosanvallon, *Le Moment Guizot*, 88.

57. André Jardin, *Histoire du Libéralisme Politique* (Paris: Hachette, 1985), 357.

58. Leon Duguit, "The Law and the State," *Harvard Law Review* 31 (November) (1917–1918), 167.

59. Jean-Claude Lamberti, *Tocqueville and the Two Democracies*, trans. Arthur Goldhammer (Cambridge, Mass., Harvard University Press, 1989), 90.

60. Holmes, *Benjamin Constant and the Making of Modern Liberalism*, 3.

61. Constant, *Conquest and Usurpation*, 58.

62. Constant, *Cours de Politique Constitutionnelle*, 2:311.

63. Larry Siedentop, "Two Liberal Traditions," in *The Idea of Freedom: Essays in Honor of Isaiah Berlin*, ed. Alan Ryan (New York: Oxford University Press, 1979), 153–74.

64. Siedentop, "Two Liberal Traditions," 162, 174.

65. Michael J. Sandel, *Liberalism and the Limits of Justice* (Cambridge, U. K., Cambridge University Press, 1982).

66. Siedentop, "Two Liberal Traditions," 174.

67. Constant, "Principles of Politics," 255. Here, Constant approvingly relays the sentiment of a friend, whom he identifies as M. Degerando.

68. Constant, *Conquest and Usurpation*, 75.

69. Guizot discusses the importance of religion and the religious spirit to political stability. See *Democracy in France,* chap. 7. Tocqueville, of course, is famous for his attention to mores and religious spirit.

70. Constant, *Cours de Politique Constitutionnelle*, 1:282.

71. Cited by Dodge, *Benjamin Constant's Philosophy of Liberalism*, 62.

72. I borrow this idea from Lamberti, who used it to describe the Doctrinaires' position on sovereignty. See *Tocqueville and the Two Democracies*, 73.

73. Guizot, *Democracy in France*, 28.

74. The typical liberal response to this line of argumentation accuses critics of undermining personal liberty for the sake of some totalizing, romantic ideology. The problem with this reaction is that it fails to address the gap in the liberal account of sovereign power. Rather than defend her own position, the liberal attacks her critic, and, while the attack might be perfectly legitimate, it does nothing to remedy the problem inherent in liberalism itself.

75. Constant, *Cours de Politique Constitutionnelle*, 282.

Chapter 7

Tocqueville and the Compatibility of the Particular and the General

Rousseau found the chief threats to freedom in civil society and the best resources for resisting them in the democratic sovereign. Conversely, liberals like Constant and Tocqueville emphasize the dangers of sovereign power and look to civil society for ways to combat these dangers.[1] Where Rousseau saw selfishness, *amour-propre,* and various relationships of dependence, liberals see a space for creativity, self-assertion, and the exercise of basic freedoms. In the right to associate, Tocqueville famously discovered a safeguard against tyranny in America. This discovery came as something of a surprise to Tocqueville, given his experience with French associations, which he viewed as tyrannical and productive of servility rather than civic-mindedness. Moreover Rousseau, whose writings Tocqueville claimed to ponder daily, described particular associations (Rousseau might say factions) as a great threat to freedom. If generality is the path to freedom, particularity must be an obstacle to it.

Despite Tocqueville's overall affinity for Rousseau, he does not accept this Rousseauean teaching. He argues that secondary associations simultaneously generate allegiance to the general will and protect against the general will's despotic tendencies. Many contemporary theorists understandably, though probably overoptimistically, pin their hopes on this Tocquevillian insight because it offers the possibility of reconciling individual autonomy and civic virtue. If we have learned anything from Rousseau, it should be that we must be skeptical about claims to transcend this tension. Still, Tocqueville's account of association serves as a useful corrective to Rousseau's almost blanket dismissal of all particularity.

For all of his profundity, we can say that Rousseau made at least two mistakes: he was overly sanguine about sovereign power (as we saw in the previous chapter) and he was overly pessimistic about forces operating in civil society (as we will see in this chapter). Constant and Tocqueville allow us to reevaluate Rousseau's excesses and prepare the ground for a revised version of the general will.

Unlike Constant, Tocqueville never undertook a systematic analysis of the general will. Nevertheless, he invokes the term from time to time, and there are reasons to believe that he envisioned something like Rousseau's general will as the key to freedom in democratic times. John Koritansky goes so far as to claim that "the final solution to the problem of democracy on the level of democracy is, in a word, the 'general will.' If Tocqueville does not actually use that expression his whole analysis points to it."[2] No doubt Tocqueville's portrait of democratic citizenship resembles Rousseau's—the emphasis on equality, self-government, mores, and religion—but Tocqueville also departs from Rousseau, especially with regard to the dangers of particular associations. Rousseau and Tocqueville both emphasize civil society as a site of despotism, but they diverge with regard to the appropriate response to this kind of anti-freedom. This chapter describes the pathologies that Tocqueville attributed to civil society in democracies and analyzes what I call his Rousseauean (patriotism and religion) and non-Rousseauean (partial association) responses to these pathologies. I conclude that Tocqueville's account of partial association serves both as a corrective to Rousseau's blanket repudiation of it and as a useful adaptation of Rousseauean republicanism to large, differentiated societies.

Before going further, I should explain my use of the term "civil society," given the proliferation of meanings assigned to it. I use the term "civil society" to designate a social space, between the intimate sphere and the official apparatus and institutions of the state. It encompasses both the commercial and noncommercial interactions of citizens within this space. Civil society, in this chapter, lacks any normative or ethical connotation, referring only to a sphere of human activity.

I. TOCQUEVILLE AND ROUSSEAU

Like Rousseau, Tocqueville aspired to show people how they could be free under the conditions of modernity. Just as Rousseau and Constant understood modernity through a juxtaposition with antiquity, Tocqueville was preoccupied with his own historical distinction—between aristocratic and democratic times. However, unlike Constant, who purged himself of nostalgia for bygone eras, Tocqueville followed Rousseau in invoking an idealized picture of the past as an indictment against the present. Both Tocqueville and Rousseau lamented the withering away of conditions they viewed as crucial to freedom, and both looked for ways to recuperate in the present what they viewed as valuable about the past.

Whereas Constant, for the most part, jettisoned the freedom of the ancients in favor of the freedom of the moderns, Rousseau and Tocqueville aspired to the preservation and/or revival of the past. Tocqueville had no illusions about a return to aristocracy, but he hoped to find ways of preserving its impulse to greatness within the constraints of democracy. It should come as no surprise then, that Tocqueville's political theory reproduces many of the paradoxes that characterize

Rousseau's thought. Tocqueville writes, "Our contemporaries are ever a prey to two conflicting passions: they feel the need of guidance, and they long to stay free. Unable to wipe out these two contradictory instincts, they try to satisfy them both together."[3] This is Tocqueville's way of describing the tension I have invoked throughout the book—between popular will and rational will.

Rousseau's greatness lies in the way he illustrates the ineluctable character of tensions like this one. Rousseau makes clear that all societies committed to egalitarian politics must strive for (though they can never fully achieve) a reconciliation of popular will and rational will. Rousseau's answer to this problem is a general will that requires the subordination of particular interests. Tocqueville, on the other hand, envisions some mixture of generality and particularity, based primarily on empirical observations of one thriving republic. He is more optimistic about the sources of freedom in modern societies, finding sites of freedom in places where Rousseau saw only corruption.

II. TOCQUEVILLE AND DEMOCRACY

If Tocqueville is more optimistic than Rousseau about the possibility for freedom in modern times, he is more pessimistic about democracy. Whereas Rousseau's political solution to the problems of modernity was radical democracy, Tocqueville viewed democracy itself as a potential threat to freedom in modern times. However, given the historical circumstances, it will end up being the case that only resources made available by democracy will be capable of mitigating the problems generated by democracy.[4]

Though ultimately not antidemocratic, Tocqueville expressed misgivings about what he took to be the inexorable progress of democracy. In the first volume of *Democracy in America,* Tocqueville emphasizes the relationship between democracy and Bonapartism. Tocqueville's acuity for the study of history is well known, particularly with respect to the events of the Revolution. While he admired the revolutionaries' dedication to individual liberty, he criticized them for centralizing administrative power and he deplored the way they used the general will to justify oppression. In the second volume, Tocqueville describes a soft despotism that even legitimate democratic regimes might produce. Contemporary democrats, quick to appropriate Tocqueville as an ally, should consider this fragment from a passage Tocqueville called "My instinct, my opinions."

> For democratic institutions I have an intellectual preference, but I am by instinct an aristocrat, which is to say that I despise and fear the mob. I passionately love liberty, legality, respect for rights, but not democracy: that is my innermost feeling. . . . Liberty is the first of my passions: that is the plain truth.[5]

While Tocqueville did not attempt to resist democracy, it cannot be said that he embraced it either. Rather, he believed that some kind of liberal democracy, with unifying mores and a civil religion, was the only viable alternative to Bonapartist democracy on one side and the soft tyranny of democratic individualism on the other. "And if we must finally reach a state of complete equality, is it not better to let ourselves be leveled down by freedom rather than by a despot?" (*DA*, 315). Tocqueville believed that the conditions of modernity would only permit freedom in a democratic context; there could be no choice between aristocracy and democracy—only between liberal democracy and democratic despotism (*DA*, 314).[6] Unlike previous French liberals, Tocqueville envisioned a new form of democracy as the proper response to the abuses of democracy that characterized the Revolution and Empire.

This is not to suggest that Tocqueville viewed democracy as nothing more than an unfortunate inevitability. He maintained, as he put it, "an intellectual preference" for democracy—for its noble aim, its emphasis on self-rule, and its capacity to generate and distribute wealth. He took particular solace in the version of democracy he found in America, which encouraged the "manly and proud virtues" and had successfully tempered democracy with laws, religion, and mores. Nonetheless, there could be no time for complacency because American democracy, though it provides an alternative to Bonapartism, risks degenerating into its own brand of despotism.

III. SOURCES OF DESPOTISM IN DEMOCRATIC SOCIETIES

In volume 1 of *Democracy*, Tocqueville emphasizes the democratic regime, specifically the ways in which American democracy resists despotism. In volume 2, he analyzes the psychology of democratic citizens, drawing conclusions about democracy that transcend the American context. Here, the chief threat to freedom is no longer Bonapartist dictatorship but an inward despotism, legitimated by democratic consent. "I do not reproach equality for leading men astray with forbidden delights, but I do complain that it absorbs them in the quest of those permitted completely" (*DA*, 534).[7] Tocqueville distinguishes between the right to liberty and the way that right is exercised. A strong doctrine of rights provides the safest protection against Bonapartist tyranny, but it does nothing to prevent democratic citizens from becoming apathetic, materialistic, isolated, and degraded. Tocqueville writes, "if a despotism should be established among the democratic nations of our day, it would probably have a different character. It would be more widespread and milder; it would degrade men rather than torment them" (*DA*, 691).

Tocqueville introduces the word "individualism" (which does not appear in volume 1) to designate this democratic tendency. Individualism risks a kind of despotism that has little in common with the despotism of the Terror and Empire, resembling Rousseau's *amour-propre* more than any type of illegitimate regime. Perhaps Tocqueville exaggerated the risks of disengaged citizens pursuing trivial pleasures. As Edward Banfield notes, modern societies have shown how "the pursuit of happiness, even when it leads to paltry pleasures, is compatible with the maintenance of freedom and justice."[8] However, even if we dispute the gravity of the pathology Tocqueville identified, few would disagree with the essence of Tocqueville's diagnosis. Moreover, if one is at all persuaded by Tocqueville's analysis, it becomes clear that the study of freedom in democratic societies cannot be detached from questions of moral psychology. Indeed, Tocqueville introduces volume 2 of *Democracy* by saying that he intends to describe the "opinions, feelings, and instincts" of the democratic majority (*DA*, 417).

Tocqueville associated individualism with democracy because of the way democracy destroys the social hierarchies and norms that previously guided personal interaction. "Democracy makes man forget his ancestors and all his ties so that he is thrown back on himself alone" (*DA*, 508). Having vitiated external standards of meaning, democratic citizens must construct worldviews of their own and they must do so on their own. This produces an unacceptable level of restlessness (which accounts for Tocqueville's emphasis on the importance of religion). Though the social hierarchies and customs of aristocracy did not support the interests of all equally, they did provide a framework for social interaction. As Franklin Rudolf Ankersmit writes, "in aristocracy social meaning has an outside to which it refers or which it reflects that is absent in democracy; social meaning in democracy lacks the clarity, precision and articulation it used to have in aristocracy."[9] Without a framework within which they can define their preferences, Tocqueville fears democratic citizens will become apathetic, isolated, and degraded.

"Such folk think they are following the doctrine of self-interest, but they have a very crude idea thereof, and the better to guard their interests, they neglect the chief of them, that is, to remain their own masters"(*DA*, 540). Tocqueville invokes a Rousseauean kind of freedom, according to which individuals may follow their personal discretion yet remain in free. Individualism is a "misguided judgment" (*DA*, 506) that Tocqueville attributes to the subordination of liberty to equality and describes as egoism in the place of virtue. Individualism "disposes each citizen to isolate himself from the mass of his fellows and withdraw into the circle of family and friends" (*DA*, 506). This, in and of itself, does not sound so bad, but Tocqueville believes that this phenomenon sacrifices civic-mindedness to egoism.

Individualism risks tyranny in two ways, according to Tocqueville: Individuals are personally threatened by a combination of isolation and conformity, and society as a whole becomes vulnerable to a usurpation of political power. Tocqueville worried that "democracy might extinguish that freedom of the mind which a democratic social condition favors;" he worried that "the human spirit might bind itself in tight fetters to the general will of the greatest number" (*DA*, 436). In their relentless pursuit of equality, Tocqueville feared that citizens' desire for freedom would wither. America was lucky for several reasons, according to Tocqueville, not the least of which was its fortune to have been founded by men who loved freedom more than equality. Equality is noble and dangerous at the same time—noble because it respects the dignity and independence of each individual, but dangerous because it leaves individuals isolated in the face of the majority (*DA*, 435).[10]

These isolated individuals lack independence of mind, and, for that reason, cannot be described as free, according to Tocqueville. Moreover, disengaged, politically apathetic, and, most importantly, unorganized citizens lack the power to resist encroachment on their freedom. Men are both independent and weak in a democracy, because they are neither under the control of anyone nor organized into associations; consequently, they look toward the state, which accrues more and more power (*DA*, 672). For Rousseau, concentrating power in the whole was the only remedy for the threats to freedom prevalent in civil society. Tocqueville identifies slightly different dangers in civil society and, consequently, proposes slightly different solutions.

IV. TOCQUEVILLE'S ROUSSEAUEAN RESPONSES

Tocqueville and Rousseau share a focus on civil society as a possible site of oppression. However, whereas Rousseau emphasized the relationships of dependence that develop in civil society, Tocqueville's primary unit of analysis was the individual, specifically the psychological implications of social equality. In this section, I discuss what we might call Tocqueville's "Rousseauean responses" to the problem of individualism. Because both Rousseau and Tocqueville think about the threats to freedom in civil society, neither is satisfied with a purely formal conception of rights. For these thinkers, freedom involves self-rule as well as the absence of external interference because mere noninterference leaves individuals vulnerable to oppression from forces within civil society and the soft despotism of individual isolation. If threats to freedom can come from all spheres of society, then our understanding of freedom itself must be multifaceted. Tocqueville's conception of freedom includes elements borrowed both from his liberal predecessors and from Rousseau. He accepts the liberal program of individual liberty, a right to property, and basic noninterference for industry. However, he also describes a process by which political participation conditions citizens to harmonize their private will with the general will.

Tocqueville stands somewhere in between Rousseau and the liberals; he thinks of politics as more than an instrument but stops short of elevating citizenship to the heights it reaches in Rousseau. For Tocqueville, greatness seems to lie only partially in citizenship itself; mainly, it lies in the great deeds performed by free souls. Still, freedom for Tocqueville comprises more than formal liberties and rights. It includes the personal obligation to secure one's independence against sovereign power, threats posed by forces in civil society, and threats that develop within the individual herself. To be free, people must "remain their own masters," as Tocqueville puts it, which, to use Rousseau's word, means that they must avoid relationships of "dependence." Consequently, freedom becomes entangled with virtue for Tocqueville (as it did for Rousseau), in that citizens must take an interest in the fate of their community if they are to preserve their independence.

This type of freedom requires what I have described as an awkward synthesis of voluntarism and virtue. For Rousseau, democracy was the foundation of this synthesis. For Tocqueville, democracy generates as many problems as it does solutions. In fact, although they have the unfortunate disadvantage of catering only to the few, aristocratic societies secure freedom better than democratic ones. Neither aristocracy nor democracy guarantee freedom for either Rousseau or Tocqueville, but unlike Rousseau, Tocqueville occupies himself with the threats to freedom that are specifically characteristic of democracy. Broadly speaking, the problem is that moral ties must replace the political ties that break down through individualism. As is the case with all regimes, democracy depends on the availability of a moral authority, a set of general principles to which the population can adhere. In aristocracy, the rigid social networks and norms of behavior provided that stable, if inegalitarian, authority. Democracies must call upon something to replace these institutions and, for Tocqueville, religion and patriotism offer the most promise. General ideas of this kind are the prerequisite to social flourishing and a constituent part of human nature. Tocqueville writes, "one can then say that all religions derive an element of strength which will never fail from man himself, because it is attached to one of the constituent principles of human nature" (*DA*, 297).

In the absence of religious authority and an aristocratic social structure (the principal losers in Revolutionary France), individuals will awkwardly grope for social meaning. Tocqueville's general critique of the French Revolution follows the trajectory of this argument. His description of the Revolution can be broadly summarized as follows: Once aristocratic social hierarchies and the authority of the church were undermined, power became increasingly centralized in the state apparatus, with deleterious implications for human liberty. Tocqueville breaks from rationalist liberals in his embrace of religion. "It is true that any man accepting an opinion on trust from another puts his mind in bondage. But it is a salutary bondage that allows him to make good use of freedom" (*DA*, 434). Bondage can be salutary for Tocqueville if it points the soul away from the self-absorbed pursuit of wealth and luxury and toward a higher morality. For all of Tocqueville's worries about conformity and the way individual minds will bind themselves to the general will, he ultimately favors certain species of conformity, specifically religion and patriotism. It is not conformity itself that poses a threat for Tocqueville, but a certain kind of democratic conformity that is staved off, ironically, by a nobler conformity.

This noble conformity breeds civic virtue through solidarity on matters of collective concern. Without solidarity, there can be no collective action, and without collective action, there can be no freedom in democratic societies. Here, we see clearly Tocqueville's Rousseauism. The threats to freedom come from forces in civil society, chiefly individual isolation, such that recapturing freedom requires active participation in the general will. However, Tocqueville stops slightly short of Rousseau's claim that freedom itself lies in participation in the general will. For Tocqueville, a sense of collective purpose becomes a prerequisite to individual flourishing—an instrument of liberty to be deployed against the soft tyranny of individualism.

"Look where you will, you will never find true power among men except in the free concurrence of their wills. Now, patriotism and religion are the only things in the world which will make the whole body of citizens go persistently forward toward the same goal" (*DA*, 94). For Tocqueville, the question is not so much whether citizens will have dogmatic beliefs, but what those dogmatic beliefs will be. Democracies will likely choose between self-absorbed egoism and either religion, patriotism, or a combination of the two. Given the inevitability and, indeed, the desirability of dogmatism, Tocqueville recommends some combination of religion and patriotism.

Democracy opens the political arena unconditionally (if only to those with full citizenship), necessitating a religious doctrine that conditions citizens to pursue more than self-aggrandizement. Religion educates citizens to an enlarged view. It restrains the "excessive and exclusive taste for well-being which men acquire in times of equality" (*DA*, 448). The obvious objection to grounding democracy on religious belief is that the dictates of individual autonomy and free conscience mandate that individuals have the option to reject a religious worldview. Tocqueville recognized this tension, and one of the things that appealed to him about America was the way Americans could incorporate the spirit of religion and the spirit of freedom, where others could not (*DA*, 47). Somehow Americans had identified liberty with Christianity from the outset, such that it became "almost impossible to get them to conceive of one without the other" (*DA*, 293). This state of mind epitomizes what Tocqueville called "salutary bondage," and it explains why Tocqueville, who clearly understood the difficulty of instilling virtue, was hardly concerned with the problem in America.[11] Tocqueville used America as an image of reconciliation, even transcendence, of the tension between popular will and rational will that is captured by the term *volonté générale*. Americans voluntarily willed the conditions for their own freedom, obviating the need for Rousseau's various mechanisms of social indoctrination. Tocqueville offers a paradox to which an idealized America is the solution: "I doubt whether man can support complete religious independence and entire political liberty at the same time. I am led to think that if he has no faith he must obey, and if he is free he must believe" (*DA*, 444).

If democracy must accommodate religion, it is no less true that religion is itself in need of democratization. One of the things Tocqueville admires about the American clergy is that they "are aware of the intellectual domination of the majority, and they treat it with respect. . . . They try to improve their contemporaries but do not quit fellowship with them. Public opinion is therefore never hostile to them but rather supports and protects them" (*DA*, 449). Tocqueville's view of the

Church in America contrasts with his view of religion in *The Ancien Régime*. In France, the Church "had become a political body in defiance of its vocation and its nature," and, because its attempts at capturing sovereign power were illegitimate, Tocqueville called it the "most odious . . . of all political bodies."[12] In America, religion buttressed rather than threatened the democratic majority, building on the principle of "self-interest rightly understood" by commingling the things of this world with those of the next. Tocqueville's democratic religion closely resembles Rousseau's civil religion, despite Tocqueville's embrace of Christianity. Both Tocqueville and Rousseau favor a chastened religiosity that primarily emphasizes the concept of an afterlife and of a God who favors those individuals who respect the rights of others.

Tocqueville parts with Rousseau over the issue of a state-sponsored religion, along the lines of the civil religion that Rousseau described. Tocqueville believed this statist model to be unworkable and undesirable, opting instead for an associative approach. Tocqueville esteems personal autonomy too much and statism too little to embrace the idea of a state-sponsored religion. Moreover, in large, diverse societies, a monolithic religious authority would surely undermine personal liberty. Without state sponsorship, Tocqueville recognizes that religion may lose its sway over citizens' souls, but reliance on a statist religion compromises fundamental human liberties in large, diverse societies. The Americans resolved this paradox by living under strict laws that were voluntarily imposed. However, this is a bit of fortune that cannot always be expected. Tocqueville's associative religion may respect personal autonomy more than Rousseau's statism, but it also depends on a fortuitous confluence of forces that cannot be expected in most societies. Here, we have the reason for Tocqueville's pessimism. He acknowledges a weakening of religion's hold on individual spirits while worrying that politics cannot flourish without the nonpolitical foundation religion provides.

Neither can the state coerce religious enthusiasm:

> So long as a religion derives its strength from sentiments, instincts and passions, which are reborn in like fashion in all periods of history, it can brave the assaults of time, or at least it can only be destroyed by another religion. But when a religion chooses to rely on the interests of this world, it becomes almost as fragile as all earthly powers. . . . Hence any alliance with any political power whatsoever is bound to be burdensome for religion. It does not need their support in order to live, and in serving them it may die.[13]

Tocqueville finds himself committed problematically to the basic separation of church and state and to religion as a foundation for political freedom. The general will requires some moral authority to temper the excesses of popular will. Tocqueville accepted the victory of the principle of popular sovereignty, however, without some conception of divine justice, he worried that there would be little to constrain tyrannical majorities and even less to prevent self-isolated individualism.

Once the hold of religion has weakened, the onus falls upon the state to provide the moral authority needed for citizens to think beyond their personal space. Fortunately, just as there was a natural tendency toward religion, "there is a patriotism which mainly springs from the disinterested, undefinable, and unpondered [sic] feeling that ties a man's heart to the place where he was born."[14] From this "unpondered" feeling, societies can cultivate "another sort of patriotism more rational than that; less generous, perhaps less ardent, but more creative and more lasting, it is engendered by enlightenment, grows by the aid of laws and the exercise of rights, and in the end becomes, in a sense, mingled with personal interest."[15] Tocqueville's "rational patriotism" synthesizes voluntarism and virtue in a way that epitomizes the idea of the general will.

Like Rousseau, Tocqueville argues that individuals have a political right to participate in government, and that if they are to put that political right to good use, they must have a strong national identity. Patriotism, therefore, conditions the will to take the public interest into account. Moreover, there is reason to be more optimistic about the sway of patriotism in democratic times, because, unlike religious enthusiasm, which tends to wane in democracies, patriotism is intensified through democratic participation. "I do say that the most powerful way, and perhaps the only remaining way, in which to interest men in their country's fate is to make them take a share in its government."[16] According to Tocqueville, then, patriotism influences the nature of popular participation and is itself influenced by it. This felicitous case of mutual causality generates a political culture capable of reconciling private interest with the general will. The American "sees the public fortune as his own, and he works for the good of the state, not only from duty or from pride, but, I dare almost say, from greed."[17] Tocqueville, like Rousseau, is skeptical about the capacity of reason alone to generate a robust sense of citizenship in most individuals. Something emotional or subconscious must supplement individual ratiocination if democratic societies are to pursue the public interest. Consequently, Tocqueville is convinced that "the interests of the human race are better served by giving every man a particular fatherland than by trying to inflame his passions for the whole of humanity."[18] Like Rousseau's cosmopolitans who love everyone in order to love no one, Tocqueville worries that cosmopolitan citizens "will perceive only from a viewpoint that is distant, aloof, uncertain, and cold."[19]

Twentieth-century developments have convinced many contemporary liberals that, more often than not, patriotism poses a threat to basic liberties. Tocqueville was a liberal in that he viewed individual liberty as the ultimate end of any social order, but he was also something of a nationalist in that he believed social stability and prosperity depend on the availability of a moral discourse that orients individuals beyond themselves.[20] Joshua Mitchell writes that the cornerstone of Tocqueville's liberalism is that "political freedom rests upon nonpolitical foundations."[21] These nonpolitical foundations pose their own threats to freedom when they are exclusionary and/or coercive, which explains why many liberals avoid discussing them. Tocqueville, like Rousseau, believed that the risks they posed were less serious than the cost of ignoring their role. But Tocqueville and Rousseau face a theoretical problem as well—namely, how the state can involve itself in the moral education of its citizens without violating their personal freedom. Tocqueville's attempts to synthesize religion and patriotism with voluntarism illustrate once more what we have described as the inexorable tension between rational will and popular will. Egalitarian societies cannot afford to ignore either, but neither can they emphasize one without risking the other—or so we have argued up to this point.

V. TOCQUEVILLE'S NON-ROUSSEAUEAN RESPONSE

Perhaps Tocqueville has a resource for transcending the tension between rational will and popular will—a resource that Rousseau did not perceive. As we have seen, Tocqueville and Rousseau share a concern for the threats to freedom posed by forces within civil society. However, unlike Rousseau, who saw only threats to freedom in the sphere of particularity, Tocqueville found sources of freedom there as well. Moreover, following the liberals, he worried far more than Rousseau did about the threats to freedom posed by public power and, more specifically, about the risks to personal liberty associated with deploying state power against particularity. Whereas for Rousseau, rationalizing popular will always meant generalizing it, Tocqueville embraced a certain type of particularity as the foundation of good citizenship. Rousseau writes, "private interest deceives us. It is only the hope of the just which never deceives."[22] Elsewhere, he adds, "Far from there being an alliance between private interest and the general good, they are mutually exclusive in the natural order of things."[23]

Tocqueville responds, "Public spirit in the Union is but the aggregate of provincial patriotism. . . . Every citizen of the United States may be said to transfer the concern inspired in him by his little republic into his love of the common motherland"(*DA*, 158, 160).[24] In America, Tocqueville discovered a species of association different from the one he and Rousseau had come to know in France. Whereas in France, particular interest connoted inegalitarian, hereditary status and/or attempts by the Church to infiltrate political decision making, in America, Tocqueville found partial societies that did not threaten political stability or favor the subordination of one group to another. In America, partial societies did not aspire to the usurpation of public authority, nor did their members view their allegiance to a partial association as conflictual with their allegiance to the larger political community. On the contrary, according to Tocqueville, identification with a partial association strengthened the citizen's attachment to the larger society.[25]

For Tocqueville, the general will is not defined in opposition to particular will as it was for Rousseau. He favored (and believed it was theoretically consistent to favor) both strong particularist identities and a strong collective identity.[26] Indeed, Tocqueville argued that a nation cannot "live, much less prosper, without a high degree of centralization of government."[27] However, he distinguished between administrative centralization and governmental or political centralization.[28] Administrative centralization "only serves to enervate the peoples that submit to it, because it constantly tends to diminish their civic spirit."[29] It removes from citizens' hands the power to meet their needs and, thereby, encourages passivity. The appropriate antidote to administrative centralization is partial association, through which citizens can recuperate the power to control their own lives, to "remain their own masters," in Tocqueville's words. Political centralization, on the other hand, is the prerequisite to national unity, the basis for the "motherland's presence" to be "felt everywhere" (DA, 95). By buttressing political centralization while undermining administrative centralization, Tocqueville combines Federalist and Anti-Federalist arguments.[30] Tocqueville preserves the Rousseauean claim that there must be unity in matters that concern the nation as a whole; however, he shrinks the sphere of national interest such that a substantial measure of political power would devolve to the local level.

Tocqueville's dual allegiance to political centralization and particular association makes sense if we remember the problem to which he was reacting—individualism. Without a unified national or general will, individuals would become isolated and eventually enslaved. However, with only a unified general will, a similar kind of slavery might occur, as the human mind binds itself to the general will. Democratic societies are particularly vulnerable to this latter tendency because they tend toward uniformity, which leaves individuals ready to "trust the mass" and "public opinion becomes more and more mistress of the world" (DA, 435). The elimination of the intermediate associations of the old regime exacerbates this problem since individuals are left with only the state as a source of identification beyond their families and themselves. Describing the Revolution, Tocqueville wrote, "When all the intermediate powers which could balance or mitigate the unlimited power of the King had been destroyed, the parliament alone remained."[31] Democracies must not only tolerate particular association but encourage it: first, because democracies have their origin in the purging of previous associations and, second, because they tend toward uniformity by their nature. In the absence of aristocratic bodies, only citizen associations can balance and check concentrations of state power and the hegemony of the general will.

As noted above, individualism risks tyranny in two ways: first, by leaving society open to a usurpation of political power and, second, through a self-imposed despotism of individual isolation. On Tocqueville's account, association offers democracies a safeguard against both of these threats to freedom. With regard to the first, Tocqueville writes, "freedom of association has become a necessary guarantee against tyranny of the majority" (DA, 192). Tocqueville assumes that associations will be relatively small, along the lines of the townships used to administer law in New England, as opposed to the large associations like the Church and aristocracy that dominated in France. When associations are small, they do not threaten the sovereignty of the majority, but they can, according to Tocqueville, "hold back tyranny" (*DA*, 192). Without them, even a tiny faction or single individual could sweep into power (*DA*, 192); with them, even the great power of the majority can be constrained. Associations preserve the liberty of all by defending their particular rights against the excessive demands of the majority. Power is generated by numbers, particularly in a democracy. When citizens are isolated, they are powerless and, therefore, unable to resist excesses of sovereign power.

In addition to providing a check on public power, associations cultivate virtues necessary to the flourishing of any society. The citizen "gets to know those formalities without which freedom can advance only through revolutions, and becoming imbued with their spirit, develops a taste for order, understands the harmony of powers, and in the end accumulates clear, practical ideas about the nature of his duties and the extent of his rights" (*DA*, 70). This type of association mitigates the democratic tendency toward individualism and materialism by cultivating certain virtues and dispositions. For Tocqueville, the efficiency and/or the success of political association matters far less than the fact that it orients the individual beyond oneself. When Tocqueville describes political activity in America, he often mentions seemingly nonpolitical activities like building churches and planning roads and schools.[32] The act of associating itself takes precedence over the actual activities carried out. People often manage public affairs badly, but it expands their horizons to be politically active (*DA*, 233–34).[33] This enlarged view is not a natural byproduct of democracy; on the contrary, democracies desperately require association because they tend by their nature to encourage individualism.

In associations, citizens realize that they are not self-sufficient—that they depend on others and, therefore, have duties and obligations toward others. "Citizens who are bound to take part in public affairs must turn from the private interests and occasionally take a look at something other than themselves. As soon as common affairs are treated in common, each man notices that he is not as independent of his fellows" (*DA*, 510). This dependence produces the enlarged view that Rousseau thought possible only in the general association of society as a whole. While Rousseau felt any partial society would pursue its own interest at the expense of the rest of society, Tocqueville believed that an enlarged worldview could be cultivated in particular associations and that this worldview would translate into fidelity to the general will at the level of the larger society. Civic virtue, for Tocqueville, is nourished by any political participation, whether it be participation in the general will or participation in the partial associations of civil society. Voluntary associations lead Americans to see the connection between self-interest and the common good. Members "learn to submit their own will to that of all the rest"(*DA*, 522)—a lesson which is smoothly carried over to the general society. For Tocqueville, turning away from private interests is the necessary starting point for civic virtue; the political space in which this activity occurs is of far less consequence than that it actually take place.

For Rousseau, democracy is the solution to the political problems of the modern era. For Tocqueville, democracy is both the solution to and the source of many of the problems in modern politics. Consequently, unlike Rousseau, he offers strategies for mitigating democracy's harmful tendencies. He embraced formal limitations on sovereign power, following previous liberals, and focused on informal associations as a remedy for democratic individualism. In aristocracies, individuals were held firmly together, but democratic revolutions destroy the old solidarities and must find new sources of unity. To quote Pierre Manent, "The goal of associations is to reknit the social fabric that equality of conditions tends to unravel."[34] Tocqueville explains,

> I am firmly convinced that one cannot found an aristocracy anew in this world, but I think that associations of plain citizens can compose very rich, influential, and powerful bodies, in other words, aristocratic bodies. By this means many of the greatest political advantages of an aristocracy could be obtained without its injustices and dangers (DA, 697).

Tocqueville found sources of freedom where Rousseau saw only the possibility of oppression. Rousseau undoubtedly exaggerated the oppressive tendencies of particular association, but we should also note that Tocqueville's celebration of association is premised upon an idealized view of civil society. As Yael Tamir puts it, "not all civil society is civic-minded. Some associations have the contradictory effect; they threaten social cohesion, erode the social capital, frustrate social equality and equal opportunity, and violate individual rights."[35] If our model is the New England township, we might adopt a favorable view of association similar to Tocqueville's. If, on the other hand, we think about the variety of associations and the different types of membership, we might become more ambivalent. We might consider the ways in which membership in an association can fuel narcissism, a feeling of impotence in the face of a complex system, militarism and vigilantism, and conspiratorial thinking.[36] Think for example of the militias that have become increasingly active in America's civil society. Think of residential community associations and small support groups, which have their advantages but probably do little to cultivate civic-mindedness or Tocqueville's enlarged view of one's role in society.

In fact, Tocqueville made just this kind of distinction between good and bad association. He distinguished, for example, between "'American' associations that allow for and encourage independent behavior and 'French' associations that are tyrannical within themselves, thus producing passive and servile behavior instead of training members in the use of their energies for the sake of common enterprises."[37] Given their mutual disdain for French particularity, perhaps Tocqueville and Rousseau are closer than one might think on the question of association. The hard battles fought against the political dominance of the Church and the system of aristocracy produced in France the view that freedom of association procures no more than the right to make war on the government (*DA*, 194). Tocqueville attributes this view to a lack of experience with political liberty. In free societies like the United States, an association is usually "an educated and powerful body of citizens which . . . by defending its private interests against the encroachments of power . . . saves the common liberties" (*DA*, 697). In contrast, for Rousseau, the idea of partial association conjured images of aristocrats, the Catholic Church, or the very wealthy, deploying their power in a way that subordinated the general will to their particular interest. As we noted in chapter 3, Rousseau was actually quite willing to tolerate particularity in areas that did not pose a direct threat to popular sovereignty and, by extension, the sovereignty of the general will. Similarly, Tocqueville shared Rousseau's concern for the divisiveness of association, noting that unbridled association was possible in America only because "differences of view are only matters of nuance" (*DA*, 194).[38] Just as Rousseau should not be read as the great enemy of particularity, we should not assume that Tocqueville celebrated association unconditionally.

Nonetheless, associations were, at best, tolerable for Rousseau, whereas Tocqueville discovered reasons to positively encourage them. Whereas Rousseau believed that attachment to a particular association would generally undermine social cohesion, Tocqueville believed citizens' attachment to particular communities could translate into an attachment to the community as a whole. Given the appropriate context and the right type of association, Tocqueville believes that particular will can bolster the general will. Moreover, associations can serve as the basis of freedom, understood as self-rule. In large societies, the decentralization of administrative authority offers individuals the opportunity to control their affairs. "Without local institutions a nation may give itself a free government, but it has not got the spirit of liberty" (*DA*, 63). Citizens will come to rely on the government for everything and succumb to the pressures of conformity. In short, they will fail to remain their own masters.

CONCLUSION

Tocqueville, I think it is safe to say, was a Rousseauean. He shared Rousseau's emphasis on forces in civil society, as well as much of his teachings on patriotism, religion, and the general will. He also diagnosed a psychological pathology (individualism) which is reminiscent of Rousseau's *amour-propre* and has equally devastating effects on human liberty. Even Tocqueville's non-Rousseauean response to this problem (partial association) emerges from a Rousseauean appreciation of the tensions that characterize egalitarian politics—tensions between voluntarism and virtue, between popular will and rational will, between private interest and the general will. Tocqueville's more nuanced account of partial association serves as a useful corrective to Rousseau's blunt repudiation of it. Yet, it can be read as an extension of Rousseauean republicanism as well because it emerges from within the framework of a political theory committed to a Rousseauean general will.

In this sense, Tocqueville's celebration of partial association might just as well be called "neo-Rousseauean" as "non-Rousseauean." Tocqueville's reconsideration of particularity can be read as an attempt to adapt Rousseau's general will to large, diverse societies. The general will, as Rousseau envisioned it in *The Social Contract,* could only survive in a small, homogeneous, self-sufficient community. Tocqueville accepted Rousseau's general will as an ideal of citizenship, with its inherent tension between popular and rational will and its embrace of civic virtue as the remedy to self-absorbed individualism. However, he unsettles two concepts that were monolithic for Rousseau: public power, which Rousseau believed would always serve freedom (so long as the general will was sovereign), and partial association, which Rousseau believed would usually undermine it. For Tocqueville, partial association, properly exercised, offers resources for directing self-interested individuals toward the common good and can act as a check on abuses of public power. Moreover, association is the modern individual's best chance to master her own destiny and realize Rousseau's ideal of freedom as self-rule. As for Rousseau's concerns about the divisiveness of partial association, Tocqueville differentiates between different kinds of association, much as he differentiates between free and despotic assertions of public power. Rousseau's general will yielded a blunt embrace of public power as the appropriate antidote to oppression and a blunt repudiation of association for its divisiveness. Tocqueville, in adapting Rousseau's general will to a large, diverse society, differentiates between good and bad uses of public power and good and bad patterns of association.

For both Tocqueville and Rousseau, the self-absorbed pursuit of private wealth and pleasure produces citizens without the resources, personal or collective, to ward off despotism. Rousseau embraced an austere collectivism as the only remedy to this problem. For Tocqueville, the antidote lies in political association, broadly understood, whether it be the association of all citizens or some segment of that larger association. As one contemporary thinker frames the problem, "our singular citizenship and our pluralized culture have a common enemy; both are threatened by a radicalized ideology of individualism and anti-politics of privatization."[39] While sensitive to the dangers posed by political faction, Tocqueville felt large, diverse, democratic societies were threatened less by their differentiation than by their tendency toward self-absorbed individualism. Moreover, he felt that allegiance to certain types of partial association would strengthen citizens' allegiance to the larger society and reinforce the supremacy of the general will.

Tocqueville's differentiated view of both public power and partial association offers a framework for thinking about republican citizenship in modern societies. He preserves the essence of Rousseau's teaching on the general will but adapts it to large, diverse societies. One might wish to ask if, in the process of adaptation, the essence of Rousseau's republicanism is corrupted. I do not believe this to be the case; however, it would be a mistake to assume that associative life is the riddle of republican citizenship solved. In other words, what Tocqueville offers is not a transcendence of the tensions that characterize egalitarian politics, but a more flexible, historically sensitive way of thinking about them. Though they do provide a useful resource, associations do not resolve the tension between popular will and rational will. Associations have the potential to cultivate the virtues necessary to the liberty and stability of democratic societies, however, they can also encourage factionalism, xenophobia and racism, narcissism, militarism and vigilantism, and a feeling of political impotence, among other things. Anyone enthused about the prospects of association should remember that even Tocqueville had a differentiated view of it. Just as we have learned to be sensitive to the variety of ways in which public power can be deployed, we must be sensitive to the variety of associative possibilities in civil society. Tocqueville's celebration of association for its power to enlighten self-interest does not resolve the tension between popular will and rational will; rather, it provides it with a new context. Tocqueville successfully refutes Rousseau's blanket condemnation of partial association, but liberal democracies must still ask whether the associations they have contribute to factionalism or unity, to the interests of the few at the expense of the rest, or to the interests of the few in conjunction with the rest. Moreover, they cannot rely on associations alone to foster citizenship. It should be obvious that some pragmatic combination of public power and partial association—of general and particular—are necessary to secure the conditions for a flourishing liberal democracy.

NOTES

1. Whether or not Tocqueville ought to be considered a liberal is a perpetual question for Tocqueville scholars. Tocqueville considered himself a "new" kind of liberal, but as we shall see in sections IV and V, Tocqueville's republicanism runs as deep as his liberalism. Moreover, he made no secret of his fondness for aristocracy. Rather than force Tocqueville into any one of these political camps, this chapter considers the role that each of them plays in what must be read as an original political theory.

2. John C. Koritansky, *Alexis de Tocqueville and the New Science of Politics: An Interpretation of Democracy in America* (Durham, N.C.: Carolina Academic Press, 1986), 87.

3. Tocqueville, *Democracy in America* (New York: Harper Perennial, 1969), 693 (hereafter cited as *DA* in the text with the page number. All subsequent quotations from this source are from the edition cited). Pierre Manent concludes his book on Tocqueville as follows: "It is difficult to be a friend of democracy, but it is necessary to be a friend of democracy. Such is the teaching of Tocqueville. . . . It is true that democracy is in a very real sense the enemy of human grandeur, but the enemies of democracy are much more dangerous enemies of this grandeur." See Pierre Manent, *Tocqueville and the Nature of Democracy* (Lanham, Md.: Rowman & Littlefield, 1996), 129.

4. It should be noted that Tocqueville understands democracy to mean more than popular sovereignty or even popular political participation. He uses democracy to denote "the general equality of social conditions" as well as the "sovereignty of the majority," as noted by Edward C. Banfield, "The Illiberal Tocqueville," in *Interpreting Tocqueville's* Democracy in America, 240. Tocqueville introduces the idea of "social state" as a category of analysis and describes the Americans' social state as democratic. In this sense, democracy denotes a tendency toward equality that undermines, even eliminates, social hierarchy.

Tocqueville's liberalism, as with that of Constant and the Doctrinaires, emerges as a response to what Guizot called the "victory of the democratic force." Cited by John Marini, "Centralized Administration and the 'New Despotism,'" in *Interpreting Tocqueville's Democracy in America*, 255.

5. Tocqueville, pt. 1 of *Oeuvres complètes* (Paris: Gallimard, 1985), 3:87.

6. Tocqueville writes, "I find those very blind who think to rediscover the monarchy of Henry IV or Louis XIV. For my part, when I consider the state already reached by several European nations and that toward which all are tending, I am led to believe that there will soon be no room except for either democratic freedom or the tyranny of the Caesars."

7. Tocqueville, *Democracy in America*, 534.

8. Banfield, "The Illiberal Tocqueville," 254.

9. Franklin Rudolf Ankersmit, "Tocqueville and the Sublimity of Democracy, Part I: Content," *La Revue Tocqueville/The Tocqueville Review* 14, no. 2 (1993): 177.

10. Though Rousseau also worried about a kind of self-absorbed individualism (which he called *amour-propre*), he did not acknowledge the dangers of conformism that accompany a robust general will. Social differences for Rousseau were either politically inconsequential (and therefore neutral) or politically destructive. The oppressive nature of the political factions that dominated Rousseau's political landscape convinced him that faction was the chief threat to political freedom. Moreover, he never found any use for particularity within a republic, even with regard to the social differences that he felt should be tolerated. Tocqueville, on the other hand, offers resources for distinguishing between the kinds of social differences and particular associations that support freedom and those that undermine it.

11. See Joshua Mitchell, *The Fragility of Freedom* (Chicago: The University of Chicago Press, 1995), 132.

12. Tocqueville, *The Ancien Régime*, trans. John Bonner (London: Dent & Sons, 1988), 120.

13. Tocqueville, *The Ancien Régime*, 298.

14. Tocqueville, *The Ancien Régime*, 235.

15. Tocqueville, *The Ancien Régime*, 235.

16. Tocqueville, *The Ancien Régime*, 236.

17. Tocqueville, *The Ancien Régime*, 237.

18. Tocqueville, *The European Revolution & Correspondence with Gobineau* (New York: Doubleday Anchor, 1959), 170 (hereafter cited as *The European Revolution*).

19. Tocqueville, *The European Revolution*, 170. Tocqueville adds, "Man has been created by God (I do not know why) in such a way that the larger the object of his love the less directly attached he is to it. His heart needs particular passions; he needs limited objects for his affections to keep these firm and enduring. There are but few who will burn with ardent love for the entire human species," 169.

20. See Stéphane Dion, "La conciliation du libéralisme et du nationalisme chez Tocqueville," *La Revue Tocqueville/The Tocqueville Review* 14, no. 1 (1995).

21. Mitchell, *The Fragility of Freedom*, 206.

22. Rousseau, *Émile*, 313.

23. Rousseau, *Geneva Manuscript*, 160.

24. Constant explains the argument (paraphrasing the word of a friend he identifies as M. Degerando): "Particular ties rather than weakening the general tie, strengthen it. In the gradation of sentiments and ideas, we care first for our family, then for our town, for the

province, and finally for the state. If you break the intermediate links, you will not shorten the chain, you will destroy it." See Constant, *Political Writings*, 255.

25. Michael Walzer explains why this might occur. "There is considerable evidence . . . that people active in their churches are readily recruited for political action. By contrast, individuals who are privately absorbed are likely to be inactive both in their particularist communities and in the larger community." See Walzer, *What It Means to Be an American*, 11.

26. Walzer writes, "The stronger the particularist identities of men and women are, the stronger their citizenship must be. For then, though individuals will be divided ('hyphenated'), the nation of nationalities, the social union of social unions, will be held together. I am inclined to think this is a good response to those advocates of multiculturalism who are really local nationalists, less interested in the negotiation of difference than in the aggrandizement of their particular group." Waltzer, *What It Means to Be an American*, 10–11.

27. Tocqueville, *Democracy in America*, 88.

28. Tocqueville writes, "Certain interests, such as the enactment of general laws and the nation's relations with foreigners, are common to all parts of the nation. There are other interests of special concern to certain parts of the nation, such, for instance, as local enterprises. To concentrate all the former in the same place or under the same directing power is to establish what I call governmental centralization. To concentrate control of the latter in the same way is to establish what I call administrative centralization." Tocqueville, *Democracy in America*, 87.

29. Tocqueville, *Democracy in America*, 87.

30. Robert P. Kraynak, "Tocqueville's Constitutionalism," *American Political Science Review* 81, no. 4 (December 1987): 1193.

31. Tocqueville, *The European Revolution*, 68.

32. See Delba Winthrop, "Rights: A Point of Honor," in *Interpreting Tocqueville's Democracy in America*, 406.

33. Here, Tocqueville refers specifically to participation in local government. For purposes of this chapter, I have assumed local government to fall within the sphere of civil society and have discussed it as a form of particular association. One could certainly debate the advantages and disadvantages of thinking about local government in this way. I have followed Tocqueville in describing local government as a kind of particular association. Others might view it as a manifestation of popular sovereignty and, therefore, a locus for the general will.

34. Manent, *Tocqueville and the Nature of Democracy*, 25.

35. Yael Tamir, "Revisiting the Civic Sphere," in *Freedom of Association*, ed. Amy Gutmann (Princeton, N.J.: Princeton University Press, 1998), 215.

36. See Nancy Rosenblum, *Membership and Morals: The Personal Uses of Pluralism in America* (Princeton, N.J.: Princeton University Press, 1998).

37. Daniel A. Bell, "Civil Society versus Civic Virtue," in *Freedom of Association*, 240–41.

38. Tocqueville also writes, "One must understand that unlimited political freedom of association is of all forms of liberty the last which a people can sustain. If it does not topple them over into anarchy, it brings them continually to the brink thereof. For these reasons I certainly do not think that a nation is always in a position to allow its citizens an absolute right of political association." Tocqueville, *Democracy in America*, 524.

39. Walzer, *What It Means to Be an American*, 11.

Chapter 8

Conclusion:
Citizenship as the General Will

Rousseau insists that it is citizens and not men who make the general will. This is one way Rousseau conveys the fundamental paradox of egalitarian politics — that sovereign power must be both popular and rational. Institutional and procedural approaches to political theory appeal to pre-political sources of authority in order to justify a particular set of constraints on popular will. Of course, actually sovereign citizens may or may not adopt particular institutions or procedures designed to rationalize or constrain popular will. Moreover, in democratic societies "politics always trumps principle,"[1] in the sense that the people will be the ultimate source of authority. They will choose the ways in which they constrain their own deliberations, which is a way of saying that their deliberations are essentially unconstrained.

Given this circumstance, Rousseau makes politics, first and foremost, about the creation of citizens who "appreciate the healthy maxims of politics."[2] There is, of course, a sense in which this pushes the same problem back one step, for we must immediately ask who or what will determine the "healthy maxims of politics." I have argued that the fundamental political lesson of Rousseau's political theory lies not in the answer it gives to this question but in the fact that it makes this ambiguity central. Rather than push aside the question of citizenship by reducing it to a status, Rousseau recognizes that civic-minded citizens provide the only reliable safeguards against tyranny. Correspondingly, he forces himself to imagine the ways in which popular will might be rationalized, consistent with a respect for the dignity of individuals.

When citizenship is conceptualized as a status and politics is understood in formal or procedural terms, certain difficulties arise. Appeals must be made to sources of authority that stand above or outside the deliberation of an actually existing sovereign body. Even if these trumps on popular will could be made theoretically consistent with the principle of popular sovereignty, they cannot empirically prevent a sovereign body from dispensing with them. Purely formal or

167

procedural approaches to political theory try to escape the inescapable—namely, the fact that egalitarian societies require a set of abstract principles of justice and legitimacy with which they can never be entirely secure. Formal or procedural constraints on popular will cannot be grounded in anything other than popular will. This paradox need not be the end of discussion; on the contrary, Rousseauean republicanism originates with this paradox.

As I have repeated throughout the book, whatever one's abstract principles of justice or legitimacy, one will want to consider the social and cultural prerequisites to the flourishing of those principles. It is also the case that abstract principles of justice and legitimacy must emerge from the underlying social and cultural character of a given society. These principles must surely be subjected to philosophical scrutiny, however, political theory cannot be only about the philosophical justification of a set of principles. It must also be about the viability of those principles. This, I believe, is the fundamental methodological difference between republicanism and formal or procedural theories like political liberalism and deliberative democracy. Think, for example, of liberal and republican arguments on behalf of rights. Where liberals will justify rights on noncontingent, ahistorical grounds, republicans will typically understand them as instruments for securing the goals of a given society at a given place and time.

Anti-republicans often argue that the republican approach imperils freedom by tying abstract questions of justice and legitimacy to the vagaries of political deliberation. This criticism ought not be denied. However, one must also consider the ways in which freedom can be imperiled when abstract principles of justice and legitimacy are declared antecedent to political deliberation. We might, in addition, repeat the brutal empirical fact that it is ultimately democratic majorities that will choose whether or not to embrace a set of abstract principles. Once we acknowledge these points, we will want to think about citizenship. Institutional approaches can accomplish a lot, but they cannot substitute for an emphasis on the values, character, and virtues of citizens. As I noted in the introduction, this approach to citizenship has undergone something of a revival in recent years. In concluding my argument, I want to emphasize ways in which citizenship understood via the general will should be appealing to those interested in the contemporary revival of citizenship.

Augustin Cochin attributes the French Revolution's slide into terror to the revolutionaries' eagerness "to cause rather than to defend."[3] In the aftermath of Robespierre and Napoleon (as in the aftermath of Hitler and Stalin), it is not difficult to surmise the reasons for the appeal of an institutional approach to politics and a repudiation of the republican ideal of citizenship. We must not underestimate the risks involved in a revival of citizenship, nor should we jettison institutional constraints on the abuse of public power. Republicans must find a way to "avoid zealotry without succumbing to stasis," in the words of Benjamin Barber. "It must show itself capable of working even when its users fail to follow directions properly."[4]

The ability to contain bad rulers has been the strength of liberal theory. It focuses not on cultivating the best society, but instead, on avoiding the worst one. The idea of an expansive tutelary apparatus designed to foster high citizenship must succumb to liberal fears of an overweening state. Yet, one cannot worry only about state power. William Galston writes, "A government too weak to threaten our liberties may by that very fact be too weak to secure our rights, let alone advance our shared purposes. Conversely, a government strong enough to be effective may be difficult if not impossible to control."[5] Indeed, liberals like Galston now acknowledge that while public power must be limited, it ought not be so limited that it cannot promote the virtues necessary to the practice of citizenship.

How can the advantages of liberal constraints on public power be accepted without undermining society's ability to resist nonpublic threats to personal freedom? This is the fundamental question for which modern-day republicanism seeks an answer. No entirely satisfying answer to this question will be possible, since resisting the abuse of power itself requires concentrations of power and these concentrations of power might also be abused. Containing public power has its advantages, but it risks allowing forces of oppression to run free in civil society. Empowering public institutions, on the other hand, risks oppression by an intrusive state in the name of cultivating virtue and securing the common good. Republicans must carve out a space between perfectionism and proceduralism wherein civic virtue can be encouraged without coercion. Rousseau believed that this challenge could be met by a general will that emerged from the will of every citizen. If the public endorsement of a conception of citizenship reflected the voice of the entire community, voluntarism and virtue could be reconciled. Of course, the model will always be imperfect because there will never be unanimity within the community, but it does, at least, demonstrate the theoretical compatibility of republican citizenship and individual autonomy.

Republicanism also suggests a deeper understanding of individual autonomy, one that moves beyond noninterference or voluntarism, beyond the notion that autonomy entails doing as one wishes without external constraint. Autonomy, understood in this voluntarist sense, can generate self-defeating patterns of behavior that ultimately undermine true autonomy or freedom. The doctrine of unfettered individual choice has shown itself to be quite compatible with the actual surrender of important choices to large bureaucracies and economic and technological forces.[6] While the individual's rights, property, and privacy are secured, justice and self-rule are often sacrificed. Judith Shklar advances one overriding aim for her "liberalism of fear": "to secure the political conditions that are necessary for the exercise of personal freedom."[7] The republican will not disagree; however, she will emphasize the threats to personal freedom that emerge in civil society—threats that liberal institutions may not have the power to challenge. Securing the conditions for personal freedom cannot be accomplished without attending to both the state and civil society.

Though proceduralism has historically been an ally of the left, suspicions continue to grow that proceduralism has allowed democratic power to be displaced by market forces, consumerist culture, and political tribalism. As John Dryzek writes, "Liberal democracy requires public-spirited *homo civicus* as well as narrowly selfish *homo economicus,* and to the extent the former is displaced by the latter, politics in liberal democratic societies becomes increasingly problematic."[8] These contemporary assaults on democratic power undermine individual freedom in ways poorly captured by the standard liberal understanding of autonomy. Jürgen Habermas describes a process by which "economic imperatives have gradually become independent of all else, and . . . politics has gradually become a matter of administration."[9] Ronald Beiner attacks consumerism for the way it "thoroughly privatizes individuals and renders them incapable of experiencing anything genuinely public."[10] Eammon Callan asks us to imagine a wealthy and peaceful society, with rights to participation, freedom of expression, equal protection, and so on, but within which almost no one votes, the political parties are controlled by essentially the same elites, citizens shun contact with anyone different from themselves and want only to satisfy their desires, or else they commit themselves so rigidly to a particular doctrine that dialogue with those who are not like-minded is thought to be repellent or futile.[11] There is something inaccurate about describing individuals as autonomous in any of these cases. As Michael Sandel puts it, "we can have all of our needs met and still be a nation of slaves."[12]

For individuals to be truly autonomous, they can no more be subjected to sources of oppression originating in civil society than they can be subjected to coercion by the state. Moreover, it makes as much sense to say that democracy is the prerequisite to autonomy as it does to claim that autonomy is the natural condition of humankind. Both noninterference and self-rule capture aspects of autonomy. In Rousseauean terms, free individuals are those who live under laws that they have given themselves. For Rousseau, autonomy is not only something given but also something attained, when conditions are structured such that the general will becomes sovereign. For men who have entered society, full autonomy is only possible once the conditions for democratic rule have been established.

T. H. Green captures the point: "Thus, though of course there can be no freedom among men who act not willingly but under compulsion, yet on the other hand the mere removal of compulsion, the mere enabling a man to do as he likes, is in itself no contribution to true freedom."[13] Rousseau connects citizenship to freedom, because, unless citizens take an active part in law making, they cannot be considered free. In addition, unless they are willing to subordinate their private interest to their civic interest, to stand in solidarity with their fellow citizens, and to defend the common liberty, they will be free in name only. Republicanism strives to cultivate these qualities in citizens without compromising personal liberty.

Proceduralists generally avoid the question of the character of citizens, which effectively reduces citizenship to a status.[14] This account of citizenship, while necessary, is far from sufficient, regardless of one's abstract principles of justice and legitimacy. Whatever the content of these principles, there will always be a gap between the principles themselves and the fidelity of the citizenry to those principles. This is a gap that must either be borne reluctantly or addressed through the formation of citizens. The "formative project," as Michael Sandel calls it, stands in tension with personal liberty but is also necessary for it.

Of course, politicizing the values, beliefs, and virtues of citizens carries substantial risks. The Jacobins repudiated passive citizenship in favor of the formative project, but they demonstrated much more clearly how that project undermines freedom than how it supports it. Rousseau and Tocqueville, on the other hand, provide resources for thinking about the ways in which citizenship and personal liberty are interdependent. There is, for example, a love of common liberty and feeling of solidarity, which we might call patriotism or civic consciousness. It risks pathologies like nativism or xenophobia, but, as Charles Taylor writes, "whatever the malign effects of patriotism, the benign ones have been essential to the maintenance of liberal democracy."[15] When the anti-civic forces of the market and *homo economicus* are undermining public life, patriotism can be the impulse for a recuperation of self-rule. We might think also of association, which, as we saw in chapter 7, offers citizens both the opportunity to control their own destinies and the power to safeguard their rights. It should also be possible to outline an approach to civic education that encourages students to take an interest in public affairs without undermining their progress toward self-definition.[16] Finally, one might support policy changes such as campaign finance reform, which transfer power from the hands of corporate and bureaucratic elites to the democratic public.

All of this must occur within a society far too diverse to approximate the general will, as Rousseau envisioned it. Rousseau's political philosophy grows out of, and depends upon, the assumption that, in any political community, there will be a set of shared interests that makes up the substance of the general will. As we saw in chapter 2, Rousseau posits this early on in *The Social Contract*. On Rousseau's account, without a set of shared interests, politics can never produce even a minimum of freedom. Moreover, unless these shared interests run deep, political freedom will never be more than minimal. However, if we focus less on Rousseau's austere prerequisites to the sovereignty of the general will and more on the basic tensions it embodies and the strategies it suggests, we can find resources for dealing with many of the challenges we face. Citizenship will unlikely become the primary identity in modern times, as it was (perhaps) for the ancients. However, it might become something more than a status, without requiring the total alienation of oneself to the whole. Even for Rousseau, the general will did not require a transformation of identity; rather, it embodied the self-defined interest that individuals have qua citizens as opposed to the private interest they have qua men. Though Rousseau hoped that this will would become entirely hegemonic, we need not take this step in order to recognize the importance of attending to the public interest. Citizenship requires occasional sacrifices, but, for the most part, it demands only that citizens work to secure their public interest as well as their private one.

Contemporary diversity precludes the kind of republicanism that insists that citizenship be the dominant identity for all members of society; it does not preclude the possibility of conceptualizing citizenship as something more than a status. Citizenship can be understood as a practice while remaining consistent with pluralism; similarly, citizenship can be understood as a shared identity, consistent with a respect for pluralism. Indeed, the circumstance of pluralism may actually contribute to the need for a common identity that can generate bonds of solidarity between otherwise sectarian groups and individuals. The real issue is not whether republicanism is "hostile to cultural pluralism," as Richard Dagger writes, "but at what point the centrifugal tendency of pluralism ceases to add a healthy measure of diversity and begins to pull the polity apart."[17] Pluralism poses a challenge to a revival of citizenship, but it also contributes to its necessity. Moreover, without a common identity to pull people together, the problem of exclusion becomes incoherent. Unless there exists some common culture, some general will, there will be nothing to which previously excluded individuals might gain entry.[18]

Neither should we valorize pluralism in a way that allows it to trump the claims of citizenship in all cases. Michael Lind has shown how America's valorization of pluralism has allowed questions of social justice to go unaddressed.[19] Diversity must be acknowledged, but societies also need some way to find commonality in the midst of diversity. Without this commonality, it becomes that much less likely that citizens will be disposed to take an interest in the welfare of those to whom they might otherwise feel no connection. Emphasizing citizenship generates this orientation toward commonality. Maurizio Viroli writes, "A good republic . . . does not need cultural or moral or religious unity; it needs another sort of unity, namely a political unity sustained by the attachment to the ideal of the republic."[20] This attachment produces a tendency among citizens to understand their particular interest via the common interest. It increases the odds that public decisions will be made more on the basis of public interests than private ones. In Rousseauean terms, it increases the likelihood that the sovereign will shall be the general will and not the will of all.

Even if our contemporary circumstances preclude the perfect realization of Rousseau's general will, his political theory can still speak to us in profound ways. Rousseau's dual commitment to voluntarism and virtue can only be satisfied under the most fortuitous of circumstances. Almost all actually existing societies will encounter this dual commitment as a paradox. Does that paradox demonstrate the incoherence of Rousseau's thought, or does it reflect the very character of politics in a modern context? Perhaps, we can answer yes on both counts. To the extent that Rousseau claims to have reconciled voluntarism and virtue or popular will and rational will, the general will does become incoherent. It is an incoherence, though, that embodies a problem that is at the very core of modern politics. Modern societies attempt to both respect popular decision making and ensure its rationality. This produces a predicament: societies require a set of constraints on popular will with which they can never feel totally secure. Rousseau accepts, even relishes, this problem. He does not attempt to elude it by positing a universal faculty of reason, as Kant does, or by appealing to the authority of natural law in the tradition of previous social contract theorists. Instead, Rousseau accepts the fact that there is an inevitable tension between voluntarism and virtue at the center of egalitarian politics. He devised the general will as a reconciliation of this tension. Unfortunately, his articulation of the general will does not produce this kind of reconciliation. Instead, Rousseau's general will illustrates the very intractability of the tension between voluntarism and virtue, and demonstrates the importance of thinking about abstract principles of justice and legitimacy in conjunction with the social and cultural prerequisites to the flourishing of those principles.

NOTES

1. Benjamin Barber, *A Passion for Democracy*, 167.
2. Rousseau, *The Social Contract*, 69.
3. Augustin Cochin, *L'Esprit du Jacobinisme*, 12.
4. Barber, *A Passion for Democracy*, 38–37.
5. William A. Galston, *Liberal Purposes*, 12.
6. For analysis of this kind see John S. Dryzek, *Democracy in Capitalist Times: Ideals Limits, and Struggles* (New York: Oxford University Press, 1996); Barber, *Jihad vs McWorld: How Globalism and Tribalism Are Reshaping the World* (New York: Ballantine, 1995); and Ronald Beiner, *What's the Matter with Liberalism?* (Berkeley and Los Angeles: University of California Press, 1992).
7. Judith Shklar, "The Liberalism of Fear," in *Liberalism and the Moral Life*, ed. Nancy L. Rosenblum (Cambridge, Mass.: Harvard University Press, 1989), 21.
8. Dryzek, *Democracy in Capitalist Times*, 13.
9. Habermas, "Citizenship and National Identity: Some Reflections on the Future of Europe," in *Theorizing Citizenship*, ed. Robert Beiner (Albany, N.Y.: SUNY Press, 1995), 267.
10. Beiner, *What's the Matter with Liberalism?*, 126.
11. Callan, *Creating Citizens*, 2–3.
12. Sandel, *Democracy's Discontent: America in Search of a Public Philosophy* (Cambridge, Mass.: Harvard University Press, 1996), 214.
13. Thomas Hill Green, "Lecture on Liberal Legislation and Freedom of Contract," in *Works of Thomas Hill Green*, ed. R. L. Nettleship (London: Longmans, Green and Co., 1891), 3:371.
14. The pervasiveness of this view of citizenship is evidenced by the Oxford English Dictionary's definition of it as "the position or status of being a citizen, with its rights and privileges," *Oxford English Dictionary*, 2d ed., s.v. "citizenship."
15. Charles Taylor, "Cross-Purposes: The Liberal-Communitarian Debate," in *Liberalism and the Moral Life*, ed. Nancy L. Rosenblum (Cambridge, Mass.: Harvard University

Press, 1989), 175. For a similar view of patriotism, see David Miller, *On Nationality* (Oxford, U.K.: Clarendon, 1995); Maurizio Viroli, *For Love of Country: An Essay on Patriotism and Nationalism* (Oxford, U.K.: Clarendon, 1995); Herbert Croly, *The Promise of American Life* (Cambridge, Mass.: Harvard University Press, 1965); John Stuart Mill, "Coleridge," in *Utilitarianism and Other Essays*, ed. Alan Ryan (London: Penguin, 1987); and John Schaar, *Legitimacy in the Modern State* (New Brunswick, N.J.: Transaction, 1981).

16. See, for example, Morris Janowitz, *The Reconstruction of Patriotism: Education for Civic Consciousness* (Chicago: University of Chicago Press, 1983); Miller, *On Nationality*; and Galston, "Civic Education in the Liberal State."

17. Dagger, *Civic Virtues*, 181.

18. Ronald Beiner, "Why Citizenship Constitutes a Theoretical Problem in the Last Decade of the Twentieth Century," 10.

19. Michael Lind, *The Next American Nation* (New York: Simon & Schuster, 1995).

20. Viroli, *For Love of Country: An Essay on Patriotism and Nationalism*, 13.

Bibliography

Abensour, Miguel. "La Philosophie Politique de Saint-Just." *Annales Historiques de la Révolution Française* 23 (January–March 1951): 1–32.

Ackerman, Bruce. *Social Justice in the Liberal State*. New Haven, Conn.: Yale University Press, 1980.

Affeldt, Steven G. "The Force of Freedom: Rousseau on Forcing to Be Free." *Political Theory* 27 (June 1999): 299–333.

Allen, Glen O. "*Le Volonté de tous and le volonté général:* A Distinction and Its Significance." *Ethics* 71 (July 1961): 263–75.

Ankersmit, Franklin Rudolf. "Tocqueville and the Sublimity of Democracy, Part I: Content." *The Tocqueville Review* 14 (1993): 173–200.

——. "Tocqueville and the Sublimity of Democracy, Part II: Form." *The Tocqueville Review* 15 (1944): 193–217.

Arendt, Hannah. *On Revolution*. London: Penguin, 1965.

Aulard, Alphonse. *Les Orateurs de la révolution, la Législative et la Convention*. 2 vols. Paris: E. Cornely, 1906–07.

Baczko, Bronislaw. *Rousseau: Solitude et Communauté*. Paris: Mouton, 1974.

——. *Lumières et L'Utopie*. Paris: Payot, 1978.

——. "Le contrat social des français: Sieyès et Rousseau." In *The French Revolution and the Creation of Modern Political Culture*, vol.1 *of The Political Culture of the Old Regime*. Edited by Keith Michael Baker. Oxford, U.K.: Pergamon Press, 1987.

Bader, Veit. "Citizenship and Exclusion: Radical Democracy, Community, and Justice. Or, What Is Wrong with Communitarianism?" *Political Theory* 23 (May 1995): 211–45.

Baker, Keith Michael. *Inventing the French Revolution*. London: Cambridge University Press, 1975.

——. *Condorcet: From Natural Philosophy to Social Mathematics*. Chicago: University of Chicago Press, 1975.

——. *The French Revolution and the Creation of Modern Political Culture*. New York: Pergamon Press, 1994.

——, ed. "Representation." In *The French Revolution and the Creation of Modern Political Culture*, vol. 1 of *The Political Culture of the Old Regime*. Oxford, U.K.: Pergamon Press, 1987.

Banfield, Edward C. "The Illiberal Tocqueville." In *Interpreting Tocqueville's* Democracy in America. Edited by Ken Masugi. Lanham, Md.: Rowman & Littlefield, 1991.

Barante, Prosper de. *La vie politique de M. Royer-Collard: ses discours et ses écrits.* 2 vols. Paris: Didier, 1861.

Barber, Benjamin. *Superman and Common Men.* New York: Praeger, 1971.

——. "Rousseau and the Paradoxes of the Dramatic Imagination." *Daedalus* 107 (Summer 1978): 79–92.

——. *Strong Democracy: Participatory Politics for a New Age.* Berkeley: University of California Press, 1984.

——. *Jihad vs McWorld: How Globalism and Tribalism are Reshaping the World.* New York: Ballantine, 1995.

——. *A Passion for Democracy.* Princeton, N.J.: Princeton University, 1998.

Barère, Bertrand. *Memoirs of Bertrand Barère.* London: H. S. Nichols, 1896.

Barny, Roger. *Les Contradictions de l'Idéologie Révolutionnaire des Droits de l'Homme.* Annales Littéraires de l'Université de Besançon. Paris: Diffusion les Belles Lettres, 1993.

——. *Le Droit Naturel à l'Épreuve de l'Histoire.* Annales Littéraires de l'Université de Besançon. Paris: Diffusion les Belles Lettres, 1995.

Barry, Brian. "The Public Interest." In *Political Philosophy.* Edited by Anthony Quinton. London: Oxford University Press, 1967.

——. *Justice as Impartiality.* Oxford, U.K.: Clarendon, 1995.

Barth, Hans. "Volonté générale et volonté particulière chez J. J. Rousseau." In *Rousseau et la Philosophie Politique.* Paris: Presses Universitaires de France, 1965.

Bastid, Paul. *Benjamin Constant et sa doctrine.* Paris: A. Colin, 1966.

——. *Sieyès et sa pensée.* Paris: Hachette, 1970.

Baynes, Kenneth. *The Normative Grounds of Social Criticism: Kant, Rawls, and Habermas.* Albany, N.Y.: SUNY Press, 1992.

Beiner, Ronald. *What's the Matter with Liberalism?* Berkeley: University of California Press, 1992.

——. "Machiavelli, Hobbes, and Rousseau on Civil Religion." *The Review of Politics* 55 (Fall 1993): 617–38.

——. "Why Citizenship Constitutes a Theoretical Problem in the Last Decade of the Twentieth Century." In *Theorizing Citizenship.* Edited by Ronald Beiner. Albany, N.Y.: SUNY Press, 1995.

Bell, Daniel A. "Civil Society versus Civic Virtue." In *Freedom of Association.* Edited by Amy Gutmann. Princeton, N.J.: Princeton University Press, 1998.

Bellah, Robert. *Habits of the Heart: Individualism and Commitment in American Life.* Berkeley: University of California Press, 1985.

Benhabib, Seyla. *Situating the Self.* New York: Routledge, 1992.

——. "Deliberative Rationality and Models of Democratic Legitimacy." *Constellations* 1 (April 1994): 26–52.

——. "The Embattled Public Sphere: Hannah Arendt, Jürgen Habermas, and Beyond." *Theoria* (December 1997): 1–24.

Berkowitz, Peter. *Virtue and the Making of Modern Liberalism.* Princeton, N.J.: Princeton University Press, 1999.

Berlin, Isaiah. "Two Concepts of Liberty." In *Four Essays on Liberty.* Oxford, U.K.: Oxford University Press, 1969.

Blankenhorn, David. "The Possibility of Civil Society." In *Seedbeds of Virtue: Sources of Competence, Character, and Citizenship in American Society*. Edited by Mary Ann Glendon and David Blankenhorn. Lanham, Md.: Madison Books, 1995.

Bloom, Allan. Introduction to *Émile or On Education*. New York: Basic, 1979.

———. "Jean-Jacques Rousseau." In *History of Political Philosophy*. Edited by Leo Strauss and Joseph Cropsey. Chicago: University of Chicago Press, 1987.

———. "The Education of Democratic Man." In *Jean-Jacques Rousseau*. Edited by Harold Bloom. New York: Chelsea House, 1988.

Blum, Carol. *Rousseau and the Republic of Virtue*. Ithaca, N.Y.: Cornell University Press, 1986.

Bohman, James. "Survey Article: The Coming of Age of Deliberative Democracy." *The Journal of Political Philosophy* 6 (1998): 400–25.

Bonald, Louis de. *Oeuvres complètes*. Paris: L. Migne, 1859.

Bonaparte, Napoleon. *Letters of Napoleon*. Edited and translated by J. M. Thompson. Oxford, U.K.: Basil Blackwell, 1934.

Bourricaud, François. "The Rights of the Individual and the General Will in Revolutionary Thought." In *Liberty/Liberté: The American and French Experiences*. Edited by Joseph Klaits and Michael H. Haltzel. Washington, D.C.: Woodrow Wilson Center Press, 1991.

Brint, M. E. "Jean-Jacques Rousseau and Benjamin Constant: A Dialogue on Freedom and Tyranny." *The Review of Politics* 47 (July 1985): 323–46.

Brinton, Crane. *A Decade of Revolution: 1789–1799*. New York: Harper and Row, 1934.

———. *The Jacobins: An Essay in the New History*. New York: Russell & Russell, 1961.

Burke, Edmund. *Reflections on the Revolution in France*. Indianapolis: Hackett, 1987.

Callan, Eamonn. *Creating Citizens: Political Education and Liberal Democracy*. Oxford, U.K.: Clarendon, 1997.

Cassirer, Ernst. *The Question of Jean-Jacques Rousseau*. Bloomington: Indiana University Press, 1963.

Chambers, Simone. "Discourse and Democratic Practices." In *The Cambridge Companion to Habermas*. Edited by Steven K. White. New York: Cambridge University Press, 1995.

Champion, Edmé. *J. J. Rousseau et la Révolution française*. Paris: A. Colin, 1909.

Charney, Evan. "Political Liberalism, Deliberative Democracy, and the Public Sphere." *American Political Science Review* 92 (March 1998): 97–110.

Charvet, John. "Individual Identity and Social Consciousness in Rousseau's Philosophy." In *Hobbes and Rousseau*. Edited by Maurice Cranston and Richard S. Peters. Garden City, N.J.: Anchor, 1972.

———. *The Social Problem in the Philosophy of Rousseau*. London: Cambridge University Press, 1974.

———. "Rousseau, the Problem of Sovereignty and the Limits of Political Obligation." In *Rousseau and Liberty*. Edited by Robert Wokler. Manchester, U.K.: Manchester University Press, 1995.

Chateaubriand, François-René de. 1961. *The Memoirs of Chateaubriand*. Translated by Robert Baldick. New York: Knopf, 1961.

Chevallier, Jean-Jacques. *Histoire des Idées Politiques*. Paris: Université de Paris, Institut d'Études Politiques, 1964.

Cladis, Mark S. "Lessons from the Garden: Rousseau's Solitaires and the Limits of Liberalism." *Interpretation* 24 (Winter 1997): 183–200.

Cobban, Alfred, *Rousseau and the Modern State*. Hamden, Conn.: Archon Books, 1961.
———. *Aspects of the French Revolution*. New York: George Braziller, 1968.
———. *The Social Interpretation of the French Revolution*. London: Cambridge University Press, 1968.
Cochin, Augustin. *L'Esprit du Jacobinisme: Une Interpretation Sociologique de la Révolution Française*. Paris: Presses Universitaires de France, 1979.
Cohen, Joshua. *Associations and Democracy*. London: Cambridge University Press, 1968.
———. "Reflections on Rousseau: Autonomy and Democracy." *Philosophy and Public Affairs* 15 (Summer 1968): 275–97.
Cohen, Paul. *Freedom's Moment*. Chicago: University of Chicago Press, 1997.
Condorcet, Jean-Antoine-Nicolas de Caritat. *Reflections on the English Revolution of 1688, and That of the French, August 19, 1792*. London: J. Ridgway, 1792.
———. *Condorcet: Selected Writings*. Indianapolis: Bobbs-Merrill, 1976.
Constant, Benjamin. *Cours de Politique Constitutionnelle*. 2 vols. Paris: Librairie de Guillaumin, 1872.
———. *Oeuvres*. Paris: Librairie Gallimard, 1957.
———. *Political Writings*. New York: Cambridge University Press, 1988.
———. "Principles of Politics Applicable to All Representative Governments," "The Spirit of Conquest and Usurpation and their Relation to European Civilization," and "The Liberty of the Ancients Compared with That of the Moderns." In *Benjamin Constant: Political Writings*. Edited by Biancamaria Fontana. New York: Cambridge University Press, 1988.
Cooper, Laurence. *Rousseau, Nature, and the Problem of the Good Life*. University Park, Penn.: Pennsylvania State University Press, 1999.
Cranston, Maurice. "Rousseau's Theory of Liberty." In *Rousseau and Liberty*. Edited by Robert Wokler. Manchester, U.K.: Manchester University Press, 1995.
Crocker, Lester. "Rousseau et la voie du totalitarisme." In vol. 5 of *Annales de Philosophie Politique*. Paris: Presses Universitaires de France, 1965.
———. "Rousseau's *soi-disant* Liberty." In *Rousseau and Liberty*. Edited by Robert Wokler. Manchester, U.K.: Manchester University Press, 1995.
Croly, Herbert. *The Promise of American Life*. Cambridge, Mass.: Harvard University Press, 1965.
Dagger, Richard. *Civic Virtues: Rights, Citizenship, and Republican Liberalism*. New York: Oxford University Press, 1997.
Dahl, Robert. "The City in the Future of Democracy." *American Political Science Review* 61 (December 1967): 953–70.
Danton, Georges Jacques. *Speeches of Georges Jacques Danton*. New York: International Publishers, 1928.
Darnton, Robert. *The Great Cat Massacre and Other Episodes in French Cultural History*. New York: Vintage, 1985.
David, Marcel. *Fraternité et la Révolution française*. Paris: Aubier, 1987.
Derathé, Robert. *Jean-Jacques Rousseau et la science politique de son temps*. Paris: J. Vrin, 1970.
———. *Le rationalisme de Jean-Jacques Rousseau*. Geneva: Slatkine Reprints, 1979.
———. "Les Réfutations du *Contrat social* en France dans la première moitié du dix-neuvième siècle." In *Reappraisals of Rousseau: Studies in Honour of R. A. Leigh*. Edited

by Simon Harvey, Marian Hobson, David Kelley, and Samuel S. B. Taylor. Manchester, U.K.: Manchester University Press, 1980.

Derrida, Jacques. *Of Grammatology*. Baltimore, Md.: Johns Hopkins University Press, 1976.

Diderot, Denis. *Political Writings*. New York: Cambridge University Press, 1992.

Dion, Stéphane. "La conciliation du libéralisme et du nationalisme chez Tocqueville." *The Tocqueville Review* 16 (1995): 219–27.

"Declaration of the Rights of Man and Citizen, 27 August, 1789." *A Documentary Survey of the French Revolution* ed., New York: Macmillan, 1951.

Dodge, Guy. *Benjamin Constant's Philosophy of Liberalism*. Chapel Hill, N.C.: The University of North Carolina Press, 1980.

Donohue, William A. "Tocqueville's Reflections on Safeguarding Freedom in a Democracy." *The Tocqueville Review* 6 (1984): 389–97.

Drescher, Seymour. *Tocqueville and England*. Cambridge, Mass.: Harvard University Press, 1964.

———. *Dilemmas of Democracy: Tocqueville and Modernization*. Pittsburgh: University of Pittsburgh Press, 1968.

Dryzek, John S. *Discursive Democracy: Politics, Policy, and Political Science*. New York: Cambridge University Press, 1990.

———. *Democracy in Capitalist Times: Ideals Limits, and Struggles*. New York: Oxford University Press, 1996.

Duguit, Leon. "The Law and the State." *Harvard Law Review* 31 (November 1917): 1–185.

Dworkin, Ronald. *Taking Rights Seriously*. London: Gerald Duckworth, 1977.

———. Liberalism." In *Public and Private Morality*. Edited by Stuart Hampshire. London: Cambridge University Press, 1978.

———. "Foundations of Liberal Equality." *Tanner Lectures on Human Values* 11:3–119. Salt Lake City: University of Utah Press, 1990.

Ellenburg, Stephen. *Rousseau's Political Philosophy: An Interpretation from Within*. Ithaca, N.Y.: Cornell University Press, 1976.

Elshtain, Jean. *Democracy on Trial*. New York: Basic, 1995.

Elster, Jon. *Political Psychology*. New York: Cambridge University Press, 1993.

———. Introduction to *Deliberative Democracy*. Edited by Jon Elster. New York: Cambridge University Press, 1998.

Fehér, Ferenc. *The Frozen Revolution: An Essay on Jacobinism*. New York: Cambridge University Press, 1987.

Fermon, Nicole. "The Female Fulcrum: Rousseau and the Birth of Nationalism." *The Philosophical Forum* 28 (Fall–Winter, 1996–97): 21–41.

Ferry, Luc, and Alain Renaut. *Philosophie politique, Des droits de l'homme a l'idée républicaine*, in vol. 3 of *Philosophie Politique*. Paris: Presses Universitaires de France, 1985.

Fetscher, Irving. "Rousseau, auteur d'intention conservatrice et d'action révolutionnaire," in vol. 5 of *Annales de Philosophie Politique*. Paris: Presses Universitaires de France, 1965.

Fishkin, James S. *Democracy and Deliberation: New Directions for Democratic Reform*. New Haven, Conn.: Yale University Press, 1991.

Fontana, Biancamaria. *Benjamin Constant and the Post-Revolutionary Mind*. New Haven, Conn.: Yale University Press, 1991.

Forsyth, Murray. *Reason and Revolution: The Political Thought of the Abbé Sieyès.* New York: Holmes & Meier, 1987.

Friedlander, Eli. "Chambery, 12 June 1754: Rousseau's Writing on Inequality." *Political Theory* 28 (April 2000): 254–72.

Friedrich, Carl. "Law and Dictatorship in the *Contrat Social.*" In vol. 5 of *Annales de Philosophie Politique*. Paris: Presses Universitaires de France, 1965.

Furet, François. *Interpreting the French Revolution.* London: Cambridge University Press, 1981.

———. *Revolutionary France, 1770–1880.* Cambridge, U.K.: Basil Blackwell, 1995.

———. "Rousseau and the French Revolution." In *The Legacy of Rousseau*. Edited by Clifford Orwin and Nathan Tarcov. Chicago: University of Chicago Press, 1997.

Furet, François, and Ran Halévi, eds. Vol. 1 of *Orateurs de la Révolution française*. Paris: Gallimard, 1989.

Furet, François, and Mona Ozouf, eds. *A Critical Dictionary of the French Revolution.* Cambridge, Mass.: Harvard University Press, 1989.

———. *Le siècle de l'avènement républicain.* Paris: Gallimard, 1993.

Furet, François, and Denis Richet. *The French Revolution.* London: Weidenfeld & Nicholson, 1970.

Gagnebin, Bernard. "L'Influence de Rousseau sur la Déclaration des droits de l'homme et du citoyen." In *Reappraisals of Rousseau*. Edited by Simon Harvey, Marian Hobson, David Kelley, and Samuel S. B. Taylor. Manchester, U.K.: Manchester University Press, 1980.

Galston, William A. "Civic Education in the Liberal State." In *Liberalism and the Moral Life.* Edited by Nancy L. Rosenblum. Cambridge, Mass.: Harvard University Press, 1989.

———. "Civil Society and the 'Art of Association'." *Journal of Democracy* 11 (January 2000): 64–70.

———. *Liberal Purposes: Goods, Virtues, and Diversity in the Liberal State.* New York: Cambridge University Press, 1991.

———. "Liberal Virtues and the Formation of Civic Character." In *Seedbeds of Virtue*. Edited by Mary Ann Glendon and David Blankenhorn. Lanham, Md.: Madison Books, 1995.

———. "Diversity, Toleration, and Deliberative Democracy." In *Deliberative Politics: Essays on Democracy and Disagreement*. Edited by Stephen Macedo. New York: Oxford University Press, 1999.

Gargarella, Roberto. "Full Representation, Deliberation, and Impartiality." In *Deliberative Democracy*. Edited by Jon Elster. New York: Cambridge University Press, 1998.

Gauchet, Marcel. Preface to *De la liberté chez les modernes.* Paris: Librairie Générale Française, 1980.

———. *La révolution des pouvoirs.* Paris: Gallimard, 1995.

Gildin, Hlail. *Rousseau's Social Contract.* Chicago: University of Chicago Press, 1983.

Gordon, Dan. *Citizens without Sovereignty.* Princeton: N.J.: Princeton University Press, 1994.

Gourevitch, Victor. "Recent Work on Rousseau." *Political Theory* 26 (August 1998): 536–55.

Grant, Ruth. *Hypocrisy and Integrity.* Chicago: University of Chicago Press, 1997.

Green, Thomas Hill. *Works of Thomas Hill Green.* London: Longmans, Green, 1891.

Grimsley, Ronald. "Rousseau and the Problem of Happiness." In *Hobbes and Rousseau*. Edited by Maurice Cranston and Richard S. Peters. Garden City, N.Y.: Anchor, 1972.

————. *Jean-Jacques Rousseau*. Totowa, N.J.: Barnes & Noble Books, 1983.

Groethuysen, Bernard. *Philosophie de la Révolution française*. Paris: Gallimard, 1956.

————. *J.-J. Rousseau*. Paris: Gallimard, 1983.

Grofman, Bernard, and Scott L. Feld. "Rousseau's General Will: A Condorcetian Perspective." *American Political Science Review* 83 (June 1988): 567–76.

Gueniffey, Patrick. *Le nombre et la raison*. Paris: Éditions de l'École des hautes études en sciences sociales, 1993.

Guilhaumou, Jacques. *La langue politique et la Révolution française*. Paris: Meridiens/Klincksieck, 1989.

Guizot, François. *Democracy in France*. New York: D. Appleton & Company, 1849.

————. *The History of Civilization in Europe*. London: Penguin, 1997.

Gutmann, Amy. *Democratic Education*. Princeton, N.J.: Princeton University Press, 1999.

Gutmann, Amy and Dennis Thompson. *Democracy and Disagreement*. Cambridge, Mass.: Harvard University Press, 1996.

Habermas, Jürgen. *The Philosophical Discourse of Modernity*. Cambridge, Mass.: MIT Press, 1987.

————. "Toward a Communication-Concept of Rational Collective Will-Formation. A Thought-Experiment." *Ratio Juris* 2 (July 1989): 144–54.

————. *Moral Consciousness and Communicative Action*. Cambridge, Mass.: MIT Press, 1990.

————. "Citizenship and National Identity: Some Reflections on the Future of Europe." In *Theorizing Citizenship*. Edited by Ronald Beiner. Albany, N.Y.: SUNY Press, 1995.

————. "Reconciliation through the Public Use of Reason: Remarks on John Rawls's Political Liberalism." *The Journal of Philosophy* 92 (March 1995): 109–31.

————. *Between Facts and Norms*. Cambridge, Mass.: MIT Press, 1996.

Halevi, Ran. "La modération à l'épreuve de l'absolutisme: De l'Ancien Régime à la Révolution française." *Le Débat* 109 (March-April 2000): 73–98.

————. "L'idée et l'événement: sur les origines intellectuelles de la Révolution française." *Le débat* 38 (January–March 1986): 145–63.

Hampsher-Monk, Iain. "Rousseau and Totalitarianism—with Hindsight?" In *Rousseau and Liberty*. Edited by Robert Wokler. Manchester, U.K.: Manchester University Press, 1995.

Hampson, Norman. *The Life and Opinions of Maximilien Robespierre*. London: Gerald Duckworth, 1974.

————. *Will and Circumstance: Montesquieu, Rousseau, and the French Revolution*. London: Gerald Duckworth, 1983.

————. "The Idea of the Nation in Revolutionary France." In *Reshaping France: Town, Country and Region during the French Revolution*. Edited by Alan Forrest and Peter Jones. Manchester, U.K.: Manchester University Press, 1991.

Hegel, G. W. F. *The Philosophy of History*. New York: Dover, 1956.

————. *Philosophy of Right*. Oxford, U.K.: Oxford University Press, 1967.

————. *Hegel's Phenomenology of Spirit*. Oxford, U.K.: Oxford University Press, 1977.

Hendel, Charles William. *J. J. Rousseau, Moralist*. 2 vols. Oxford: Oxford University Press, 1934.

Hennis, Wilhelm. "In Search of the 'New Science of Politics.'" In *Interpreting Tocqueville's* Democracy in America. Edited by Ken Masugi. Lanham, Md.: Rowman & Littlefield, 1991.

————. "Tocquevilles 'neue politische wissenschaft.'" In *Aspekte der kultursoziologie*. Edited by Justin Stagl. Berlin: Reimer, 1982.

Higonnet, Patrice. *Goodness beyond Virtue: Jacobins during the French Revolution.* Cambridge, Mass.: Harvard University Press, 1998.

Hobbes, Thomas. *Leviathan.* Edited by C. B. MacPherson. London: Penguin, 1968.

Hobsbawm, Eric. *Echoes of the Marseillaise.* New Brunswick, N.J.: Rutgers University Press, 1990.

Hoffmann, Paul. "Benjamin Constant: Critique de Jean-Jacques Rousseau." *Revue d'Histoire Littéraire de la France* 82 (January–February 1982): 23–40.

Hoffmann, Stanley. "Du 'Contrat Social,' ou le Mirage de la Volonté Générale." *Revue Internationale d'Histoire Politique et Constitutionelle* (October–December 1954), 293–95.

———. *Rousseau, la guerre et la paix."* In vol. 5 of *Annales de Philosophie Politique.* Paris: Presses Universitaires de France, 1965.

Holmes, Stephen. "Two Concepts of Legitimacy: France After the Revolution." *Political Theory* 10 (May 1982): 165–83.

———. *Benjamin Constant and the Making of Modern Liberalism.* New Haven, Conn.: Yale University Press, 1984.

———. "Constant and Tocqueville: An Unexplored Relationship." *Annales Benjamin Constant* 12 (1991): 29–41.

Hont, Istvan. "The Permanent Crisis of a Divided Mankind: 'Contemporary Crisis of the Nation State' in Historical Perspective." In *The Crisis of the Nation State.* Edited by John Dunn. Oxford: Basil Blackwell Publishers, 1995.

Hulliung, Mark. *The Autocritique of Enlightenment.* Cambridge, Mass.: Harvard University Press, 1994.

Hunt, Lynn. 1984. *Politics, Culture and Class in the French Revolution.* Berkeley: University of California Press, 1984.

———. "The 'National Assembly.' " In *The French Revolution and the Creation of Modern Political Culture.* Vol. 1 of *The Political Culture of the Old Regime.* Edited by Keith Michael Baker. Oxford, U.K.: Pergamon Press, 1987.

Isaac, Jeffrey C. "Republicanism vs. Liberalism? A Reconsideration." *History of Political Thought* 9 (Summer 1998): 349–77.

Isnard, Achille Nicolas. *Observations sur le principe qui a produit les revolutions de France, de Genève et d'Amérique.* Évreux: Imprimerie de la veuve Malassis, 1789.

Jacques, Daniel. *Tocqueville et la modernité.* Montreal: Boreal, 1995.

Janowitz, Morris. *The Reconstruction of Patriotism: Education for Civic Consciousness.* Chicago: University of Chicago Press, 1983.

Jardin, André. *Histoire du Liberalisme Politique.* Paris: Hachette, 1985.

Jaume, Lucien. "Peuple et individus dans le débat Hobbes-Rousseau: d'une représentation qui n'est pas celle du peuple à un peuple qui n'est pas représentable." In *La représentation.* Edited by François d'Arcy. Paris: Économica, 1985.

———. "Citoyenneté et souveraineté: le poids de l'absolutisme." In *The French Revolution and the Creation of Modern Political Culture.* Vol. 1 of *The Political Culture of the Old Regime.* Edited by Keith Michael Baker. Oxford, U.K.: Pergamon Press, 1987.

———. *Le discours jacobin et la démocratie.* Paris: Fayard, 1989.

———. "Le Jacobinisme de Jean-Jacques Rousseau: Influence ou mode de légitimation?" In *Jean-Jacques Rousseau and the Revolution.* Edited by Jean Roy. Ottawa, Canada: North American Association for the Study of Jean-Jacques Rousseau, 1991.

Johnston, Steven. *Encountering Tragedy: Rousseau and the Project of Democratic Order.* Ithca, N.Y.: Cornell University Press, 1999.

Jones, W. T. "Rousseau's General Will and the Problem of Consent." *Journal of the History of Philosophy* 25 (January 1987): 105–30.

Jordan, David. *The Revolutionary Career of Maximilien Robespierre.* New York: Free Press, 1985.

Jouvenel, Bertrand de. Introduction to *Du Contrat Social.* Geneva: Éditions du Cheval aile, 1947.

——. "Rousseau, évolutionniste et pessimiste." In vol. 5 of *Annales de Philosophie Politique.* Paris: Presses Universitaires de France, 1965.

——. "Rousseau's Theory of the Forms of Government." In *Hobbes and Rousseau.* Edited by Maurice Cranston and Richard S. Peters. Garden City, N.Y.: Anchor, 1972.

Julliard, Jacques. *La Faute à Rousseau.* Paris: Seuil, 1985.

Kekes, John. *The Morality of Pluralism.* Princeton, N.J.: Princeton University Press, 1993.

Kelly, Christopher, " 'To Persuade without Convincing': The Language of Rousseau's Legislator." *The American Journal of Political Science* 32 (May 1997): 321–35.

——. "Rousseau and the Case for (and against) Censorship." *The Journal of Politics* 59 (November 1997):1232–51.

Kelly, Christopher and Roger Masters. "Human Nature, Liberty and Progress: Rousseau's Dialogue with the Critics of the *Discours sur l'inégalité.*" In *Rousseau and Liberty.* Edited by Robert Wokler. Manchester, U.K.: Manchester University Press, 1995.

Kelly, George Armstrong. "Liberalism and Aristocracy in the French Restoration." *Journal of the History of Ideas* 26 (October–December 1965): 509–30.

——. 1986. "Constant and His Interpreters: A Second Visit." *Annales Benjamin Constant* 6 (1986): 81–89.

——. "The Jacobin and Liberal Contributions to the Founding of the Second and Third French Republics (with an Epilogue on America)." In *Liberty/Liberté: The American and French Experiences.* Edited by Joseph Klaits and Michael H. Haltzel. Washington, D.C.: Woodrow Wilson Center Press, 1991.

——. *The Humane Comedy: Constant, Tocqueville and French Liberalism.* New York: Cambridge University Press, 1992.

Kendall, Willmoore. Introduction to *The Government of Poland.* Indianapolis: Hackett, 1985.

Keohane, Nannerl. *Philosophy and the State in France.* Princeton, N.J.: Princeton University Press, 1980.

Knee, Philip. "Religion et souveraineté du peuple: de Rousseau à Tocqueville." *Canadian Journal of Political Science* 23 (June 1990): 211–32.

Koritansky, John C. *Alexis de Tocqueville and the New Science of Politics: An Interpretation of Democracy in America.* Durham, N.C.: Carolina Academic Press, 1986.

Kraynak, Robert P. "Tocqueville's Constitutionalism." *American Political Science Review* 81 (December 1987): 1175–95.

Kymlicka, Will, and Wayne Norman. "Return of the Citizen: A Survey of Recent Work on Citizenship Theory." In *Theorizing Citizenship.* Edited by Ronald Beiner. Albany, N.Y.: SUNY Press, 1995.

Lakanal, Joseph. *Rapport sur J-J. Rousseau fait au nom du comité d'instruction publique.* Paris: De l'Imprimerie Nationale, 1794.

Lakoff, Sanford. "Liberty, Equality, Democracy: Tocqueville's Response to Rousseau." In *Lives, Liberties and the Public Good: New Essays in Political Theory for Maurice Cranston.* Edited by George Feaver. Houndmills, Basingstoke, Hampshire, U.K.: Macmillan, 1987.

Lamberti, Jean-Claude. "La liberté et les illusions individualistes selon Tocqueville." *The Tocqueville Review* 8 (1986–87): 153–64.

——. *Tocqueville and the Two Democracies.* Cambridge, Mass.: Harvard University Press, 1989.

Landes, Joan. *Women and the Public Sphere.* Ithaca, N.Y.: Cornell University Press, 1988.

Lane, Robert E. "Markets and Politics: The Human Product." *British Journal of Political Science* 2 (January 1981): 1–16.

Lawler, Peter Augustine. *The Restless Mind: Alexis de Tocqueville on the Origin and Perpetuation of Human Liberty.* Lanham, Md.: Rowman & Littlefield, 1993.

——. "Tocqueville on the Doctrine of Interest." *Government and Opposition* 30 (Spring 1995): 221–39.

Leroy, Maxime. *Histoire des Idées Sociales en France.* 3 vols. Paris: Gallimard, 1946.

Levine, Andrew. *The Politics of Autonomy: A Kantian Reading of Rousseau's Social Contract.* Amherst: University of Massachusetts Press, 1976.

——. *The General Will: Rousseau, Marx, Communism.* New York: Cambridge University Press, 1993.

Lind, Michael. *The Next American Nation.* New York: Free Press, 1995.

Lively, Jack. *The Social and Political Thought of Alexis de Tocqueville.* Oxford, U.K.: Clarendon, 1962.

MacAdam, James I. "Rousseau and the Friends of Despotism." *Ethics* 71 (October 1963): 34–43.

Macedo, Stephen. *Liberal Virtues.* Oxford, U.K.: Clarendon, 1990.

MacIntyre, Alisdair. "Is Patriotism a Virtue?" In *Theorizing Citizenship.* Edited by Ronald Beiner. Albany, N.Y.: SUNY Press, 1995.

MacPherson, C. B. *The Political Theory of Possessive Individualism.* Oxford, U.K.: Oxford University Press, 1962.

Maistre, Joseph de. *The Works of Joseph de Maistre.* New York: Schocken Books, 1971.

——. *Considérations sur la France.* Genève: Éditions Slatkine, 1980.

Manent, Pierre. *An Intellectual History of Liberalism.* Princeton, N.J.: Princeton University Press, 1994.

——. *Tocqueville and the Nature of Democracy.* Lanham, Md.: Rowman & Littlefield, 1996.

Manin, Bernard. "On Legitimacy and Political Deliberation." *Political Theory* 15 (August 1987): 338–68.

Marini, John. "Centralized Administration and the 'New Despotism.'" In *Interpreting Tocqueville's* Democracy in America. Edited by Ken Masugi. Lanham, Md.: Rowman & Littlefield, 1991.

Marshall, T. H. *Citizenship and Social Class.* London: Pluto, 1992.

Massin, Jean. *Robespierre.* Paris: Alinéa, 1988.

Masters, Roger. *The Political Philosophy of Rousseau.* Princeton, N.J.: Princeton University Press, 1968.

——. "The Structure of Rousseau's Political Thought." In *Hobbes and Rousseau.* Edited by Maurice Cranston and Richard S. Peters. Garden City, N.J. : Anchor, 1972.

——. Introduction to *On the Social Contract with Geneva Manuscript and Political Economy.* New York: St. Martin's Press, 1978.

Mayer, J. P. *Political Thought in France from the Revolution to the Fifth Republic.* London: Routledge & Paul, 1961.

Mazauric, Claude. "Les choix économiques et sociaux: Préliminaires." In *Robespierre: Dans la Nations artésienne à la République et aux Nations*. Edited by Jean-Pierre Jessenne, Gilles Deregnaucourt, Jean-Pierre Hirsch, and Hervé Leuwers. Lille: Centre d'Histoire de la Région du Nord et de l'Europe du Nord-Ouest, 1993.

McCarthy, Thomas. *Ideals and Illusions*. Cambridge, Mass.: MIT Press, 1996.

McDonald, Joan. *Rousseau and the French Revolution, 1762–1791*. London: Althone Press, 1965.

Mélonio, Françoise. *Tocqueville and the French*. Charlottesville, Va.: University Press of Virginia, 1993.

———. "Nations et Nationalismes." *The Tocqueville Review* 18 (1997): 61–75.

Melzer, Arthur. *The Natural Goodness of Man: On the System of Rousseau's Thought*. Chicago: University of Chicago Press, 1990.

———. "The Origin of the Counter-Enlightenment: Rousseau and the New Religion of Sincerity." *American Political Science Review* 90 (June 1996): 344–60.

Meynier, Albert. *Jean-Jacques Rousseau, révolutionnaire*. Paris: Schleicher, 1912.

Mill, John Stuart. "Tocqueville on Democracy in America (Vol. II)." In *Essays on Politics and Culture*. Edited by Gertrude Himmelfarb. Glouchester, Mass.: P. Smith, 1973.

———. "Coleridge." In *Utilitarianism and Other Essays*. Edited by Alan Ryan. London: Penguin, 1987.

Miller, David. "Citizenship and Pluralism." *Political Studies* 43 (September 1995): 432–50.

———. *On Nationality*. Oxford, U.K.: Clarendon Press, 1995.

———. "The Left, the Nation-State, and European Citizenship." *Dissent* (Summer 1998): 47–51.

Miller, James. *Rousseau: Dreamer of Democracy*. New Haven, Conn.: Yale University Press, 1984.

Mitchell, Joshua. *The Fragility of Freedom*. Chicago: University of Chicago Press, 1995.

Montesquieu, Charles de. *The Spirit of the Laws*. New York: Cambridge University Press, 1989.

Morgenstern, Mira. *Rousseau and the Politics of Ambiguity*. University Park: Pennsylvania State University Press, 1996.

Mornet, Daniel. *Les Origines intellectuelles de la Révolution française*. Paris: A. Colin, 1954.

Mouffe, Chantal. Preface to "Democratic Politics Today." In *Dimensions of Radical Democracy: Pluralism, Citizenship, Community*. Edited by Chantal Mouffe. London: Verso, 1992.

Nagel, Thomas. *Equality and Partiality*. Oxford, U.K.: Oxford University Press, 1991.

Nauta, Lolle. "Changing Conceptions of Citizenship." *Praxis International* 12 (1992): 20–33.

Neuhouser, Frederick. "Freedom, Dependence, and the General Will." *The Philosophical Review* 102 (July 1993): 363–95.

Nicolet, Claude. *L'idée républicaine en France*. Paris: Gallimard, 1994.

Nisbet, Robert. *Twilight of Authority*. New York: Oxford University Press, 1975.

Nussbaum, Martha, et al. "Patriotism or Cosmopolitanism." *Boston Review* 19 (October–November 1994): 3–34.

O'Donovan-Anderson, Michael. "Wittgenstein and Rousseau on the Context of Justification." *Philosophy and Social Criticism* 22 (1996): 75–92.

Oldfield, Adrian. "Citizenship: An Unnatural Practice?" *Political Quarterly* 61 (April–June 1990): 177–87.

O'Neill, Onora. "Political Liberalism and Public Reason: A Critical Notice of John Rawls' *Political Liberalism.*" *The Philosophical Review* 106 (July 1997): 411–28.

Ozouf, Mona. *Festivals and the French Revolution.* Cambridge, Mass.: Harvard University Press, 1988.

———. *L'homme régénéré.* Paris: Gallimard, 1989.

Palmer, R. R. *Twelve Who Ruled.* Princeton, N.J.: Princeton University Press, 1941.

Pangle, Thomas. *The Ennobling of Democracy: The Challenge of the Postmodern Age.* Baltimore: Johns Hopkins University Press, 1992.

Pasquino, Pasquale. "Emmanuel Sieyès, Benjamin Constant et le 'Gouvernement des Modernes.' " *Revue Française de Science Politique* 37 (April 1987): 214–29.

———. "Citoyenneté, égalité et liberté chez J.-J. Rousseau et E. Sieyès." *Cahiers Bernard Lazare* 121–22 (1988): 150–60.

———. "The Constitutional Republicanism of Emmanuel Sieyès." In *The Invention of the Modern Republic.* Edited by Biancamaria Fontana. New York: Cambridge University Press, 1994.

Pateman, Carole. *Participation and Democratic Theory.* London: Cambridge University Press, 1970.

———. *The Sexual Contract.* Stanford, Calif.: Stanford University Press, 1988.

Patterson, Orlando. 1999. "The Liberal Millenium." *The New Republic* (November 8): 55–63.

Pettit, Philip. *Republicanism: A Theory of Freedom and Government.* New York: Oxford University Press, 1997.

Plamenatz, John. *Man and Society: A Critical Examination of Some Political and Social Theories from Machiavelli to Marx.* London: Longmans, Green, 1963.

———. "Ce qui ne signifie autre chose sinon qu'on le forcera d'être libre." In *Hobbes and Rousseau.* Edited by Maurice Cranston and Richard S. Peters. Garden City, N.Y.: Anchor, 1972.

Quinet, Edgar. *La Révolution.* 2 vols. Paris: Librairie Internationale, 1869.

Rawls, John. *A Theory of Justice.* Cambridge, Mass.: Harvard University Press, 1971.

———. *Political Liberalism.* New York: Columbia University Press, 1993.

———. "Reply to Habermas." *The Journal of Philosophy* 92 (March 1995): 132–80.

———. "The Idea of Public Reason Revisited." *University of Chicago Law Review* 64 (Summer 1997): 765–807.

Raz, Joseph. *The Morality of Freedom.* Oxford, U.K. Clarendon, 1996.

Reedy, W. Jay. "The Relevance of Rousseau to Contemporary Communitarianism: The Example of Benjamin Barber." *Philosophy and Social Criticism* 21 (1995): 51–84.

Reichardt, Rolf. *Reform und Revolution bei Condorcet.* Bonn: Rohrscheid, 1973.

Reinhardt, Mark. *The Art of Being Free.* Ithaca, N.Y.: Cornell University Press, 1997.

Rémusat, Charles de. *Politique Libérale.* Paris: Librairie Nouvelle, 1875.

Richter, Melvin. "Toward a Concept of Political Illegitimacy: Bonapartist Dictatorship and Democratic Legitimacy." *Political Theory* 10 (May 1982): 185–214.

———. "Tocqueville, Napoleon, and Bonapartism." In *Reconsidering Tocqueville's Democracy in America.* Edited by Abraham S. Eisenstadt. New Brunswick, N.J.: Rutgers University Press, 1988.

———. "Rousseau and Tocqueville on Democratic Legitimacy and Illegitimacy." In *Rousseau and Liberty*. Edited by Robert Wokler. Manchester, U.K.: Manchester University Press, 1995.

Riley, Patrick. *Will and Political Legitimacy: A Critical Exposition of Social Contract Theory in Hobbes, Locke, Rousseau, Kant, and Hegel*. Cambridge, Mass.: Harvard University Press, 1982.

———. *The General Will before Rousseau*. Princeton, N.J.: Princeton University Press, 1986.

———. "Rousseau's General Will: Freedom of a Particular Kind." In *Rousseau and Liberty*. Edited by Robert Wokler. Manchester, U.K.: Manchester University Press, 1995.

Ripstein, Arthur. "Universal and General Wills, Hegel, and Rousseau." *Political Theory* 22 (August 1994): 444–67.

Robespierre, Maximilien. *Discours et Rapports*. Paris: Charpertier et Fasquelle, 1908.

———. *Oeuvres*. 10 vols. Paris: Leroux, 1910.

———. *Speeches of Maximilien Robespierre*. New York: International Publishers, 1927.

———. *Textes Choisis*. 3 vols. Paris: Éditions Sociales, 1958.

Roche, Daniel. *France in the Enlightenment*. Cambridge, Mass.: Harvard University Press, 1998.

Rosanvallon, Pierre. *Le Moment Guizot*. Paris: Gallimard, 1985.

———. *Le Sacre du Citoyen: Histoire du Suffrage Universel en France*. Paris: Gallimard, 1992.

Rosenblatt, Helena. *Rousseau and Geneva*. New York: Cambridge University Press, 1997.

Rosenblum, Nancy L. *Membership and Morals: The Personal Uses of Pluralism in America*. Princeton, N.J.: Princeton University Press, 1998.

Rousseau, Jean-Jacques. *The Confessions*. London: Penguin, 1953.

———. *Oeuvres complètes*. Edited by Bernard Gagnebin and Marcel Raymond. Paris: Gallimard, 1959.

———. *Politics and the Arts, Letter to M. D'Alembert on the Theatre*.Translated by J. M. Cohen. Ithaca, N.Y.: Cornell University Press, 1960.

———. *Oeuvres*. Edited by Michel Launoy. Paris: Seuil, 1967.

———. *The Political Writings of Jean-Jacques Rousseau*. Edited by C. E. Vaughn. Cambridge, U.K.: Cambridge University Press, 1971.

———. *On the Social Contract with Geneva Manuscript and Political Economy*. Edited by Roger Masters. New York: St. Martin's Press, 1978.

———. *Émile*. Translated by Allan Bloom. New York: Basic, 1979.

———. *Reveries of a Solitary Walker*. Translated by Peter France. London: Penguin, 1979.

———. *The Government of Poland*. Translated by Willmoore Kendall. Indianapolis: Hackett, 1985.

———. *The First and Second Discourses*. Edited by Victor Gourevitch. New York: Harper and Row, 1986.

Roussel, Jean. *Jean-Jacques Rousseau en France après la Révolution, 1795–1830*. Paris: A. Colin, 1972.

Rudé, George. *Robespierre: Portrait of a Revolutionary Democrat*. London: Collins, 1975.

Ryan, Alan. "The Liberal Community." In *Democratic Community*. Edited by John W. Chapman and Ian Shapiro. New York: New York University Press, 1993.

Sa'adah, Anne. *The Shaping of Liberal Politics in Revolutionary France.* Princeton, N.J.: Princeton University Press, 1990.

Saint-Just, Louis Antoine. *Théorie Politique.* Paris: Seuil, 1976.

———. *Oeuvres complètes.* Paris: G. Lebovici, 1984.

Sandel, Michael J. *Liberalism and the Limits of Justice.* New York: Cambridge University Press, 1982.

———. *Democracy's Discontent: America in Search of a Public Philosophy.* Cambridge, Mass.: Harvard University Press, 1996.

Scanlon, T. M. "Rights, Goals and Fairness." In *Public and Private Morality.* Edited by Stuart Hampshire. New York: Cambridge University Press, 1978.

———. "Contractualism and Utilitarianism." In *Utilitarianism and Beyond.* Edited by Amartya Sen and Bernard Williams. New York: Cambridge University Press, 1982.

Schaar, John. *Legitimacy in the Modern State.* New Brunswick, N.J.: Transaction Books, 1981.

Schama, Simon. *Citizens.* New York: Vintage, 1989.

Schmidt, James. "Cabbage Heads and Gulps of Water: Hegel on the Terror." *Political Theory* 26 (February 1998): 4–32.

Schwartz, Joel. *The Sexual Politics of Jean-Jacques Rousseau.* Chicago: University of Chicago Press, 1984.

Schwartz, Joseph. *The Permanence of the Political.* Princeton, N.J.: Princeton University Press, 1995.

Scott, John T. "Rousseau and the Melodious Language of Freedom." *The Journal of Politics* 59 (August): 803–29.

Shklar, Judith N. *Men and Citizens.* London: Cambridge University Press, 1969.

———. "Rousseau's Images of Authority." In *Hobbes and Rousseau.* Edited by Maurice Cranston and Richard S. Peters. Garden City, N.J.: Anchor, 1972.

———. "General Will." In vol. 2 of *Dictionary of the History of Ideas*, 275–81. Edited by Philip P. Wiener. New York: Charles Scribner's Sons, 1973.

———. "Jean-Jacques Rousseau and Equality." *Daedalus* 107 (Summer 1978): 13–25.

———. "The Liberalism of Fear." In *Liberalism and the Moral Life.* Edited by Nancy L. Rosenblum. Cambridge, Mass.: Harvard University Press, 1989.

Siedentop, Larry. "Two Liberal Traditions." In *The Idea of Freedom: Essays in Honor of Isaiah Berlin.* Edited by Alan Ryan. New York: Oxford University Press, 1979.

Sieyès, Emmanuel. *Écrits politiques.* Paris: Éditions des Archives Contemporaines, 1985.

Singer, Brian. *Society, Theory and the French Revolution.* Houndmills, Basingstoke, Hampshire, U.K.: Macmillan, 1986.

Skinner, Quentin. "The Idea of Negative Liberty." In *Philosophy in History.* Edited by Richard Rorty, J. B. Schneewind, and Quentin Skinnner. New York: Cambridge University Press, 1984.

———. "On Justice, the Common Good and the Priority of Liberty" In *Dimensions of Radical Democracy.* Edited by Chantal Mouffe. New York: Verso, 1992.

———. "The Paradoxes of Political Liberty." *The Tanner Lectures on Human Values* 15 (1994): 227–50.

———. *Liberty before Liberalism.* New York: Cambridge University Press 1998.

Smith, Steven B. *Hegel's Critique of Liberalism.* Chicago: The University of Chicago Press, 1989.

Soltau, Roger. *French Political Thought in the Nineteenth Century.* New York: Russell & Russell, 1959.

Spitz, Jean-Fabien. *La liberté politique: essai de généalogie conceptuelle*. Paris: Presses Universitaires de France, 1995.

Starobinski, Jean. *Jean-Jacques Rousseau: Transparency and Obstruction*. Chicago: University of Chicago Press, 1971.

———. "The Accuser and the Accused." In *Jean-Jacques Rousseau*. Edited by Harold Bloom. New York: Chelsea House, 1988.

Starzinger, Vincent. *The Politics of the Center: The Juste Milieu in Theory and Practice, France and England 1815–1848*. New Brunswick, N.J.: Transaction Books, 1991.

Steinberger, Peter J. "The Impossibility of a 'Political' Conception." *The Journal of Politics* 62 (February 2000): 147–65.

Stephens, H. Morse, ed. *Orators of the French Revolution*. 2 vols. Oxford, U.K.: Clarendon Press, 1892.

Stewart, John Hill, ed. "Declaration of the Rights of Man and Citizen." In *A Documentary Survey of the French Revolution*. New York: Macmillan, 1951.

Strauss. Leo. *Natural Right and History*. Chicago: University of Chicago Press, 1957.

———. "On the Intention of Rousseau." In *Hobbes and Rousseau*. Edited by Maurice Cranston and Richard S. Peters. Garden City, N.J.: Anchor Books, 1972.

Strong, Tracy. *Jean-Jacques Rousseau: The Politics of the Ordinary*. Thousand Oaks, Calif.: Sage, 1994.

Taine, Hippolyte. *The Origins of Contemporary France*. Chicago: University of Chicago Press, 1974.

Talmon, Jacob. *The Origins of Totalitarian Democracy*. Boulder, Colo.: Westview, 1985.

Tamir, Yael. "Revisiting the Civic Sphere." In *Freedom of Association*. Edited by Amy Gutmann. Princeton, N.J.: Princeton University Press, 1998.

Taylor, Charles. *Philosophy and the Human Sciences: Philosophical Papers 2*. London: Cambridge University Press, 1985.

———. "Cross Purposes: The Liberal-Communitarian Debate." In *Liberalism and the Moral Life*. Edited by Nancy L. Rosenblum. Cambridge, Mass.: Harvard University Press, 1989.

Terchek, Ronald J. *Republican Paradoxes and Liberal Anxieties: Retrieving Neglected Fragments of Political Theory*. Lanham, Md.: Rowman & Littlefield, 1997.

Thibaud, Paul. "Rousseau-Tocqueville: Un Dialogue sur la Religion." *The Tocqueville Review* 18 (1997): 47–59.

Thompson, Dennis F. "Democratic Theory and Global Society." *The Journal of Political Philosophy* 7 (1999): 111–25.

Thompson, J. M. *Robespierre*. New York: Basil Blackwell, 1988.

Tocqueville, Alexis de. *The European Revolution & Correspondence with Gobineau*. Translated by John Lukacs. Garden City, N.Y.: Doubleday Anchor Books, 1959.

———. *Oeuvres complètes*. Edited by J. P. Mayer. Paris: Gallimard, 1967.

———. *Democracy in America*. Edited by J. P. Mayer. New York: Harper Perennial, 1969.

———. *The Recollections of Alexis de Tocqueville*. Edited by J. P. Mayer. Westport, Conn.: Greenwood Press, 1979.

———. *Journey to America*. Edited by J. P. Mayer. Westport, Conn.: Greenwood, 1981.

———. *The Ancien Régime*. Translated by John Bonner. London: J. M. Dent & Sons, 1988.

Todorov, Tzvetan. *Frêle bonheur*. Paris: Hachette, 1985.

———. *Benjamin Constant: la passion democratique*. Paris: Hachette, 1997.

Trachtenberg, Zev. *Making Citizens: Rousseau's Political Theory of Culture*. New York: Routledge, 1993.

Valensise, Marina. *François Guizot et la culture politique de son temps*. Paris: Gallimard, 1991.

Vaughan, C. E. Introduction to *The Political Writings of Jean-Jacques Rousseau*. Cambridge: Cambridge University Press, 1915.

Vincent, Andrew, and Raymond Plant. *Philosophy, Politics and Citizenship: The Life and Thought of the British Idealists*. Oxford, U.K.: Basil Blackwell, 1984.

Viroli, Maurizio. *Jean-Jacques Rousseau and the "Well-Ordered Society."* New York: Cambridge University Press, 1988.

———. *For Love of Country: An Essay on Patriotism and Nationalism*. Oxford, U.K.: Clarendon, 1995.

Waldron, Jeremy. "Judicial Review and the Conditions of Democracy." *The Journal of Political Philosophy* 6 (1998): 335–55.

Walzer, Michael. *Obligations: Essays on Disobedience, War, and Citizenship*. Cambridge, Mass.: Harvard University Press, 1970.

———. *Radical Principles: Reflections of an Unreconstructed Democrat*. New York: Basic, 1980.

———. *Spheres of Justice*. New York: Basic, 1983.

———. "Citizenship." In *Political Innovation and Conceptual Change*. Edited by Terence Ball, James Farr, and Russell L. Hanson. New York: Cambridge University Press, 1989.

———. *What It Means to Be an American*. New York: Marsilio, 1992.

Wenar, Leif. "*Political Liberalism:* An Internal Critique." 106 *Ethics* (October 1995): 32–62.

Wingrove, Elizabeth Rose. *Rousseau's Republican Romance*. Princeton, N.J.: Princeton University Press, 2000.

Winthrop, Delba. "Rights: A Point of Honor." In *Interpreting Tocqueville's* Democracy in America. Edited by Ken Masugi. Lanham, Md.: Rowman & Littlefield, 1991.

Wokler, Robert. "Rousseau's Perfectibilian Libertarianism." In *The Idea of Freedom: Essays in Honour of Isaiah Berlin*. Edited by Alan Ryan. New York: Oxford University Press, 1979.

———. "Rousseau's Two Concepts of Liberty." In *Lives, Liberties, and the Public Good: New Essays in Political Theory for Maurice Cranston*. Edited by George Feaver and Frederick Rosen. Houndmills, Basingstoke, Hampshire, U.K.: Macmillan, 1987.

———. "Rousseau and His Critics on the Fanciful Liberties We Have Lost." In *Rousseau and Liberty*. Edited by Robert Wokler. Manchester: Manchester University Press, 1995.

———. "Contextualizing Hegel's Phenomenology of the French Revolution and the Terror." *Political Theory* 26 (February 1998): 33–55.

Zetterbaum, Marvin. *Tocqueville and the Problem of Democracy*. Stanford, Calif.: Stanford University Press, 1967.

Index

Lakanal, Joseph, 73
Lamberti, Jean-Claude, 138, 146n73
Landes, Joan, 98n55
Legislator, 55–57, 78, 108
LePeletier, Louis Michel, 102
liberalism, 125, 127, 137, 138, 147; and
    citizenship, 1, 15–16, 168–69;
    distinguished from political liberalism,
    22n24; English vs. French, 139–40;
    and the French Revolution, 118–19;
    and republicanism, 4, 25n73, 92, 96n7,
    168–69; sovereignty and, 140–42,
    145n46, 145n50, 146n75; and the
    tension between popular will and
    rational will, 23n35, 24n39. *See also*
    political liberalism.
Lind, Michael, 172
Locke, John, 19, 33, 38, 103
Louis XIV, 84, 126
Louis XVI, 74–76, 111
Louis-Philippe, 137

McAdam, James I., 130
Machiavelli, Niccolò, 73
Malouet, Pierre-Victor, 81–82, 99n72
Maistre, Joseph de, 126
Manent, Pierre, 160, 163n3
Manin, Bernard, 112, 123n74
Marat, Jean-Pierre, 102, 112
Marshall, T. H., 5–6
McDonald, Joan, 72, 74, 96n8
Michelet, Jules, 103
Mill, J. S., 140
Mirabeau, Marquis de, 64
Mirabeau, Comte, 75–76, 81–82, 97n17,
    97n18, 99n72, 116
Mitchell, Joshua, 156
monarchists, 74
Montesquieu, Charles de, 79, 102–3,
    116–18
Mornet, Daniel, 72
Mouffe, Chantal, 5
Mounier, Jean-Joseph, 75

Nagel, Thomas, 10, 23n35
Nassau, Anne-Paulina-Adrienne de, 129

natural law, 31, 45n17

Ozouf, Mona, 109, 112, 115

Palmer, R. R., 109
paradox, 50–51, 107–8, 148–49, 167–68,
    172
partial association, 147–48m, 157–63,
    165n38, 164n10, 164n24, 171
patriotism, 171; Tocqueville on, 152–57
le peuple, 81–83, 91–92, 99n82, 112, 115
Plato, 19, 56
pluralism, 6, 7, 20, 60–65, 162, 171–72
Poland, 88, 115–16
political liberalism, 7–10, 23n25; and
    citizenship, 23n25; contrasted with
    deliberative democracy, 10–12, 14; and
    the tension between popular will and
    rational will, 7–10, 23n32
popular will: tension with rational will,
    2–20, 21n9, 27, 51, 53, 81, 85–87,
    89–95, 107, 118, 127, 143, 149, 154,
    157, 161–63, 167–68, 172–73
privilege, 84, 101, 103
proceduralism, 169–70
procedures, 133–34, 143
the public/private distinction, 33, 41,
    109–10, 114, 119, 129

Quinet, Edgar, 72

rational will. *See* popular will
Rawls, John, 7–12, 14, 16, 23n29, 23n32,
    23n35
Reign of Terror, 73–73, 91–95, 109–20,
    122n60
religion: Rousseau on, 57–58; Tocqueville
    on, 152–56
Rémusat, Charles de, 137
representation, 77–81, 87–89, 92, 133–34
republicanism, 1, 21n12, 27, 102, 118,
    120, 137, 143, 168–70; and
    deliberative democracy, 18–19; and
    liberalism, 4, 16, 25n73, 26n74, 92,
    96n7; and pluralism, 6–7;
Restoration liberalism, 125–43

rights, 4, 113–15
Riley, Patrick, 52, 54
Robespierre, Maximilien de, 61, 90–92;
and the distinction between popular
will and rational will, 85–86; and *le
peuple*, 81; Restoration liberals' view
of, 126–28; and Rousseau, 71, 73; and
the Terror, 109–18; and virtue, 103–05,
121n25
Rousseau, 65–66, 69n70; on citizenship,
1–2, 6–7, 53–60, 167–73; and
deliberative democracy, 12–13, 19; on
freedom and its connection to morality,
51–53; and the French Revolution,
71–95, 101–19, 121n18, 122n60; on
the general will, 2, 27–44, 49–51,
67n6, 68n27; on particularity, 60–65,
69n67, 157–63; and Restoration
liberalism, 125–43, 143n2, 144n5,
144n17; and Tocqueville, 147–63,
164n10
Rosenblatt, Helena, 31
royal veto, 75–77, 88, 99n72
Royer-Collard, Pierre Paul, 136, 138
Rudé, George, 117

Saint-Just, Louis-Antoine, 85, 102, 104,
107, 110–13, 116, 120n11, 121n18
Sandel, Michael, 139, 170, 171
self-government. *See* civic freedom
self-interest, rightly understood, 155
Shklar, Judith, 29, 53, 55, 61, 169
Siedentop, Larry, 139–40
Sieyès, Immanuel, 77–84, 89–93, 98n34,
103, 113
Singer, Brian, 89
single will, 61; *On the Social Contract*,
72; and legitimacy, 27–28
social contract, 30–33, 41
Soltau, Roger, 137, 143n2, 144n5

sovereignty, 125–43; of reason, 134–36
Starobinski, Jean, 47n45, 55, 57, 58,
67n10
Strauss, Leo, 108
Strong, Tracy, 67n10

Taine, Hippolyte, 116
Talmon, Jacob, 96n1, 96n7, 110
Tamir, Yael, 160
Taylor, Charles, 171
Terchek, Ronald, 16
Third Republic, 120
Tocqueville, Alexis de, 147–63, 171; on
centralization, 158, 164n28, 165n28,
165n33; on democracy in general,
149–50, 163n3, 163n4; on freedom,
152–53; on the French Revolution,
104; on individualism, 150–52; on
partial association, 157–63, 165n38; on
patriotism, 156–57, 164n19; on
religion, 153–56; and Restoration
liberalism, 144n22, 146n70; status as a
liberal, 163n1
Todorov, Tzvetan, 53
Trachtenberg, Zev, 48n49

Ultras, 134–46

Vaughn, C.E., 38, 47n39
Vergniaud, Pierre, 77
Viroli, Maurizio, 172
virtue, 15–16, 51, 56, 101–05, 109–13,
118, 140
volonté une (single will), 103, 110, 119

Waldron, Jeremy, 25n59
Walzer, Michael, 4,6, 22n19, 165n25,
165n26
will of all, 2, 39–40, 44, 47n40, 85–87,
94, 133, 143, 172

About the Author

Jason Neidleman was educated at UCLA and at Harvard University, where he received a Ph.D. in political science. He teaches a wide variety of subjects to a wide variety of students: philosophy at South Suburban College, political theory at De-Paul University, and reading, writing, math, social studies, and French to students of all ages in the Chicago public school system. He writes on modern and contemporary political theory, with particular emphasis on eighteenth- and nineteenth-century continental political thought. Jason Neidleman lives with his wife in the Ukrainian Village in Chicago.